— THE —

FATAL
LOVER

MATA HARI AND THE MYTH
OF WOMEN IN ESPIONAGE

— THE —
FATAL
LOVER

MATA HARI AND THE MYTH
OF WOMEN IN ESPIONAGE

JULIE WHEELWRIGHT

A JULIET GARDINER BOOK

C&B

COLLINS & BROWN

FOR WALLY

First published in Great Britain in 1992
by Collins & Brown Limited
Mercury House
195 Knightsbridge
London SW7 1RE

Copyright © Collins & Brown 1992

Text copyright © Julie Wheelwright 1992

British Library Cataloguing-in-Publication Data:
A catalogue record for this book
is available from the British Library

ISBN 1 85585 105 9 (hardback edition)
ISBN 1 85585 128 8 (paperback edition)

Typeset by Falcon Graphic Art Limited
Printed and bound in Great Britain by The Bath Press

CONTENTS

ACKNOWLEDGEMENTS

T HIS BOOK HAS HAD MANY MIDWIVES since I first began to contemplate the rich myths
surrounding Margaretha Zelle MacLeod, aka Mata Hari. A friend had suggested I
read the interview between Madame Zelle and the head of Scotland Yard, Basil Thomson,
at the Public Record Office. Like many people, I knew the name and had a vague notion of
Mata Hari as a spy of the *film noir* variety. But when I opened the file, I was struck full-force
by her cool demeanour, her calculated replies, her distressed notes for help and an exotic list
of her luggage. I wanted to know more. But learning more convinced me that no one had yet
solved the mystery of why she remained such a powerful and enduring cultural icon. Why had
I remembered her name yet nothing of her story?

Between those early explorations and the book's completion, I have had help from many
friends and colleagues who have contributed everything from research skills to advice and
insightful comments. Among them, I'd like to thank: Juliet Gardiner, my editor, for her
enthusiasm and encouragement in bringing my ideas into focus; Julian Putkowski, who acted as
my research assistant, for his steady flow of books, newspaper articles, references and thoughts;
Sam Waagenaar for speaking with me about Mata Hari at his flat in Rome; Andrea Stewart for
her suggestions on initial drafts; Dianne Dugaw for research at the Houghton Library; Peter
Colebrook, Rudolf Dekker, Mike Dockerill, Susan Grayzel, Nick Hiley, Jonneke Krans, John
Maclaren, Steve McClure, Dr Simon Wesley and Professor Robin Winks for supplying references; Alan Rolfe for sharing his reminiscences about his sister Lilian; Margaret Clark for her
considerable patience while copy-editing the manuscript; and my agent Rachel Calder for her
much-appreciated support.

I am also greatly indebted to those friends who helped with the translation of documents
and newspaper articles, without which the story would have been greatly impoverished. I am
especially grateful to Henk Kerkwijk for deciphering the Dutch documents relating to Mata
Hari's conviction, to Lourdes Berdasco for the translation of Spanish newspaper reports and
to Harriet Brennan for several lengthy articles in French.

For financial support, and the moral support that accompanies it, I am very grateful to
the Canada Council and to its Awards Officer, Robert Richard. For their help, I would
also like to thank my Canadian friends, Bill Richardson, Susan Swan and Debbie Wilson.

Among the archivists, librarians and researchers at various institutions I have consulted,
I am grateful to: the staff at the Service Historique de l'Armée de Terre; Mrs F. van
Anrooij, at the Algemeen Rijksarchief, The Hague; J.P. de Haas at the Ministry of Foreign Affairs, Library and Archival Services, The Hague; Jelle Krol and A. Stienstra at
the Frysk Letterkundich Museum en Dokumintaesjesintrum, Leeuwarden; W. Sheckleston
at the British Consulate-General, Berlin; John K. Vandereedt, at the National Archives
and Record Administration, Washington, DC; Owen Ketherry, *The New Yorker*, New York
Public Library; Robert J. Walsh, Freedom of Information/Privacy Office; Anne Craiger,
Department of Special Collections, University of California, Los Angeles; Molly Molloy,
Hoover Library, Stanford, CA; the Houghton Library, Harvard University; the British
Library; the staff at the reading room in the Imperial War Museum; the London Library;
the Institute of Historical Research; the Victoria and Albert Theatre Museum; the Mander
and Mitchenson Theatre Collection; Max Tyler, the British Music Hall Society; the German
Historical Institute, London; Dr H. Gordon, Broadmoor Hospital; the Public Record Office
at Kew Gardens and Chancery Lane; and Frank Wintel and Peter Colebrook at Television
SouthWest.

Grateful acknowledgement is made to the following for permission to quote from previously
published material: EMI Music Publishing for 'Olga Pulloffski, The Beautiful Spy', written by
R.P. Weston and Bert Lee, copyright 1935, Francis, Day and Hunter.

I am also indebted to Wally Menteth, who neither typed nor edited my manuscript but
carried my note-laden luggage round France, and patiently lived with my obsession for the
past few years.   J.W.

INTRODUCTION

Woman, when intent on turpitude, is capable of sounding lower
depths than the vilest of the male species.

HAMIL GRANT, *Spies and Secret Service* (1915)

WHILE AWAITING TRIAL ON ESPIONAGE CHARGES at Saint-Lazare prison
in Paris, Mata Hari waged a personal campaign against its austere
conditions. In letters to Lieutenant André Mornet, the prosecuting attorney for
the Third Council of War, she complained bitterly that he denied her requests
for clean shirts, better bathing facilities and the right to send and receive letters.
'Last night I coughed blood,' she wrote in her bold, looped hand. 'I cried with fear
and nobody could hear me. Show a bit of humanity for me. The shock has upset
me so much that I no longer feel like myself. I think I'm going mad.'[1] There were
demands for her travelling bag with its toiletries – 'all the little boxes of cream
and powder' – left behind in the Elysée Palace Hotel when she was arrested on
13 February 1917. For the foremost 'Hindu' dancer of Paris, the demi-mondaine
who had graced stages from Berlin to Monte Carlo, the humiliations of prison
were intense.

'The conditions in which I have to live here are so bad, and it's so dirty,
that I don't know how I am going to bear it,' she wrote to Captain Pierre
Bouchardon, the investigating officer. 'You must realize that I am a different
woman from those around me and yet I am treated like them.' Defiance, self-
pity and arrogance characterized her mood during the long days in her cell,
broken only by interrogations about her alleged espionage activity, visits from
her lawyer Edouard Clunet and often disappointing news. Denied her freedom,
she asked Bouchardon to fulfil certain tasks: her seamstress Madame Chartier
was owed twenty or thirty francs for small repairs, the chambermaid at the
Elysée Palace needed five or six for the laundry, Madame Daludier Madiste
was due fifteen francs for the repair of a white feather boa, and had the 'big
Portuguese earrings' been found at the hotel? Finally, she protested, 'I have
never done any harm towards you. Let me go free.'

Her letters began to ramble, stringing together vague phrases yet still
conveying a powerful sense of injustice. 'You cannot imagine what this Saint-
Lazare is, in its depraved, dirty and humiliating state,' she wrote to Mornet.
'It's terrible to lock up a woman like me for five months in these conditions.'
She was unable to sleep, her body became riddled with vermin bites and her
once-brilliant black hair, which was turning grey, had been cropped according
to prison regulations. The food was so disgusting, she said, even the prison
dogs refused to eat it.[2] Reflecting her confused, weakened state, she vacillated
between using her stage name – Mata Hari or 'eye of the day', the dawn in
Malay – and her married name, Margaretha Zelle MacLeod. To Mornet, on
4 July, she demanded, 'I am suffering enormously and I'm losing such a lot of
weight that I beg you to do something ... Why, my Lieutenant, am I being
made to suffer this misery? You can question me but I am always still a woman.'[3]

None of Mata Hari's pleas moved Bouchardon, who was convinced of her guilt from the beginning of the investigation. He later claimed that she was 'a born spy, who clearly showed that she was one'.[4] Lieutenant Mornet, whom she had repeatedly asked for leniency, announced to the military court when she was sentenced on 24 July: 'The evil that this woman has done is unbelievable! This is perhaps the greatest woman spy of the century.'[5] On 15 October 1917, the morning of her execution, after hearing that her appeal for clemency had been refused, Mata Hari prepared for her final role. According to Léon Bizard, the prison doctor, she sat on the bed and put on her stockings, inadvertently revealing her legs. She dressed in a pearl-grey frock, slung a coat over her shoulders, buttoned her boots, put on a dark tricornered hat with a veil, and gloves.[6]

She wrote three letters – one to her daughter and the others to intimate friends – which were never sent. Then she was led from Saint-Lazare's notorious cell 12 for the condemned, accompanied by the military gendarmes, Sister Léonide and Sister Marie, the nuns who had remained with the prisoner for her last eighteen days, and the prison pastor, the Reverend Jules Arboux. In the chilly dawn at the Château Vincennes, she refused a blindfold and stood up straight rather than have her hands lashed to the firing post. The sergeant major who helped her was stunned by her courage and swore, 'This lady knows how to die.' She turned and thanked him as the twelve soldiers of the Fourth Zouave regiment raised their guns. She lifted her hands, blew the men a kiss and, after the shots were fired, crumpled into what one witness described as 'a heap of petticoats'.[7]

The Paris newspapers reported that she had been buried at a new cemetery in Vincennes but no one claimed her body for fear of association with a traitor.[8] Instead, her corpse was donated to the dissecting room of a Paris teaching hospital. But, like a phoenix from the ashes, her life was already passing into the realm of fantasy. Curiosity seekers flocked to the newly dug grave and, when they found it empty, provided their own explanations. There were stories that a single bullet had pierced her heart, that she had almost eluded the firing squad. Had she died at all? In Parisian cafés rumours circulated that she had startled her executioners in a desperate bid for freedom by throwing open her coat to reveal her still-dazzling naked body. Others said her bravery came from a tragic belief that her Spanish lover, Pierre Mortissac, had tried to recreate the finale of the French dramatist Victorien Sardou's play *La Tosca*, the source of Puccini's opera, where the eponymous heroine attempts to arrange her lover's mock execution. No, maintained the disbelievers, a man on horseback had ridden to the firing line, snatched Mata Hari and had disappeared into the woods with her.

The rumours infuriated American expatriate Natalie Barney, who had once paid Mata Hari to dance at her celebrated women-only parties in Paris. According to George Wickes, Barney's biographer, she hunted down the French commander of the Fourth Zouave regiment who executed Mata Hari, 'to get the exact details of her death rather than the more melodramatic account published in the popular press'.[9] Janet Flanner, who was the Paris columnist for *The New Yorker* at the time, told Wickes:

> Natalie was the one who supplied me with the information on what [Mata Hari] wore the day she was shot. She tracked down the young lieutenant or captain who had given the signal to fire, the one who said she stood so still it made him tremble. So one has an accurate story instead of that tawdry imagined sable coat over nude flesh invented by someone who wrote for the most scurrilous kind of literary weekly.[10]

For Barney, a foreigner, to dispute the rumours about Mata Hari and express shock at her execution in 1917 took great courage at a time when any criticism of the French government was tantamount to treason.[11]

Years later, Frenchmen still argued about Mata Hari's death. They spoke of friends who had visited a remote Austrian castle where a charming chatelaine, who was unmistakably the elusive dancer, had greeted them.[12] A woman who called herself Gloria MacAlister, but was said to be Mata Hari in disguise, was rescued after falling from the British steamer *Eagle* in 1929. The *Daily Mail*'s Paris correspondent claimed 'highly-placed personages' had prevented Mata Hari's death in 1917 and her secret had been safe until now.

'Wild dreams' rapidly became the staple of Mata Hari's legacy, but the verdict of her guilt remained largely unchallenged. Almost two decades after her execution, a Parisian journalist Paul Allard reinvestigated the claims of espionage used to convict her and found that even the hardened Bouchardon remembered no conclusive evidence.

> I have read everything that has been written about the famous dancer-spy – and I am just as far advanced as before. I still do not know what Mata Hari has done. In fact nobody knows what Mata Hari has done! Ask the average Frenchman, or even the more intelligent Frenchman what Mata Hari's crime was, and you discover that he does not know. He is only convinced that she was guilty, but he does not know why.[13]

During the Second World War, the myth of Mata Hari's guilt was particularly potent as the dancer Josephine Baker discovered when she applied to work in the French Resistance during the Occupation. Jacques Abtey, the head of military counter-intelligence in Paris, was at first reluctant to accept her because he remembered the story of Mata Hari. Baker convinced Abtey the similarities between the two entertainers were merely superficial. 'Whereas Mata Hari had been an adventuress drifting around the world without a home, interested above all in her own comfort,' Baker told him at a meeting in her Le Vésinet home, '[she] Josephine Baker was fiercely and to the point of self-sacrifice, devoted to France.'[14]

By 1964, the 'intelligent Frenchman' had not changed his opinion. Director Jean-Louis Richard commented on his film, *Mata Hari, Agent H21*, 'Our biggest problem was making her *sympathique*. After all, she did betray us to the Germans.'[15] In the United States, Raphael Gould, director of the American Library Service, wrote in 1954 that 'Mata Hari is universally known, so much so that the name has become literally synonymous with the word spy.'[16] When in 1965 a statue of Mata Hari was erected in her birthplace, Leeuwarden,

Holland, to commemorate the hundredth anniversary of her birth, the director of tourism George Kooijman said he still received letters condemning or praising her in equal numbers.[17] In 1990, Mata Hari appeared in an article by Jack Pleasant as the 'seductress and spy' who '[slept] with top ranking officers of the enemy and [exchanged] sexual favours for top secret information.' The quest for the reality of her existence melted in the face of an enduring fantasy of female evil.

Yet the precise nature of the crime with which Mata Hari was charged was never incorporated into the mythology. Although she was found guilty on eight charges of passing information of interest to the German naval attaché in Madrid, Arnold Kalle, in reality it had no military or political value. Neither was it ever proved that she had surreptitiously gathered news from her French, Belgian, Dutch or English lovers to sell to the enemy. Yes, she admitted to receiving money from Cramer, the German consul in Amsterdam, as an advance payment for information. But she had never supplied him with anything. Rather, Mata Hari maintained that the only 'intelligence' she had ever passed on was to Kalle; even then, it was nothing more than gossip about the Greek royal family and rumours about an Allied spring offensive which were making the rounds in Parisian cafés. As the prosecutor André Mornet would later admit, during her 1917 trial, 'there was not enough evidence to whip a cat.'[18]

Despite well-documented claims that Mata Hari was innocent of the crime for which she was executed – most notably by Sam Waagenaar in 1964 and Russell Howe in 1986 – she survives as a powerful icon of a wicked woman. But she was, and is, more. Mata Hari, who was born Margaretha Geertruida in 1876 to Antje van der Meulen and Adam Zelle in a small Frisian town, became the female espionage agent *par excellence*. She remains the measure against which all other fictional women spies have been assessed for their competence, loyalty and femininity. The demonization that followed her execution in 1917 made her a convenient pillory for women's attempts at sexual, economic and marital independence. Although she was only one of an estimated ten women and 300 men the French executed for espionage during the First World War, she alone became a household name.[19] The others, whose exploits became an integral part of Mata Hari's mythology, move like shadows behind her. She alone has carried the mantle of 'spy-seductress' but there were a dozen others who could have played the part and died at Vincennes.

Mata Hari brought together fears about the enemy alien, the wayward woman and sexual decadence. But to understand Mata Hari's significance is to explore the myth of the female spy created by war propagandists, film-makers, historians, playwrights, songwriters, and former intelligence operators turned novelists. It was the particular combination of her exotic past as a modernist dancer, her unapologetic role as a courtesan, her fabricated 'Orientalism' and her demand for public approval that worked to keep her story alive. While Mata Hari lived, she conquered the art of giving her customers what they wanted by shaping and remoulding her image to suit their expectations. Such proclivity for life-as-theatre later gave legitimacy to the espionage writers' archetype of the deceptive, irresistible vampire woman, an embodiment of female eroticism and betrayal who frequented Edwardian literature. Writers seized upon the myth and embroidered the already embellished story of Mata Hari's life. Bernard

Newman, reviewing the literature on her story in 1956, commented, 'There seems to be some peculiarity about the Mata Hari case – some malevolent influence which caused men, usually precise and reliable, to be careless and inaccurate.'[20] Sexuality had become a weapon of war.

This 'malevolent influence' is rooted in the espionage myth itself. This book is not a history of Allied military intelligence during the First World War, rather it explores the popular image of the female spy the espionage writers created, and how this reflected attitudes towards gender and sexual anxiety. Whether in historical documentation, newspaper and court reports, films or novels, the espionage myth provides the framework for understanding Mata Hari's significance. She remains the focal point, however, appearing in different forms: as a child-bride, a dancer, a spy-courtesan, a traitor, a martyr and a legend, allowing other women's lives to be viewed through the lens of this prevailing archetype.

Espionage is still regarded as an almost exclusively male world; its fiction writers, often former agents themselves, cater to a largely male audience. Although women often appear as enemy agents who use their sexuality to extract information from unknowing men, their characters rarely venture beyond the exacting boundaries of the literary form. The spy novels of the 1930s, which often used a mythic Mata Hari as their model, bear little relation to the reality of women's wartime experience as agents. Instead, these fictional portraits reveal an internal struggle: women were the vessels of domestic peacetime values, but were also deeply resented for the gains they were making, at what many men believed was their expense. The New Woman was on the move after 1918; suffrage was extended to women in Britain, America, Canada and many European countries for the first time, as they ventured into new occupations and exercised their burgeoning liberties by taking up sports and wearing trousers. The lingering fear that accompanied these changes between the sexes was often found in the predictable plots of spy novels. The sexually independent adventuress who embodies a woman's desire for what was once regarded as 'male privilege', gets her comeuppance in the dark world of espionage. In a hundred variations on the theme, Mata Hari relived her final moments at Vincennes, waving goodbye and falling into a heap of nothing more harmless than skirts.

Mata Hari was not the only dancer-courtesan to step from the international stage into the world of politics during the war. But her myth set the tone for others who followed and she became the most enduring fictional figure. Even before the war, new theories in Britain that the Germans recruited women spies from the ranks of the demi-monde had made significant inroads. Any single, foreign female in Britain – whether a German governess, tutor, student, barmaid, housewife or nurse – was immediately a target for accusations of espionage.

The parallels were clear. Whether she was an actress, prostitute, spy or a combination of all three, the fictionalized female agent extracted payment for her performance. 'The ideal type of woman spy is the Hollywood-cultivated "film vamp",' psychologist Dr Magnus Hirschfeld wrote in his 1934 essay on 'the amatory adventures' of women spies, '[who is] cold, egotistical, and vengeful, who responds to men as objects of exploitation but who exerts a demonic attraction upon [men].'[21] He argued that the female spy's mental composition so closely resembled the prostitute's that it was no wonder the best were courtesans and the rest were drawn from those who worked as singers, dancers or acrobats. Bernard Newman, who claimed to have worked with prostitutes in British intelligence during the First World War, blamed female agents for drawing on the Mata Hari legend to validate their sexuality as a weapon: 'Any woman who values her virginity would be well advised to keep away from the spy-business.'[22] Many male intelligence officers set up the conundrum that while men were expected to separate sexual experience from their emotions, women who did so were unnatural. The spy-courtesan allegedly developed this deception into a high art form.

However, Lieutenant-Colonel Oreste Pinto, who worked for the Deuxième Bureau (the French office for espionage and counterespionage which was established by General Joffre in August 1914) and later became an espionage writer, claimed female agents couldn't live up to these expectations:

> Living constantly at such a mental pitch, a woman spy very often lets her emotions get the better of her. Where men have been accustomed for years to keeping their business and their sexual lives in two separate compartments, women have not been emancipated for a sufficiently long time to have the habit – that is, if their make-up will allow them to do so. To a man with self-control, his sex life need never impinge on the job in hand. He may enjoy a sexual adventure without allowing any emotion to enter. Only a prostitute among women could do the same – and prostitutes are notoriously untrustworthy so that they could never make reliable secret agents. Some women might easily fall in love with the man on whom they have been set to spy and would then go over to the enemy, taking with them all the secret information with which they had been equipped in order to undertake the task of spying . . . women by their very nature do not make good spies.[23]

The received wisdom among spy masters during the First World War was that while women might feature in spy literature and fiction, they were a liability in the field. Major General Sir Vernon Kell, who headed Britain's first Secret Service Bureau which later became MI5, was adamant about the limited use of female agents. 'Women do not make good secret service agents,' Kell claimed in his lecture on 'security intelligence in war'. 'The difficulty with the female agent is her lack of technical knowledge of naval and military matters.' Her only successes, he added, were confined to acting as 'a scout, a judge of character, a recruiter or trainer of agents in non-technical matters.'[24]

This book is largely a history of Mata Hari's creation as the century's most important icon of female betrayal, but it is also a study of attitudes towards women's participation in this sphere of international politics. The reason espionage writers most frequently cited for a woman's decision to join the secret service was 'love of adventure' rather than money or patriotism. These are women who so passionately covet the privileges that belong exclusively to men they will use any means of access. Despite its lure of romance, the writers are always quick to point out that espionage is actually a dirty business and women are invariably soiled by their experience. Nathaniel Greenleaf, the hero of Herbert Yardley's autobiographical novel, *The Blonde Countess*, describes the ambiguity the spy-seductress roused: 'She was, he supposed, one of the highest products of civilization, the goal and flower of innumerable generations of struggling up through the mire. Despite her physical loveliness, the effect of the innumerable generations seemed to him at the moment largely in vain.'[25] Membership of this secret club usually wrecks the *femme fatale*'s chances of a domestic life or even reform and often maroons her on foreign shores.

When Mata Hari died at Vincennes in 1917 the ground was already well prepared to receive a new version of the *femme fatale* legend. From the spy novels of the late nineteenth century to the First World War propagandists and music-hall artists, Mata Hari's death was already imbued with cultural significance. It had influenced the instructions that intelligence chiefs issued to their female agents and in Britain any foreign woman, from showgirl to suburban housewife, fell under public suspicion. The 'Hunness' was everywhere 'within our midst'. But the process by which Mata Hari – the supreme spy-courtesan – rose to such cultural prominence has never been seriously addressed. This book is an attempt to fill these gaps, to uncover the life of the woman obscured by the myths and reveal her difficult, troubled, courageous and entertaining experiences. The following chapters focus on myths, texts and images: the child-bride, the 'Hindu' dancer, the spy-courtesan, the traitor and all the attendant ideological baggage of Mata Hari's legend. Above all, I hope to shed further light on the historical relationships between men and women, how they use one another in the context of war, and how the two are rarely reconciled.

CHAPTER ONE

THE CHILD-BRIDE

Perhaps it is because the French understand women and idealize them more than any other nation that those who live on the 'border-line' between crime and honesty, virtue and immorality make their headquarters in Paris.

GEORGES DU PARCQ, *Secrets of the French Police* (1934)[1]

AFTER NINE LONG YEARS OF MARRIAGE, Margaretha Zelle MacLeod had had enough.[2] In 1904 she packed her bags and headed for Paris, the city of romantics and runaways. The twenty-one-year age gap between her and her husband Rudolph MacLeod, which had once seemed irrelevant, now marked a gulf between them; they quarrelled bitterly about everything from child-rearing to the cost of Margaretha's wardrobe. Their lightning romance – they were engaged six days after meeting and married four months later – had quickly soured. Rudolph had no patience with his young wife's fascination with fashion and European society which had, at first, charmed him. Publicly and privately, he admonished her for immaturity and openly demonstrated his disappointment. The real conflict, however, stemmed from Margaretha's refusal to become the bourgeois matron that Rudolph expected. The more he exercised his authority, the stronger she rebelled. For her, all the pleasures of *la belle époque* beckoned irresistibly.

Margaretha had met Rudolph MacLeod through an advertisement in the Amsterdam newspaper, *Het Nieuw van den Dag*, that a lonely captain of the Colonial Army in the Dutch East Indies was searching for a companion while on leave in Holland. Margaretha, then living in The Hague, replied with a photograph and letter suggesting a meeting which was, eventually, arranged for 24 March 1895 at Amsterdam's Rijksmuseum. Rudolph was immediately intrigued by the dark-eyed, dark-haired nineteen-year-old who would later write him seductive letters ingenuously asking his advice on the colour of her wedding chemise and *pantalons*. Breathlessly she promised, 'Oh, how we will play!'[3] But Rudolph was almost forty, a tough, hard-bitten soldier who had enlisted in the Colonial Army at sixteen. After their courtship, he made few concessions to a young wife who did not conform to the current ideal of feminine passivity.[4]

A few weeks after the wedding, J.T.Z. de Balbian Verster, Rudolph's friend who had placed the *Het Nieuw van den Dag* advertisement for him, noticed that MacLeod had returned to his old habits; one evening Rudolph asked him to keep Margaretha company as 'he had a date with two girls'.[5] Adam Zelle, Margaretha's father, would later claim in a biography of his daughter that Rudolph spent whatever savings he had during the first weeks of his marriage, entertaining other women. Meanwhile Margaretha sat at home, increasingly frustrated that Rudolph had decided they should live with his widowed sister, 'Tante' Lavies [Dutch for Louise], whom she disliked. Life at Leidschkade 79 in Amsterdam was fractious. The only brief excitement came when Rudolph presented his young bride, resplendent in her yellow wedding gown with her thick dark hair, at a Royal Palace reception given by the Queen Regent Emma of Holland.[6]

When Rudolph's extended home leave ended, the couple embarked for the Dutch East Indies on the SS *Prinses Amalia* with their son Norman John, born five months earlier on 30 January 1897. A photograph taken aboard ship of the departing passengers on May Day that year reveals the sharp contrasts already evident between the MacLeods. Margaretha poses with her hands folded in her lap, her pale face and wide mouth alight with excitement and dreamy sensuality, while Rudolph stands behind her, ramrod straight, staring outward, neither touching nor looking at his wife. The afternoon before their departure, Margaretha claimed Rudolph had left the house and returned early the next morning without explanation.

Their arrival in Jandjong Priah, Java, did not ease the mounting tension. They settled for a year in Toempoeng on the eastern part of the island and on 2 May 1898 Margaretha gave birth to a daughter named Jeanne Louise, who would be known as Non. Rudolph's insistence on absolute authority within his family was reflected in the children's names. Norman John was named after his paternal grandfather John van Brienen MacLeod and his great-uncle Norman, a retired general; Non's namesake was Lavies – who was also Jeanne Louise.[7] It seems unlikely Margaretha would have wished her daughter to be named after a woman whom she so intensely disliked and partly blamed for ruining her early married life. Rudolph meanwhile wrote letters to his sister often expressing his fears that Margaretha's behaviour would besmirch the family's reputation.

It was only several months later, after Rudolph had been posted to Medan on Sumatra's east coast, that Margaretha began to relax. While she and the children stayed on at Toempoeng, living with another Dutch family the van Rheedes, Rudolph could only berate her by post. 'Yes, Griet,' he once wrote, 'just try to understand that when I rave and swear, this is caused principally because I am afraid for the children, for do not forget that our characters differ tremendously.'[8] At other times, she was attacked for dullness. 'You are too narrow-minded, too stupid and too superficial to ever write an interesting letter and you are no longer allowed to speak of beautiful dresses, of hairstyles or other banalities,' he raged from Medan. 'Do you understand now that I am constantly in a bad temper because of you?'

Rudolph exercised his husband's right, according to prevailing moral codes, to indulge his appetite for prostitutes while bullying Margaretha about the propriety of her behaviour. She railed against the hypocrisy but realized that her erotic appeal was her strongest weapon of revenge in arousing his jealousy and thus defying his control. 'My husband won't get me any dresses because he's afraid I will be too beautiful,' she wrote in a letter to a friend. 'It's intolerable. Meanwhile the young lieutenants pursue me and are in love with me. It's difficult for me to behave in a way which will give my husband no cause for reproaches.'[9]

These statements also reveal Margaretha's desperate need for approval. Since her husband refused to accept her as an adult and found fault with her as a wife and mother, she turned elsewhere for support. It was familiar ground to Margaretha who, at the age of fourteen, had lost her mother, her family and her home within a year. Antje Zelle died in May 1891, nine months after a legal separation from Margaretha's father who had moved the family from Leeuwarden to The Hague when his hat shop was declared bankrupt. Soon after her mother's funeral, Margaretha was sent to live in Sneek with her godfather, Mr Visser. Older men such as Heer Wybrandus Haanstra, the headmaster of a nursery-training school Margaretha attended in Leiden, offered a new kind of attention. Whatever transpired between the headmaster and his pupil, and there were conflicting reports that the fifteen-year-old Margaretha seduced or was seduced by Haanstra, she left the school without finishing her training.[10] It is difficult to believe that, however magnetic his pupil's personality, Haanstra had not exploited his authority, age and experience with this vulnerable teenager.

But the incident may have taught Margaretha that if she lacked power in most spheres of her life, her good looks and physical charm were a marketable asset. Cora Pearl, an Englishwoman who became a celebrated Parisian courtesan in Napoleon III's court, was drugged and raped by a London diamond merchant at the age of fourteen. This experience, for which she received payment of £5, marked the end of her childhood and she soon found an older man who arranged her first dancing venues in the West End. 'Remarkable women,' wrote Pearl's biographer Polly Binder, 'often build their careers on the ruins of a shattering, emotional sexual experience . . . They will not, and do not seek to, love again.'[11] Although Margaretha was probably once in love with Rudolph, their marriage had also offered a pragmatic solution to her financial insecurity. As she described her motives years later, 'I married to become happier.'[12]

The frank sensuality which made her so attractive to men, however, also made her a target for MacLeod's rage. Before the wedding she showed a remarkable sexual confidence that he appreciated but later came to equate with the behaviour of a prostitute. Addressing Margaretha in tones usually reserved for children or soldiers under his command, he sought unsuccessfully to force her into the role of passive, passionless wife. In the documented history of their relationship, Rudolph depicted Margaretha as an uncaring, unkempt slattern with a passion for material acquisition and no maternal feelings. However, read in the light of his comments and his criticism, her greatest crime was her refusal to live up to his rigid expectations.

Margaretha and the children arrived in Sumatra to join Rudolph on 26 May 1899. According to him, Norman and Non were very thin, pale and badly neglected and he immediately called for a doctor. During the two days they spent in Surabaja en route to Sumatra, Rudolph claimed Margaretha had left the children alone in a hotel so she could go shopping for dresses and gloves which she bought on credit in his name. On 10 June he wrote to Lavies explaining that he was consumed with thinking of a way in which he could get rid of his wife while keeping the children: 'It's going to be very difficult Louise. Ah! If only I had the money to buy their [the court's] consent, for the rogue takes all my money . . . if only I could get rid of her.'[13] He prayed that God would keep him alive for another twenty years to spare him the pain of having 'that creature' sully the honour of his name by raising his children badly.

Their differences deepened. Only a few weeks after their arrival, both children became seriously ill and although a Dutch doctor managed to save Non, Norman died on 27 June 1899. All the tenderness that Rudolph was unable to express to his wife, he poured into his grief for his only son. Before the burial, he cut a lock of Norman's hair and put it in an envelope with the inscription: 'Hair of my unique boy, taken from his small coffin 28 June 1899.' Pasted onto the envelope were two dates from a calendar – 27 and 28 June – marking 'the day of death and day of burial of my dear Norman'. A week after the funeral, he wrote to Lavies, 'I am profoundly unhappy and miss my little dear every minute of the day and night . . . He was so sweet, this little one, and my life is empty and arid without him.' In the midst of his misery, Rudolph decided to leave the army and return with his family to Holland.[14]

A few days later, one of the children's nurses caught cholera and on her deathbed confessed that she had been forced by a soldier to poison the family's food. But it was only Norman who ate enough of the tainted rice to be fatally stricken. The description of the nurse in Charles Heymans' biography of Margaretha, however, reveals the racist assumptions attributed to her motives: 'Docile, like all the Malaysians, even when their master and mistress are ordered to be killed, [she] had carried out the task with the refined cruelty peculiar to her race.'[15] The soldier, who was under MacLeod's command, sought revenge for disciplinary measures taken against him. Rumours among the Dutch colonists, however, said the soldier was the nurse's lover, whom MacLeod had caught and beaten. Others said that MacLeod had attempted to seduce the nurse and the soldier had poisoned the children in revenge.[16]

Whatever the reason for their son's death, the couple became further estranged. Even their move to the village of Banjoe Biroe brought little comfort since Margaretha soon fell ill with typhoid fever which lasted several months. Rudolph became increasingly abusive to his wife and on 27 May 1901 Adam Zelle received a petition in Amsterdam from a Batavian justice official asking him to witness Margaretha MacLeod's petition for divorce on the grounds of maltreatment. Although nothing came of this, MacLeod's behaviour continued to deteriorate according to Dr Roelfsema, the medical officer for Preanger province in which the MacLeods lived. 'During the year and a half I used to know the MacLeod family,' he wrote to the Amsterdam newspaper *Algemeen Handelsblad* in 1930, 'the conduct of Mrs MacLeod, notwithstanding the many rude insults she had to endure in public from her husband, was perfectly correct . . . Her marriage to the uneven tempered and excitable MacLeod was doomed to failure.'

In a 1932 interview with Sam Waagenaar, Dr Roelfsema described a typical scene at the MacLeods' home in Sindanglaja. Margaretha had been speaking about Europe but when the subject turned to Paris, MacLeod became excited and shouted at her, 'What the hell! If you want that much to go to Paris, why don't you just go and leave me alone!' On another occasion, Dr Roelfsema recalled a party where Margaretha was dancing as her husband looked on from the sidelines; as she and her partner passed Rudolph, Margaretha said, 'Hello, darling.' Rudolph snarled back, 'You go to hell, bitch.'[17] Despite MacLeod's concern about his wife's public behaviour, he often humiliated her in front of friends. Such scenes added to her deep, bitter resentment, sealing the failure of their marriage.

Adam Zelle later documented Margaretha's allegations of her husband's mental and physical abuse in a biography published in 1906. Calling it 'a history of the life of my daughter and my grievances against her ex-husband', Zelle reprinted a few of the anguished letters Margaretha had sent him from Java. On 3 August 1901 she wrote that Rudolph could no longer control himself during his attacks of rage; he had recently threatened to kill her, waved a loaded revolver in front of her and spat in her face. He had taken to hitting her, without the slightest provocation, taunting her to, 'fight back a little if you dare!'

Even more sinister was Margaretha's description of a skin disease that he passed on to her and Non, covering their bodies in sores. The doctors in Batavia, she claimed, had warned MacLeod that he no longer had the right to be married. Margaretha said that he wanted a divorce so he could marry another woman, that Dutch people in the town began to avoid him and his debts became so large that the police raided their home.[18] Rudolph, in his letters home, called her 'a villain of the lowest order', who in exasperation would scream that she 'spat in the face of his hypocrisy and his egotism'. During an especially violent argument, when he was about to walk out with Non, he claimed that she pretended to fear for her life and picked up his revolver. Later, he said, she invented stories about the incident, and he dismissed the claim that he had threatened her.[19]

Adam Zelle's biography was biased towards his daughter and both tended to dramatize events; he maintained that Margaretha's childhood was spent in an old château in Cammingha and that her grandmother and namesake was the Baroness Margaretha van Wijnbergen – neither of which were true. However, Margaretha's description of her husband's violence is consistent with the rage revealed in his letters. An independent source – de Balbian Verster who was a long-standing friend of Rudolph's – confirms that he visited prostitutes after his marriage. His harsh letters condemning Margaretha for her stupidity also bear the hallmarks of an abuser. But according to the prevailing ideology the family was sacrosanct and Rudolph could behave as he liked. Church and state divided women into virginal wives – who needed protecting – and prostitutes, who were the vehicles of male sexual urges. Since Margaretha had demonstrated her sexual confidence from the start, in Rudolph's eyes she had sullied her role as wife and must be controlled.

Like most officers' wives, Margaretha had few real options; financially she was completely dependent on Rudolph and even if her neighbours in Sindanglaja sympathized with her situation, they could do little to help. Meanwhile, Rudolph's campaign of rage continued as he littered his letters to Lavies with descriptions of his wife as 'a stinking wretch', a 'beast', a 'bloodsucker' with 'the totally depraved nature of a scoundrel'. He once ended with his fantasy that, 'I sometimes laugh all over when I think that someone might marry her, only to find out that he sold himself down the river as I did.'[20]

Even if Rudolph had not brandished a gun, he appeared to wish for his wife's death openly. During an epidemic, he wrote to Lavies: 'ah, if only the epidemic would free me from this creature, I would be happy again. Sometimes I can't control myself with this coquine around me; but how can I rid myself of her? With or without scandal, it's the same to me.'[21] Margaretha maintained that after the family returned to live in Amsterdam at the end of 1901 Rudolph began to drink heavily; he beat her, refused to give her any money and would slap her or spit in her face if she complained. On 26 August 1902 he left their apartment at 188 Van Breestraat with Non to post a letter and never returned.

Margaretha was greatly distressed that Rudolph had taken her daughter. She promptly sold whatever possessions she could and four days later contacted Mr Eduard Philips, a public prosecutor, to petition for divorce and the custody of her daughter. Zelle's 1906 biography contains a copy of the divorce settlement, authorizing Rudolph to pay 100 florins a month towards his wife's rent. With this assurance, Margaretha left her aunt's house, where she had been staying, and moved into a hotel. Rudolph, however, pleaded poverty and never paid, but in retaliation ran an advertisement in the Amsterdam newspapers warning merchants against supplying goods or services to his estranged wife.[22] There was a brief reconciliation which ended badly and finally Margaretha turned her sights elsewhere. She found no work in Amsterdam or The Hague and, as she later told a journalist, Paris seemed the obvious solution. But why Paris? 'I don't know,' she replied, 'I thought all women who ran away from their husbands went to Paris.'[23]

Her first attempts at employment as an artist's model in Paris were a miserable failure and she returned penniless to an aunt and uncle of MacLeod's in Nijmegen. But once Rudolph heard about this arrangement, the uncle was forced to ask Margaretha to leave. In 1904 she took her second journey to Paris and found work this time at the riding school in the rue Benouville run by Monsieur Molier. A canny businessman, he advised her that with her exquisite body and charm she could become a dancer.[24] This time she looked up the French diplomat she had met the previous year at The Hague. Henry Jean-Baptiste Joseph de Marguérie had recognized her talents, thought her very intelligent and a talented singer. Through his acquaintances, he introduced Margaretha into the salons which would lead to her dancing debut.[25]

At this time, the leading dancers in European theatres were assumed to be *cocottes* and well-bred ladies who took to the stage were forever banished from polite circles. In London, Lady Constance Stewart-Gordon might be praised in the *Lady's Realm* for stag-hunting in Scotland, shooting big game in Ceylon and bagging wild hogs in Texas, but she was ostracized from society for her theatrical dancing. Lady Diana Cooper who knew her as the star of London's Bath Club, where her 'Greek boy's body' made her a champion swimmer, remembered the scandal when Constance took to the 'halls' to compete with Isadora Duncan. '. . . though she was severely criticised for her audacity and lack of art,' wrote Cooper, 'I still believed in her.'[26]

Margaretha was soon to join the ranks of women who lived on the 'borderline' between virtue and crime described by the French espionage writer Georges du Parcq. By the prevailing moral conventions of the period, she was now a fallen woman who had so failed her husband and child that she had been deserted. MacLeod's 'bloodsucker' who would transform herself into Salome was ready to shed her ill-suited identity as obedient army wife. The new Margaretha – now Lady MacLeod, later Mata Hari – intended to take full advantage of those attributes that turned the young lieutenants' heads in Java. Her rebirth as an exotic, erotic dancer from the mysterious East would plumb the depths of nineteenth-century fantasy about the Orient with all its dangerous, enticing associations. In time, it would also make her the perfect target for fears about the 'enemy within', the Kaiser's vamp, who was bent on destroying the Allied nations through sexual depravity. She was never to learn that if she could reinvent her past, so could others and use it against her.

By 1905 Margaretha had begun to call herself Lady MacLeod and had made her astonishing dancing debut at Madame Kiréevsky's chic Parisian salon. Frances Keyzer, the city's correspondent for a London society magazine, *The King*, wangled an invitation to the performance at 'a carefully-selected evening party':

> Vague rumours had reached me of a woman from the Far East, a native of Java, wife of an officer, who had come to Europe, laden with perfumes and jewels, to introduce some of the richness of the Oriental colour and life into the satiated society of European cities; of veils encircling and discarded, of the development of passion as the fruits of the soil, of a burst of fresh, free life, of Nature in all its strength untrammelled by civilization.[27]

The hostess vetted the guests for Philistines as well as any 'suspicion of naughtiness' before the performance began. A door opened, and in glided a tall, dark-eyed figure, who stood motionless before a statue of the god Siva, her arms folded upon her breast beneath a garland of flowers. Adorned with 'authentic Eastern head-dress [and] breast plate of similar workmanship', she swirled different coloured veils that symbolized 'beauty, love, chastity, voluptuousness, and passion'.[28] A strange melody sounded and the dancer moved towards the Siva, then away, appealing to an evil spirit to avenge a wrong. Then as she turned back to the god, her expression softened. In a frenzy she threw flowers and feverishly tore the veils from around her hips, unclasped her belt and finally prostrated herself before the altar.

A second dance paid more obvious tribute to the dancer's Javanese experiences. She wore the veil of 'Javanese maidens' – the *slendong* – which symbolized a woman's virtue and, if stripped from her body, resulted in public dishonour. Lady MacLeod danced with an enchanted passion-flower, falling under its spell and loosening her inhibitions as well as the veil around her waist. The audience caught a tempting glimpse of the native maiden unbound. 'As the veil drops to the ground, consciousness returns,' wrote Keyzer. 'She is ashamed and covers her face with her hands.'[29] Hailed as 'intelligent', 'natural', and 'refined', reviewers predicted that Lady MacLeod would now rival Isadora Duncan whose dance displayed a 'heavy German atmosphere' after her recent stay in Berlin. If Isadora was the Vestal Virgin, Lady MacLeod was now her superior, the Venus.

Among Madame Kiréevsky's guests was Monsieur Guimet, an industrialist and owner of the Museum of Oriental Art which housed his burgeoning collection of Oriental *objets*. Lady MacLeod's performance moved him to suggest she dance at his museum, under a new name. After a long discussion, Margaretha MacLeod became Mata Hari, 'eye of the day' or 'the dawn' in Malay, another tribute to her Javanese sojourn.[30] Her married name, with its painful associations, and her troubled history were jettisoned as well as her domestic life. Like the grand courtesans who were an integral part of Parisian society, Mata Hari was becoming a woman whose past was merely another prop in her own personal theatre, altered, like her name, to fit the current scene.

The audience that flocked to watch Mata Hari stripping off her multi-coloured veils and listen to her 'Oriental' tales projected their own fantasies onto the stage. The mysterious East that Mata Hari chose to represent was 'a place of romance, exotic beings, haunting memories and landscapes and remarkable experiences'.[31] Mata Hari's performance drew upon the French obsession with the Orient's 'Fatal Woman', described by nineteenth-century European writers such as Swinburne, Baudelaire and Huysmans. Like the veils Gérard de Nerval saw everywhere in Cairo, Mata Hari's dance promised to reveal a deep, rich fund of female sexuality.[32] Cloaked in her imitation 'otherness', she offered an escape from all conventional expectations of femininity.

As Monsieur Guimet transformed his second-floor library with its shining marble floors and columns into his vision of a Hindu temple on 13 March 1905, Mata Hari was born. The lights were dimmed, incense floated through the air, the columns were adorned with garlands of flowers, and thick, rich Persian rugs softened the stone floors. 'All Paris is talking of the beautiful woman known as Mata Kari [sic],' reported *The Gentlewoman*. 'On two consecutive nights the halls and staircases leading to the circular library were filled with all that Paris contains of the artistic, scientific and literary world.'[33] Audiences learned that Mata Hari had arrived in Paris a month ago from Java where she was born of European parents and married to 'Sir George MacLeod', a colonel in the Dutch Colonial Army. Her mission in Paris was to initiate the city 'into the classical dances of her adopted country'. The reviewers were completely convinced of her 'Oriental' message and *Le Gaulois* devoted a front-page review to the evening, praising its unique depiction of 'primitive theosophies', and 'arcane rites of the Hindu'. Leaving the Musée Guimet that evening, the reviewer mused over a poem that unconsciously compared the 'virginal' Mata Hari to the 'amber bodies of the Bayadères'.[34]

Louis Dumur, who published a novel entitled *Les Défaitistes* in 1922 in which Mata Hari loomed large, was another witness to her triumphal night at Monsieur Guimet's. 'Mata Hari danced nude, her small breasts covered with two carved brass plates, held by chains. Glittering bracelets held her wrists, arms and ankles; all the rest of her was nude, fastidiously nude, from the nails on her fingers to the point of her toes.'[35] Already, admirers were assembling the requisite elements of legend.

Mata Hari had touched a raw, erotic nerve, that fed seamlessly into powerful myths about the sensuality and licentiousness of Asian women. As her fame increased, her past was transformed into a chapter more befitting a sacred Oriental temple dancer; Java and India were merely interchangeable backdrops. During 1905 Mata Hari danced thirty times in the most exclusive salons of Paris, appeared six times at the Trocadéro Theatre, and at the homes of Baron Henri de Rothschild, Cécile Sorel, the famous Comédie-Française actress, at the Grand Cercle, and the Cercle Royal.[36] Since her audiences were so delighted with 'the sight of the beautiful naked Indian woman', with each performance she became more convinced of her own re-creation. Her carefully constructed 'primitive religion' allowed sophisticated Parisian society to applaud and appreciate, as art, the unspoken thrill of watching a nude woman dancing before it.

In rewriting her history as an 'Oriental', Mata Hari also rationalized Mac-Leod's rejection and assumed a role as lost innocent. In interviews she alternated between declaring herself a native of Java with European parents, and the daughter of a temple dancer in Jaffnapatain, southern India. She claimed her mother died after giving birth to her – perhaps reflecting her feelings of desertion after Antje Zelle's death – and that she was raised by the temple priests at the Kanda Swany. They trained her as a dancer but dedicated her soul to the god of Swa, and by the age of thirteen she was dancing nude in the temple. Fortunately, a few years later, she was rescued from this life by an English officer who had seen her dance and fallen instantly in love with her.[37] The story drew on the myth of the sexually rapacious 'Oriental' who eagerly sacrified young girls to his unseemly appetite. During the period of scares about the 'white slave trade' in Britain and France, such images had a particular potency, giving Mata Hari's performance an added excitement as she literally acted out the forbidden dreams of her male audience.[38]

It is also intriguing that at a time when Parisian courts were suppressing nude dancing by other performers, Mata Hari was left alone.[39] Sarah Brown, who appeared in a nude performance at the Bal des Quat'z' Arts, was sentenced by the Lord Chancellor to fifteen days' imprisonment on charges of indecent appearances on stage at the time of Mata Hari's debut. One reviewer noted that Brown's sentence was 'outrageous' because her performance was no more pornographic than Mata Hari's; but connections with the very best of Paris society and the religious elements of her 'Hindu' performance may explain Mata Hari's protection from similar prosecution.[40] One critic commented wryly that if all India possessed such marvellous dancers then the borders of the Ganges would soon be crammed with French immigrants.[41]

'Mata Hari personifies all the poetry of India, its mysticism, its voluptuousness, its languor, its hypnotizing charm,' enthused *Le Journal*. 'To see Mata Hari in a rhythm and with attitudes that are poems of wild voluptuous grace is an unforgettable spectacle, a really paradise-like dream.' Monsieur Gaston Menier, a French chocolate manufacturer, wrote in a letter of thanks to Mata Hari after she danced at his salon in May 1905: 'you represented the true antique beauty . . . your beautiful appearance, like an Oriental dream.' Mata Hari was quick to exploit the fantasy of ideal Eastern femininity; in an interview with the St Petersburg *Journal*'s correspondent, she scorned the wigs and face powders worn by French socialites as mere artifice.

> Having remained for so long close to Nature, which is simultaneously innocent and simple, she looks upon our worldly behaviour as if it took place on a stage . . . She is astonished that women do not have the customs of her country, where women may have to suffer inferior treatment like being whipped, but where at the same time, they are superior on account of a far more stimulating and higher education.[42]

Mata Hari as the noble savage maiden could afford to spurn her more sophisticated colleagues and revel in the astonishment with which her nudity was greeted. But the sinister side of the fantasy which she acted out, like MacLeod's abuse, was the punishment such a wayward woman endured. Throughout this period, as Mata Hari became one of the highest paid dancers throughout Europe, when she was invited to dance at the Monte Carlo Opera, La Scala in Milan and Vienna's Secession Art Hall, she was ensuring her demise a decade later.

Once she had adopted the trademark of mysterious Hindu dancer, she had irrevocably crossed the thin line between virtue and crime, however much her admirers praised her unadorned beauty.

A dance critic would later comment that the secret of Mata Hari's success stemmed from having observed Java's native bayadères of the Susuhanan of Solos' and Sultan of Jogja's ballet corps. These dancers, tripping the light fantastic, enabled Mrs MacLeod to develop pseudo-Oriental poses which she performed at her own pace, adapting them to suit Western tastes. Her dances attracted attention by whispered tales of what she risked at private exhibitions. But her most daring, 'Dance of the Seven Veils', was most likely 'a quasi-idealized imitation of an Arabic stunt' which Western choreographers had witnessed in the old souks of Egypt. In its original form, a young woman would act out throwing off her clothes in a frenzy to dislodge an insect. First her inner then her outer garments were tossed aside 'in hot pursuit of the intruder, bent on murderous revenge'. However, Mata Hari left out this detail, preferring to fling off her veils until she was prostrate, as if in ecstatic rapture, and sank before a golden Buddha.[43]

Mata Hari flaunted her 'otherness' and noted with delight that, from the beginning, she was compared with Salome. After her first performance at Guimet's, a review in Le Gaulois commented that she 'danced like Salammbo before Tanit, like Salome before Herod'. By 1907 Mata Hari had become obsessed with dancing the role and wrote several letters to her agent Gabriel Astruc urging him to persuade the composer Richard Strauss to produce it for her. '[Only] I will be able to interpret the real thoughts of Salome,' she wrote to Astruc. Although she never played the role publicly, her January 1912 performance at the apartment of Prince di San Faustino at the Barberini Palace in Rome was considered a great success. In a portrait reproduced on the programme, Mata Hari appears naked except for a thin veil covering her wide hips and a medallion lying between heavy breasts; she smiles heavenward in ecstasy with St John's head at her feet. Salome, the lascivious girl from a dark paradise, gloried in her grisly prize.[44]

What separated Mata Hari from her rival Salomes, however, was her determination to continue the role of primitive princess offstage. In interviews, she reinforced the racist assumption that the cruelty of the Orient went hand in hand with overpowering lust, women from her 'native country' were whipped, and young girls who acknowledged their budding sexuality were punished for their indiscretion. The Asian woman of the Salome dance had no voice; she remained a visual exhibition which invited her male audience to revel in the sexual and the macabre. Like the nineteenth-century Orientalist paintings, she became a metaphor for the moral abandon of the East:

> ... it seemed to be a dramatically different mode of dancing from its Western counterpart. It was not a social expression only, since the woman (scantily-clad as she was pictured) was there to pleasure the onlooker, who did not participate but watched. The dance could be used as a medium that illustrated what were perceived to be the Oriental qualities. It could portray female nudity, rich and sequestered interiors, jewels, hints of lesbianism, sexual languor and sexual violence; in brief, it encapsulated the East.[45]

Since there were few Asian women living in Paris at the time within the circles in which Mata Hari moved, she easily spun her legends, contradicting the reality of her sources. Oriental or Occidental, she moved behind a constantly fluctuating mask.

Not every audience was convinced by her performance, however. The writer Colette cast a critical eye over Mata Hari at one of Natalie Barney's famous garden parties in Neuilly, just outside Paris. Following the Boston shepherdess and the Moscow herdsman, a naked Mata Hari on a white horse appeared from behind a screen of foliage. At the salon of opera star Emma Calvé the dancer had been 'sufficiently snake-like and enigmatic to produce a good effect' commented Colette who added wryly, 'The people who fell into such raptures and wrote so ecstatically of Mata Hari's person and talents must be wondering now what collective delusion possessed them.' Her steps and Hindu tales 'were of no better quality than the ordinary claptrap' accompanying the 'Indian numbers' currently in vogue at the music halls.[46]

The secret of Mata Hari's success, concluded Colette, was her willingness to reveal her slender waist, her fine, supple back, muscular loins, long thighs and slim knees. But she was disparaging about the dancer's face: 'her nose and mouth, which were both rather thick, and the rather oily brilliance of her eyes, did nothing to alter – on the contrary – our established notions of the Oriental.' The finale in the Neuilly garden that May afternoon, when the last girdle had been flung aside, 'carried the male – and a good proportion of the female – spectators to the limit of decent attention'. But, once dressed, Mata Hari 'bowed, talked and was faintly disappointing'.[47]

Colette, who was then a struggling writer, may have attacked Mata Hari – 'a transparent fraud' – because her situation was too familiar to be comfortable. After all, Colette, who was separated from her husband, a writer of pornography, and a music-hall dancer and mime artiste, was hardly in a position to scorn Mata Hari's attempt to 'act like a lady'. Perhaps she knew very well that the Dutch dancer's struggle to keep afloat in Parisian society necessitated pretensions and artfully crafted lies. Perhaps from jealousy, she delighted in overhearing a bystander announce audibly, 'She an Oriental? Don't be silly! Hamburg or Rotterdam, or possibly Berlin.'

Despite Colette's criticism, Mata Hari danced three times at Natalie Barney's home: once as an erotic Javanese dancer before a small, all-female audience and again as Lady Godiva, which gave rise to the legend that she rode through the garden on an elephant. Janet Flanner, the *New Yorker*'s correspondent, remembered that Mata Hari on a white horse 'was certainly one of the big events' at Natalie's. As Flanner defended her, 'the only woman who had that extraordinary style was Mata Hari. *There* was a woman who was equal to any event.' Ironically, Colette's disdain did not prevent her from playing the role of Mata Hari in a pantomime Natalie Barney organized in memory of the lesbian poet, Renée Vivien, who died in 1909.[48]

Mata Hari's willingness to perform at Barney's all-female parties was later used as potent evidence of her sexual depravity which indulged the espionage writers' voyeuristic fantasies. The burgeoning movement for 'homosexual emancipation' in Germany, led by social scientists such as Dr Magnus Hirschfeld, would enable Mata Hari's biographers to support the paranoic theory that sexual perversity had threatened Allied morale during the war.[49] Writers would look back on Mata Hari's success in Vienna in early 1907, and project their own anxieties onto the reception of her performances. Mata Hari had enjoyed mixed reviews, with a few critics questioning whether she was more than a talented amateur. While sceptics claimed that Mata Hari's greatest box-office draw was her nudity, nothing halted the 'aristocratic women with endless forebears' from bursting into 'thunderous ovation'.[50]

Within a few years' time, such success would become proof positive of Mata Hari's association with the 'homosexual licentiousness' that had plunged the world into war.

In 1907, however, Mata Hari was more concerned about the proliferation of competitors whose names were springing up on playbills throughout Europe than her moral influence. Colette's comment on music-hall 'Indian numbers' was an accurate jibe at what was rapidly becoming a craze for Oriental dance and its convenient rationalization for all-but-nude dancing. Mata Hari was staying at Vienna's Hotel Bristol during her performances, while Maud Allan, one of her greatest rivals, was at the Hotel National. Isadora Duncan was encamped between the two hotels when the *Neue Wiener Journal* claimed, 'Isadora Duncan is dead! Long live Mata Hari!'[51] The stage was getting crowded. Maud Allan, a Canadian dancer who had trained in San Francisco and at Berlin's Royal High School of Music, was laying claim to her own 'Dance of Innocence'. Although Allan was known for appearing on stage clothed only in a 'chic ventilation' of veils, or gold chains, she edged onto Mata Hari's territory with her classical Egyptian dance.[52]

Maud Allan rejected the restricting poses of classical ballet, to espouse a more liberated dance that allowed for spontaneous movement. 'I only know that as the music calls,' she wrote in her 1908 autobiography, 'so every muscular fiber that responds to the beating of my heart, responds to that particular voice and the tone becomes movement.'[53] Many other dancers shared her complaints as ballet performances throughout Europe 'had sunk by the end of the nineteenth century to a display merely of prettiness; pleasant, controlled steps and charming costumes . . .'[54] Allan composed steps which she claimed were inspired by Botticelli's 'Birth of Venus' to turn the artist's goddess into flesh and blood. It was, however, her heady interpretation of Salome that shot her to fame.[55]

The dancing daughter of Herod who inspired Oscar Wilde's play, Richard Strauss's 1905 opera, novels by Flaubert and Huysmans and paintings by Gustave Moreau, Albrecht Dürer, Ghirlandaio, Piazza, Van Thulden and Leclerc was the period's most potent symbol of mystified femininity – the phallic woman. The ten lines devoted to Salome's story in St Mark's gospel spawned a legend that became the most often used biblical character on the dance stage.[56] *Salome* was one of the most popular plays in Germany, dating from Max Reinhardt's 1903 stage production, and it became part of the Russian theatre's repertoire.[57] Whatever the venue or medium, Salome always reflected a complex set of male assumptions about women's lustful and deadly desires; in Huysmans' 1884 novel, she appeared as:

the symbolic incarnation of old-world Vice, the goddess of immortal Hysteria, the Curse of Beauty supreme above all other beauties by the cataleptic spasm that stirs her flesh and steels her muscles – a monstrous Beast of the Apocalypse, indifferent, irresponsible, insensible, poisoning, like Helen of Troy of the old Classic fables, all who come near her, all who see her, all who touch her.[58]

Maud Allan protested that her 'Vision of Salome' that took Europe by storm in 1908 simply enacted the first public performance of a young woman awakened to the power of her beauty. However, Allan also acknowledged that men, rather than women, better understood her aspirations.[59]

Allan's Salome was certainly influenced by her training in Berlin where the story came to be associated with the sexual liberation movement. German artists placed a new emphasis on *Leibeskultur*, or body culture, that called for a fresh appreciation of the female body freed from the restraints of corsets, belts and brassieres. But this call for *liberté* aroused ambiguous emotions. From Franz Wedekind's Lulu plays to Richard Strauss's Salome, sexual themes appeared in literature and art as a way of expressing disillusionment with contemporary values and political agendas.[60] These stories explored violence as a means of regenerating interest in life: destruction through the act of creation.

Salome was a cult hit in Europe among men and women alike, each reading the story through his or her own experience. 'Nothing in this present decade,' wrote Percival Pollard in 1908, 'has been more interesting than the successive waves of The Dance that have swept over Europe and America.' Pollard's friend Otto Julius Bierbaum had signalled its beginning in a letter from Germany in September 1908 headed, 'Munich in the Month of Saharet. And after Saharet came Isadora Duncan, and Marie Madeline and the innumerables who danced "Salome".' Both claimed the new wave of dancers peaked in Germany in 1904 and swept over America four years later.[61] Munich, then dubbed 'Athens by the Isar', hosted Duncan's Greek rhythms that inspired modernist poets to pay tribute.

While Duncan promoted herself as an American, her greatest rival, Marie Madeline, the hypnotic dancer, 'used her French extraction to incite in the Fatherland that enthusiasm for the exotic which has been growing greater every year.' Like Isadora, Madeline acted out philosophies, poems and histories, and danced literally in a trance. To prove that she was in a complete state of unconsciousness, learned academics were invited on stage to pinch her calves in mid-performance. As the interest in the newly established field of psychoanalysis took hold, hypnotic dancers became 'a veritable . . . epidemic throughout Germany'. Neither dance nor analysis, however, could make women less enigmatic. 'Is not the soul of every woman like a Sphinx,' wrote A. de Nora in his poem 'Madeline', 'that sits and smiles upon the verge of the intangible and gives us riddles none can solve?'[62]

The new dancers also inspired portrait painters to capture this new form of expression. But the women were reduced to a canvas onto which male admirers projected their desires; the dancers had no voice, no tangible essence and were almost interchangeable. As their youth faded, so did their popularity. Pollard wrote of the famous Spanish dancer Saharet, that 'every other portraitist in

Germany had painted her', but after ten years on stage, 'her vogue was already staled'. In the end, the male gaze and its interpretation of the female was all that lasted:

> Let us applaud Miss Duncan as much as we like; let us give solemn ear to all the noble lessons she would teach with her toes; but let us not imagine that she, her pupils, or her theories will live one-half as long as the portrait F.A. von Klaubach painted of her in Munich in 1902.[63]

Jules Chéret's poster of Loie Fuller, Dudley Hardy's for 'The Gaiety Girl' and Toulouse-Lautrec's Yvette Guilbert would, Pollard predicted, outlive their stars. 'Many of these dancers will live longer by what they inspired in poetry and paint than by any ever so vast vogue they may have enjoyed while alive.' The women, like glittering trinkets, shone brightly for a time and then faded; but the competition for that brief moment was fierce among the Salomes of the new century.

It was no coincidence that in 1906 an influential French journal, *Intermédiare des Chercheurs et Curieux*, placed Mata Hari's success within the context of the modern art movement. Support for nude dancing began in Paris at the *fin de siècle*, when women were invited to perform before a male audience in an artist's studio. Following these private shows, Paul Fort, director of the Théâtre des Arts, used an 1892 production of Marlowe's *Faust* to feature a woman – one of the Seven Sins – wrapped only in gauze. The theatres then made 'a series of natural transitions, substituting a costume with the appearance of a costume; a transparent veil.' Even the Opera, a family theatre, had allowed Mademoiselle Régina Badet to appear wearing only a jewelled belt and white corset. Isadora Duncan then followed with her naked legs and now there was Mata Hari whose dance was beautiful and her intention artistic.

But Mata Hari's greatest gift was her ability to make a clear distinction between the 'nude of art' and 'the nude of commerce', according to the *Intermédiare*. The generations of 1860 and 1875, who were designated purists or naturalists, had confused *'la femme nue et la courtisane'* – the nude woman and the courtesan. Modern artists had attempted to clear up the matter by demanding that the passion in the human form should be applauded rather than hidden in shame. Mata Hari provided a crucial link. Her show was 'very gracious and artistic and not at all pornographic' and she would go far because she would perform not just in exclusive salons but 'in the world before husbands accompanied by their wives'.[64] Mata Hari had even anticipated the great couturier Poiret who persuaded women to abandon the corset in 1906 – a year after 'Madame MacLeod's' debut at Monsieur Guimet's.[65]

The European dance craze, however, took several years to reach America, and Salome finally hit Broadway in January 1907. Following a performance of Strauss's opera at the Metropolitan Opera House 'the very disease of Salomania broke out in the land', as music halls took up the new classical poses. But early attempts at choreographic interpretation of the story had provoked Loie Fuller, whose 'serpentine dance' was enormously successful at New York's Columbus Theatre in 1894, to cross the Atlantic. Fuller performed Salome in Paris at the Athénée Theatre in 1907, then moved to the Théâtre des Arts and performed a ballet version entitled 'Dances of a Thousand Veils' at the Hippodrome.[66]

The following year a Loie Fuller protégée, the pre-pubescent Zoula Boncza, was heralded as 'the rage of Paris' for her portrait of a little Indian maiden charming snakes in the woods.[67]

Although Germany had been accustomed to Salome for several years, Maud Allan's first attempt at dancing in Munich on her 1903 European tour ended in a 'rebuff of a serious nature', when the Bavarian government censored it 'to preserve public morals'. Bierbaum rose to her defence but the Bavarians remained unconvinced by arguments that the audiences were interested only in Allan's artistic and aesthetic values.

In England, Oscar Wilde's play *Salome* was refused a licence in 1892 by Public Examiner Edward Pigott, who described it as 'a paroxysm of sexual despair', but Maud Allan opened in London with the Lord Chamberlain's approval.[68] Archdeacon Sinclair, however, attacked Allan after her royal command performance before Edward VII in 1908, claiming he was 'repulsed' that John the Baptist was the subject of a stage scene.[69] Maud Allan ignored her righteous critics and opened her Salome dance at London's Palace Theatre for an uninterrupted run from March to November 1908.[70] 'London raved over the Toronto girl in whom the spirit of ancient Babylon seems to have been born again,' proclaimed the *London Magazine*.

But Allan, more than any other dancer of the period, aroused controversy with her performances. A 'veteran diplomat' writing in *The New York Times* that summer, used her to illustrate the alarming growth of Bohemianism in England. '[Maud Allan] is not only accustomed to gyrate in a state of almost absolute nudity but that she has moreover inaugurated a fashion of dancing which has unfortunately found innumerable imitators on both sides of the Atlantic.' King Edward, it was rumoured, was considering a programme of radical social reform to curb such tendencies. The 'diplomat' explained that while it was perfectly acceptable for the King to visit risqué theatres in Paris or London, he protected his wife and daughters from 'any [who] by their reputation, their antecedents, their characters or their manners were calculated to offend'. English gentlemen, following the monarch's example, must safeguard 'the sanctity of the fireside', which should 'remain inviolate from the invasion of people whose notions of decency and respectability are of a distinctly inferior, and sometimes even the lowest, order'.[71]

Moral corruption, however, had spread to the highest circles of British society; at Mrs Margot Asquith's invitation Maud Allan had not only danced before the Prime Minister but also dined with him and his guests at Downing Street. Even worse were rumours that among Miss Allan's many follow-ers were several titled ladies, 'gossip pointing to the married daughter of a Ducal House renowned for her extravagances and eccentricities'. Miss Allan's 'almost entire nakedness and the repulsive contortions' of her dance were bad enough, but now she threatened the entire class structure of English society. Like the Italian artist Lina Cavalieri, she had been entertained as an equal with the aristocracy. The King was said to be equally incensed when Lina Cavalieri dined with the Duchess of Sutherland at Stafford House and afterwards performed a dance with the hostess's niece, Lady Constance Stewart-Richardson. In New York, Lady Astor was seen driving through the Manhattan streets in an open carriage with the Italian singer while Mrs

Guinness organized Lina Cavalieri's appearances in 'private theatricals and *tableaux vivants*'.[72]

The new-wave dancers meant different things to their male and female audiences. Male viewers might appreciate their form and applaud the rebellion of their naked limbs and fluid movements, but the men were disturbed when their wives or daughters imitated these steps. The dancer's threat to the 'sanctity of the fireside' offered upper-class ladies the fantasy of release from stifling social constraints. The muddying of carefully drawn divisions between 'society and the stage' held exciting potential which was irresistible to Lady Constance Stewart-Richardson or Lady Astor. The trend also signalled middle-class women's desire to step beyond the home and experience the public sphere with all of its dangers; in doing so, their husbands' control of their lives would inevitably diminish.

Maud Allan, however, took pains to distance herself from the sexual politics of this New Womanhood and the suffrage movement. Instead, she used a column in the *Daily Mail* to condemn strongly the English suffragettes, arguing that women 'can do more from an elevated position in the world of art' than with the vote. She believed women were more influenced by emotions than men and while men cared for principles, women cared for people.[73] These reassurances aimed to convince the British public that Salome dancers wanted only to express an appreciation of art, nothing more.

What the dancers could not control, however, was the way in which they would be received. Since our fantasies of desire are no more self-engendered than our bodies, an artistic performance operates within a particular set of historical and social circumstances. During the first decades of the century, artists exploded erotic themes, attempting to banish the moral sense of sin attached to sexual expression. But instead of liberation, many men gazed upon the image of Salome with fear. The pleasure-giving Eros wore a Janus face; the carefree explorer soon found himself falling into the tentacles of a woman who demands death for her unsatisfied sexual desire. As the Austrian artist Gustav Klimt revealed in his painting of a predatory Salome with clawed hands and bony face, the new freedom might easily turn into a nightmare of anxiety.[74]

Maud Allan, who received dozens of letters from male admirers, many clergymen among them, must have realized the potency of her 'Vision of Salome'. Her fans expressed respect for her artistic ability and thanked her for the emotions she had stirred within them. By emphasizing the aesthetic elements of her avant-garde performance, she managed to elevate their response from lust to discerning judgement. Allan claimed she was enacting the role of an ancient female figure who embodied Nature's most intense emotions. 'You seem to interpret [Salome's dance] as the triumph of the wildest passion, the intoxication of the power of beauty, revulsion at the crime and fascination for the ghastly evidence of it,' wrote one such clergyman on 25 June 1908.[75] Since Allan's dance ended with repentance at Salome's responsibility for John the Baptist's head, 'the wildest passion' in the piece was displayed but carefully contained.

While performing in Vienna in late 1906, Mata Hari appeared equally ingenuous about the sensation her dancing aroused. She told a correspondent for the *Deutsches Volksblatt* that the spiritual message of her performance was what most moved her audiences. 'In my dance, one forgets the woman in me so that when I offer everything and finally myself to the god . . . for only half a second entirely naked, I have never yet evoked any feelings but the interest in the mood that is expressed by my dancing.'[76] But 'the woman' in Mata Hari *was* the act and everything else the packaging. Without any professional training she had magnificently exploited the current mood of new erotic yearnings, yet to acknowledge this would have threatened her innocent appearance and widespread approval.

Allan was equally circumspect in describing her interpretation of Salome. In the first part of her dance, she acts out the cloistered life of the fourteen-year-old princess who lives in 'luxurious Oriental seclusion' until she is corrupted by the wishes of her mother, Herodias, and stepfather, Herod. He appears on stage to request that she dress in adult, jewelled robes in celebration of his birthday. Salome is oblivious to 'the circle of inflamed eyes that devour her youthful beauty' when she stumbles self-consciously into the great hall in her finery, and the music for her performance begins. She notices only Herod and Herodias. '[Salome] weaves her most ingenious witcheries of dance . . . The music dies away in a wail of passion. The little figure lies panting in obeisance before the throne.' Herod rewards her dance with a wish; manipulated by her mother, Salome requests the head of John the Baptist – who has insulted Herodias – on a plate.[77]

When the head appears before Salome, she relives the dance as a 'vision' which Allan interpreted as lost innocence. After the erotic dance in front of the favoured few – Salome's first adult performance, a realization of her sexual powers – she is given whatever she wants from the powerful male ruler. Even though the request for John's head, which in Freudian symbolism is a metaphor for castration, comes from the mother (who owns the sexual feelings the daughter cannot yet accept) Salome is both horrified and excited when it is carried out.

Allan's beguiling description of her dance is loaded with sexual imagery; Salome is fearful of the 'purple sticky stain that she has not been able to avoid'; 'she feels a strange longing' and advances towards John's head 'with ecstasy mingled with dread'. 'Every fiber of her youthful body is quivering; a sensation hitherto utterly unknown to her is awakened and her soul longs for comfort,' wrote Allan. 'Frightened lest her treasure be taken away from her before she has solved its mystery, she stands guard over it . . . What passes in those few moments through this excited, half terror-stricken, half stubborn brain makes of little Salome a woman!'[78] The final moments of the dance leave Salome wanting not to conquer, but to be conquered as a way of atoning for 'her mother's awful sin'.

Like Salome, Allan seemed unwilling to acknowledge the sexual message in her performance. However, as the protests from dance societies, archdeacons and city councils reveal, the threat implicit in *The Vision of Salome* was clearly understood. Diana Cooper, whose mother was a fan of this new 'Grecian frieze form of movement', sent her daughters to the Palace Theatre. As a young woman, Cooper thought the production very daring since the dancer appeared on stage in loose chiffon, with bare legs and pipes and cymbals. Cooper's mother, 'untrammelled by convention', ignored the critics who declared Allan's Salome 'scandalous for she was all but naked and had St John's head on a plate and kissed his waxen mouth.'[79]

Whether Allan chose to acknowledge it, her performance in thin veils, at a time when well-bred ladies never undressed before their husbands, aroused her audience sexually. While theatre managers and critics maintained that a new interest in Greek, Egyptian, Indian or biblical dances motivated their bookings for these shows, a London comedian skilfully exposed the suspicion that it was all about exposing female flesh.

Phyllis Dare appeared at the Queen's Theatre in June 1908 with a child chorus of 'tiny Maud Allans' in a satire on 'the Salome Craze'. A photo feature in *The Sketch* shows Dare dressed in a shepherdess costume, standing amidst four girls wearing heavy black wigs and enormous pearls – a send-up of Salome's costume. On stage they shrank back in mock horror at papier-mâché heads while Dare parodied Allan's serious poses:

> The latest society fashion
> Is a dancer just now on the stage;
> For she poses with infinite passion,
> And her hands, worked with art, are the rage,
>
> She is dressed in chic ventilation,
> Quite the thing for our tropical May;
> She gets many a smart invitation,
> And they're most of them framed in this way –
>
> 'Hello there Miss Allan,
> How well you have gone.
> Won't you come and bite
> And perhaps dance to-night?'[80]

That the manager of the Queen's Theatre was subsequently investigated by the Society for the Protection of Children reveals the moral fear that 'Salome' aroused. The sexual undertones of the dance that fashion writers omitted from their reviews of Allan's work also provided fuel for the sketch writers. Just as Colette mocked Mata Hari's pretensions, the music-hall parody cut through the construction of exotic Orientalism that surrounded Allan's performances.[81]

While Maud Allan's long run at the Palace was coming to an end, another American dancer, Ruth St Denis, opened at the Scala in London's West End. Accompanied by 'native Indian' musicians, with well-researched costumes, scenery and atmosphere, she offered dances, 'having the character and movement of the Orient that express the meaning and story in each act'. They included 'the Purda', 'the Street', 'the Cobras or Snake Charmer', 'the Palace', 'the Nautch Girl' and 'the Temple', which featured 'the mystic dance of the five senses'. 'Radha', which St Denis first performed in 1906, was the most daring dance 'of carnal ecstasy which she performed in bare feet, legs and midriff [which] either shocked or entranced the audience'.[82] The Scala's programme notes describe Radha, Krishna's wife and the incarnation of Vishnu, as delivering a message to her priests on a teaching from the Bhagavad Gita. Through the dance, she reminds them 'that the gratification of the senses leads to fulfilment and despair and only through their renunciation does the soul arrive at peace'.[83]

St Denis had seriously studied Hindu dancers, but had also shrewdly switched her act in New York from rapid-fire vaudeville stunts to Eastern performances that offered visual beauty and a spiritual message. 'Now that the dancing cult is so fashionable,' predicted *The Bystander*, '[St Denis] is not unlikely to prove a huge draw.' Her reception in London followed glowing reviews in Berlin, Monte Carlo and the United States and it was rumoured that she had refused £300 a week to dance at less prestigious music halls. Her commitment to the educational element led her to include benefit performances in aid of the 'Indian Relief Fund' in November 1908.

The assumptions contained in Ruth St Denis' performance were a complex critique on the status of Victorian femininity. While the Indian dances were meant to symbolize a woman who lived closer to nature, free from the physical constrictions dictated by contemporary Western fashions, 'exotic' was her only label. The dances conveniently enabled Maud Allan, Mata Hari and Ruth St Denis to move across the stage, proudly displaying their muscular bodies which upper-class women were doomed to keep forever covered. Displaying the female body on stage was to be an empowering experience for the dancer herself, providing a new venue for self-expression.

By 1932 St Denis, addressing the female students at Barnard College, suggested that if women were still barred from the political arena, the theatre offered them a voice: 'Today is woman's hour. It is a woman's chance to offset what man may be doing in the realm of politics and war. It is a woman's place to foster and develop the cultural forces of civilization.'[84] Without following in the footsteps of New Woman, these dancers held out the promise of physical and spiritual enlightenment which male audiences eroticized. But they also represented the female desire to break down the stifling limitations bourgeois society placed upon them; women fantasized too about Salome's wild limbs and John's dripping head.

The Russian dancer Ida Rubenstein added another dimension to the Salome story: the supernatural. In 1908 the young dancer, who like Maud Allan had rejected classical ballet, travelled through Syria and Palestine to research her St Petersburg production of Wilde's *Salome*. Rubenstein had channelled her passion for Greek mythology into her first theatrical success with a private production of *Antigone* with sets by the famous designer Leon Bakst. 'This young woman with her disconcerting and mysterious beauty, this mythical virgin, voluptuous yet frigidly cold, with a will of iron beneath a fragile form,' wrote André Levinson on her Antigone, '. . . became one of the muses of [Leon Bakst] . . . she held for him the all-powerful attraction of the strange, the unreal, of the supernatural.'[85] Following critical acclaim, Rubenstein planned a nude dance for *Salome*.

Ida Rubenstein's story has many striking parallels with Mata Hari's. Rubenstein, in her ambition to become a professional performer, confronted the assumption that the actress and the courtesan were interchangeable. On a trip to Paris in 1907, Rubenstein told her sister that she was going to be an actress; the horrified sister immediately enlisted the help of her husband, the famous Dr Lewinsohn, in packing Ida off to a Saint-Cloud sanatorium until her family in St Petersburg could arrange for her journey home. Ida returned and promptly married Vladimir Horowitz, an obliging, love-struck cousin who was informed shortly after the wedding that his wife would devote her full attention to learning the Salome dance.[86]

The production finally opened in the wake of protests from church and state.

26

The Holy Synod in St Petersburg tried to ban the performance but finally agreed to the actors miming Wilde's script. Copies of the text, which had been translated into Russian, were circulated, however, before the play and John the Baptist's head remained in the wings. Ida Rubenstein recreated Mata Hari's success at the Guimet as the audience watched entranced while she discarded brilliantly coloured veils to 'insinuating oriental music'. The performance caused a sensation among St Petersburg intellectuals but Ida's family was deeply embarrassed and rejected her. Ida swiftly moved on to join Sergei Diaghilev's Ballets Russes – fifty-five dancers trained in the Imperial ballet school on temporary leave from the Imperial theatres of St Petersburg and Moscow – and played Cleopatra during the company's Paris debut in May 1909.[87]

The excitement that Diaghilev's dancers had attracted began to worry Mata Hari who also noticed that Paris was now full of music-hall artistes sporting 'Oriental' costumes. She was no longer unique and the Russian dancers threatened to show up her fear that she was little more than a bold amateur. Despite her impressive record of performing at the best theatres in Paris, winning critical acclaim in Vienna, and a recent billing as a Star of Dance, she felt compelled to expose her imitators as fakes. The anxiety seemed unfounded since Mata Hari had made a personal fortune following her debut with Monsieur Guimet, and she could afford to appear at benefit concerts, including a performance on 20 September 1908 at the Pont-aux-Dames home for 'old and decayed actors and actresses'. She was the star of the afternoon, yet she could not resist commenting on her competitors.

After the now very polished 'Ketjoeboeng' flower dance, accompanied by Paul Vidal, the *chef d'orchestre* at the Paris Opera, Madame Mata Hari and a few intimate friends retired to discuss the new dance craze. Over the last three years, Mata Hari had noticed that 'ladies styling themselves "Eastern dancers" have sprung out of the ground and honour me with imitations'. These would be welcome, she added, except that none were scientifically or aesthetically accurate.

> Born in Java, in the midst of tropical vegetation, I have been taught from my earliest childhood the deep meaning of these dances which constitute a cult, a religion. Only those born and bred there become impregnated with their religious significance, and can impart to them that solemn note to which they can lay claim.[88]

In a direct attack on music-hall artistes who used snake dances in their acts, Mata Hari, who claimed to have danced all over Asia, dismissed them as limp imitators. 'The Eastern dances such as I have witnessed and learnt in my native Java,' she sniffed, 'are inspired by the flowers from which they take their poetry.' On a trip through the Russian interior the previous year, she encountered a 'pseudo Eastern dancer', whose overtures of friendship Mata Hari scorned. 'I could not help remarking to her that if there are real precious stones, there are also imitation ones.'

These remarks reveal much about how Mata Hari saw herself within the profession. She created such mystery about her past through her conflicting stories that she could easily claim an understanding of ritual Javanese dance as a birthright. To avoid the accusations of fraud that she generously heaped upon others, Mata Hari *became* whatever part she played. If she honestly believed she had been born in Java, had travelled throughout Asia and visited Russia – all of which was untrue – she could convince an audience. Her admirers ignored the obvious incongruity in her stories because they believed that 'primitive' cultures thrived on Mata Hari's 'cult' of religious body worship.

As Mata Hari amassed fame and fortune, there was another important role she came to play which later made her such a potent symbol for the espionage writers. On 26 April 1906 she was divorced from Rudolph MacLeod so he could remarry, and during that year she became mistress to Herr Alfred Kiepert. This wealthy landowner, who lived on a sprawling estate outside Berlin with his Hungarian wife, installed Mata Hari in an apartment in the west of the city. That autumn Mata Hari spent a few days with Herr Kiepert, a lieutenant in the Second Westphalian Hussars, at Jauer-Streigau, Silesia, watching the Imperial army manoeuvres.[89]

Earlier that year Mata Hari had reached new heights in her career with an engagement at Monte Carlo Opera House, dancing in Jules Massenet's ballet, *Le Roi de Lahore*. The composer looked on contentedly from the Prince of Monaco's box at her debut on 17 February and, weeks later, sent a note to her apartment in Berlin, reflecting the intimacy of their relationship. 'How happy I am to have been to see you again! Mata, Mata – I am leaving for Paris within a few minutes! Thank you, thank you – and my fervent admiration.'[90] Despite the praise showered upon her by younger men, Mata Hari was still inclined towards father figures like Massenet, then aged sixty-four, who could play the benefactor.

With her sights set on power, Mata Hari followed in the tradition of many grand Parisian courtesans, combining a stage career with a highly public private life. These sexual liaisons attempted to satisfy mutual interests; husbands maintained an active erotic life, completely separate from their marital commitments, while the courtesan enjoyed her financial independence, social prestige and perhaps even a degree of political power. *Musica*, the arts review for France, listed Mata Hari as a Star of Dance in 1908 along with Cléo de Mérode, the official mistress of Belgium's King Leopold II, and the Irish-born dancer Lola Montez, who was King Ludwig of Bavaria's lover. Montez, who had been born Eliza Gilbert and was reborn as a 'Spanish dancer from Seville' on the London stage, had set another precedent for Mata Hari. Her politics were liberal and her religion anti-clerical. Her association with King Ludwig caused 'the Jesuits to spread stories that she was a witch, an agent of the English Freemasons' and British intelligence. Ludwig responded by making Lola a countess and the canoness of a religious order.[91] While the status of a courtesan, like that of any bourgeois wife, was tied directly to her patron's, she was often able to pursue a career on the stage, in politics or even as an intellectual.

During the reign of Napoleon III the courtesan's profession had been carefully regulated and her sponsorship depended on the district in which she lived. A woman with a flat in the rue de Grammont could expect to charge her 'protector' 300 francs a month for gloves and flowers but was free to entertain other men. At the top of the hierarchy ranked the ladies in the Faubourg Saint-Honoré with a count or duke as protector who supplied them with 2,000 francs a month, a mansion, two carriages, two horses, a footman and a chef.[92] Such a lucrative market attracted women from Italy, Russia, England

and the United States who offered, among other delights, skilled conversation, wit, entertainment and superb food.

Such arrangements had survived into *fin-de-siècle* France. Since Mata Hari's first marriage had proved so disastrous, relationships with older men who were willing to support her expensive tastes and make few demands ideally suited her. Such arrangements, which rarely led to marriage, were tolerated in French society where it was assumed that men needed an outlet for their excess sexual urges. Even bourgeois women entered these ranks, as Abraham Flexner found during his research into prostitution in Berlin, London and Paris just before the First World War; the profession included women who lived in comparative luxury, with an occupation and even good social position. Courtesans in Paris were conspicuous during this period as Jean Cocteau learned when his cousin whispered to him: 'There are some grown-ups who go to bed in the daytime. The men are called *lapins* and the women are called *cocottes*.'[93] Keeping up appearances was important and *lapin* and *cocotte* made sure they were seen at famous spas, race tracks, gambling establishments and international resorts.

The courtesan in France, however, was also known for her involvement in political intrigues. The Contessa di Castiglione, whom Cora Pearl once admired in the Bois de Boulogne, was reputed to have been sent to France by Cavour to spy for Italy and instead became the mistress of Emperor Louis Napoleon when she was sixteen. It was also rumoured that the Russian-born Pavia, the wealthiest courtesan by the mid nineteenth century, was a spy for the Germans. The salons she held with her Prussian lover, Count Guido von Donnersmarch, for distinguished men only fell under particular suspicion.[94] Magnus Hirschfeld, in his post-war study on women spies, concluded that from the time of Catherine de Medici, mistresses made the crucial link between espionage and eroticism:

> The excellence of a woman spy stands in inverse relationship to the strength of her own eroticism and for this reason, the best women spies were nearly always grand cocottes, mondaines and demi-mondaines who had gone through the mill. These women all bore names of great repute which were changed as often as the occasion demanded it . . . The battlefield of these ladies is the great French bed.[95]

An actress, continued Hirschfeld, was particularly well suited to the profession of erotic espionage because she usually enjoyed a wide circle of friends, connections in high places and the ability to divorce her emotions from the task at hand. These adventuresses could be observed plying their trade in pre-war Paris, London, Bucharest or Athens.

By the outbreak of war, Mata Hari had become an established performer, well known at theatres in Paris, Vienna, Monte Carlo, Milan and Berlin. She had commanded huge audiences, bigger fees and the praise of serious artists; privately she had been the mistress of powerful men while maintaining her independence. But when the war began, her transformation from a runaway Dutch wife into the greatest living Hindu dancer had pushed her far outside the safety of bourgeois society. When national identity and outward demonstrations of patriotic devotion became tantamount to ensuring personal security, Mata Hari ignored the new rules of conduct. Instead, she continued to hold her identities close to her, like talismans against the coming retribution; her roles as *grande cocotte*, as Javanese maiden and as a theatrical eminence combined to focus suspicion upon her. All carried the seeds of their own destruction. But Mata Hari added to this deadly combination her naïve belief that yet one more role – espionage operator – would only serve her purposes.

CHAPTER TWO

THE BIRTH OF EROTIC ESPIONAGE

The scene is a military ballroom –
The gallant and fair are the dancers –
But who's the Brunette who with eyes black as jet
Fascinates all the Guards and the Lancers?

Olga Pulloffski, the beautiful spy!
The gay continental rapscallion!
Some say she's Russian and some say she's French
But her accent is Gin and Italian.
Shame on you! Shame on you! Oh fie fie!
Olga Pulloffski you beautiful spy![1]

R.P. WESTON AND BERT LEE (1935)

DURING THE WINTER OF 1907 René Puaux, special correspondent of the Paris *Temps*, met Mata Hari aboard the SS *Schleswig* sailing from Marseilles to Khartoum. Puaux was enchanted with his fellow passenger and later wrote of the encounter: 'She has renounced Siva and her cult. She has become Berlinoise, speaks German with an accent that is as un-Oriental as possible . . . Her greatest desire is to forget her brilliant career and success at Monsieur Guimet and the Trocadéro. *Damit ist fertig.* [It is finished.]' But despite various experiments at changing her image, Mata Hari never found another, more successful formula for her art. In Egypt, she observed ancient dances in villages along the Nile but returned to Paris a few weeks later to announce her plans for the new season.[2]

Although Mata Hari easily relaunched her career that winter, the phenomenal success she had once enjoyed was broken by bleak periods when she was forced to pursue engagements. Until the outbreak of war, whenever the public seemed to lose interest in Oriental exotica, Mata Hari tried to invent another, equally powerful fantasy. She often used press interviews to try out these new poses, blithely claiming, as she did to René Puaux, that she had put Monsieur Guimet's behind her. Despite brief attempts at dancing in a Spanish *tableau vivant* and in virginal, laced gowns, her real talent lay in the interpretation of one particular myth. Mata Hari, the Javanese maid who had escaped from an Indian temple and stripped naked in ecstasy before a Hindu idol, had become her only enduring role. But over the years, whenever her financial situation became precarious, Mata Hari the courtesan emerged.

In December 1907, however, Mata Hari – calling herself 'Lady' MacLeod once more – was preparing a dramatic comeback in Paris. 'I have three new Indian dances which I believe will create sensations, but owing to the difficulty of getting the public to interpret them properly, I shall give at first only one,' she told the *New York Herald* in a subtle rebuke to her imitators now packing the music halls. She was happy to be back in Paris, where her audience was more appreciative, and she planned to open at the Salle Fémina in the Champs Elysées on 1 February. Then she claimed that she would venture to London to perform that winter at the Palace Theatre. Although she would never appear on a British stage – the Palace invitation was merely wishful thinking on Mata Hari's part – Parisians still flocked to see her.

That winter, she also gave a buoyant interview to journalist Charles Doury at her temporary home, the Elysée Palace Hotel. Doury marvelled at her sumptuous gown, made of a revealing white lace, as he listened to her tales of hunting expeditions in Egypt and the Indies. She was chagrined that the music halls were now full of her imitators, who debased the noble and sacred meaning of nude dancing. From now on, Mata Hari would dance in a long, high-necked gown with a double train.[3] In May 1908, riding the crest of this new wave, she appeared at a students' reception, the *Galades Pupilles*, where she was lavishly praised for displaying 'for the pleasure of all, the forms of her superior and fascinating talent'.[4]

But whether Mata Hari's new taste for dressing up was an attempt to lure a bourgeois audience or an indication of her yearning for social acceptance, it was short-lived. During this period Mata Hari was wealthy enough to afford to take fewer engagements and perform in several benefits. At the home of her mentor, Monsieur Guimet, she appeared in honour of the Japanese ambassador Baron Kurino; in Houlgate, Normandy, she danced for a local charity and at the Théâtre Fémina, and she took part in a benefit for the Clementine Hospital in Sofia.[5]

This period of drifting ended abruptly in 1911. When Gabriel Astruc arranged a two-month engagement at the Scala Theatre, Milan, Mata Hari knew she had achieved her greatest professional success. Her fee of 3,000 francs a month for her performance of 'The Princess and the Magic Flower' in the Gluck opera *Armide* was irrefutable evidence of stardom. At La Scala she mingled with many of Europe's finest dancers. She was so inspired by the illustrious company that she pushed Astruc, who had sponsored the first Western appearance of the Ballets Russes, for an audition with its director, Serge Diaghilev. Mata Hari was so confident of her success that she had a contract drawn up in anticipation. 'The premier dancer of the Scala in Milan' would make exclusive appearances in St Petersburg for two weeks in March 1912, while reserving her right to perform elsewhere in public or private without Diaghilev's consent. The composer Reynaldo Hahn and the writer Jean Cocteau were approached for the production; the contract was detailed and only needed Diaghilev's signature.[6]

However, the venture ended in humiliation for Mata Hari. Diaghilev insisted that she work for an unpaid trial period and Leon Bakst, who auditioned her in Monte Carlo, demanded that she dance naked before him. The contract was never signed and Mata Hari returned empty-handed to Paris.[7] Despite the glowing reviews 'the premier dancer' had received in Italy, she retired to her villa in Neuilly-sur-Seine, nursing her wounded pride. 'Protect me from the *things which hurt me*, and take away my desire to work,' she wrote to the novelist and critic Louis Dumur. '. . . I want to work again and forsake my life of ease for all the worries that glory necessarily brings with it; I want to feel there is honour in what I do.'[8] Erté, the Russian-born designer who made one of his first theatrical costumes for Mata Hari, realized that what she offered her audiences had little to do with dancing. 'Her talent was not much, in fact it was not enough, so she fabricated this aura of mystery around her in order to conceal any lack of it.'[9]

During that spring and summer, Mata Hari took dancing lessons to bolster her sense of self-worth and professional standing. George Saracco, the former ballet master at the Monte Carlo opera, was engaged to give her dancing exercises, as well as training in method and treatment. Saracco also instructed her in Russian steps and a Spanish habanera – a living painting – which was to be performed against a Goya-esque backdrop. Saracco taught Mata Hari for two months, including three sessions of 'special dancing' in Monte Carlo, and then presented her with a bill for 850 francs. When Saracco's fees were still outstanding in November, he hired Edouard Marise, a debt collector. Mata Hari's lavish taste in clothes, restaurants and entertainments had rapidly exceeded her considerable savings. The furniture in the villa remained unpaid for since her lover, the financier Xavier Rousseau, had gone bankrupt. Worse still, in December she was forced to sue the Paris theatre director Monsieur Antoine for breach of contract.[10] Despite the money that she could command, her engagements were too infrequent to support her spending sprees at the jewellers, couturiers, hat-makers and saddlers.

The previous year Antoine had hired Mata Hari to perform her 'Fire Dance' in *Antar*, a five-act drama by the Syrian writer, Chekri-Ganem, which opened at Monte Carlo in January 1910. Following enthusiastic reviews Antoine decided to take the production to the Odéon in Paris and duly engaged Mata Hari again for 200 gold francs a night for fifteen performances. However, when Antoine began to notice that the dancer was too overweight for ballet and was petulant in rehearsals, he broke off the engagement.[11] Mata Hari sued for her 3,000 franc salary and 5,000 francs in damages.

According to contemporary reports, the hearing of the tribunal on 3 October 1911 had become 'very turbulent'. One newspaper recorded Mata Hari's accusations against her former employer:

> M. Antoine wanted not only the presence of a dancer of name but he also wanted to give his public an original Hindu dance of which the secret has been handed down through the ages without ever having a written tradition. In effect, I possess a real secret of the dance. This particular art and its knowledge of the ancient Hindu dances constitutes for me a precious property. M. Antoine imagined that I would rehearse in the presence of a woman expert such as Madame Mariquita to make possible another artist's interpretation of the 'fire dance', an original Hindu dance of which I have revealed the theme. Such insults constitute a serious case of prejudice.[12]

Mata Hari's testimony revealed her insecurity at being judged, and found wanting, by professional dancers. Mariquita, the mistress of ballet at the Paris Opéra-Comique whom Mata Hari accused of stealing her 'interpretation', had appeared at Antoine's request to give an expert opinion on the 'Hindu dance'.

Although the courts decided in Mata Hari's favour two years later, Monsieur Antoine paid only the outstanding salary and refused to pay damages. The trial and the withholding of funds Mata Hari had counted on resulted in a desperate attempt to keep up appearances by delaying whatever creditors she could.

As usual, she attempted to seize control of the situation and wrote urgently to Astruc enquiring if he had any wealthy friends who might be willing to act as her patron. Thirty thousand francs were needed to prevent embarrassments, such as leaving hotel bills unpaid, and 'to give me the peace of mind necessary to my art'. In exchange for such patronage, she was willing to offer everything she had, including horses and cars.[13] However, Astruc pursued more reliable methods of financial security for Mata Hari and the following year she introduced a new element into her repertoire. Through Astruc, she hired 'The Royal Hindu Musicians' under the direction of an authentic Indian artist. The young Inayat Khan was a Sufi, born in Baroda, whose great-great-grandfather was southern India's last Mogul emperor, 'the Tiger of Mysore'. His orchestra played while Mata Hari danced before selected guests, theatrical agents and critics at her villa in Neuilly. 'Lady MacLeod dances in the light of the Moon to friends' ran *The Tatler*'s headline. 'Recently her ladyship gave a wonderful *soirée d'art* in her magnificent hotel at Neuilly, near Paris, to which only a few special friends were invited. The dances which she performed were most suggestive of religious rites, and love and passion, and were brilliantly executed.' In the photos accompanying the piece, Mata Hari expertly flings diaphanous veils through the air, dressed in her customary corset, beads and bangles. She now wore her black hair in two thick 'Tamil' braids that trailed down her long back. 'Such stuff as dreams are made of,' sighed *The Tatler*'s reviewer, 'a gossamer, a breath.'[14]

The presence of Inayat Khan lent Mata Hari's 'Indian' dances enormous credibility.[15] After the performance at Neuilly, agent H.C. Buysens invited her and Khan's musicians for an audition the following week. Producer Jean Charlot, who had also seen the show, enquired at Astruc's on 21 September whether Mata Hari and Khan's musicians would tour through England and Germany. At first glance Charlot thought 'this production is . . . a little too artistic for the music hall' but he was willing to take the risk and requested postcards of all the performers.

However, nothing came of these tantalizing enquiries. On 18 September, H.B. Marinelli wrote declining an offer to take up the act after several preliminary enquiries about their possible engagement met without success. On the same day, F.O. Sénéchal from the Agence Dramatique et Littéraire Franco-Anglo-Américaine also sent apologies, turning down Mata Hari, 'and the musicians Hindu'.[16] Jean Fuller, the biographer of Khan's daughter Noor (who was a wireless operator in France for the British SOE and shot at Dachau in 1944), mentions only that Inayat Khan and his brothers played for Mata Hari on a European tour in 1912. The enterprise, however, was much more serious.

By December that year, Inayat Khan was acting as 'master of music' for Mata Hari's performance at the Université des Annales where she danced before an audience of young women and wealthy matrons. At the request of

Madame Brisson-Sarcey, she exposed a naked shoulder and was applauded for dancing 'with an enveloping and feline grace that is her secret'. Paul Olivier, music critic of *Le Matin*, had hired Mata Hari and her friend, Madame Sorga, to illustrate his lecture to the university on Javanese, Indian and Japanese temple festivals. The programme, in which Mata Hari danced 'the legend of the princess and the magic flower' and 'a prayer to the moon', proved so popular that soon afterwards the actor Lucien Guitry mounted a production of *Kismet* with a 'Hindu' piece at the Sarah Bernhardt Theatre.

But the revival of interest in Oriental dances proved temporary, forcing Mata Hari to change her tactics once again. She opened at the Folies Bergère in Paris on 28 June 1913 for a summer season in 'La Revue en Chemise' as a Spanish dancer and performed an old favourite – an Oriental 'special attraction' – in the play *Marie Marais*. 'It is the power of feminine charm at its greatest which she succeeds in expressing in these dances,' glowed the *Comoedia*'s reviewer.[17] An invitation soon came to dance in the fiftieth performance of *The Minaret*, a play at the Théâtre de la Renaissance, starring Cora Laparcerie, Harry Baur, Marcelle Yrven and Jean Worms.[18] Erté, the costume designer, met Mata Hari several times during fittings for her 'Oriental' creation for the third-act Nuptial Festival and he noticed her vulnerability.

> She was not really beautiful. She had a sensuous body, but she lacked personality and there was even something a little vulgar about her, although she would come to fittings wearing smart, classically tailored suits. She was always even-tempered and easy to get along with ... Mata Hari acted out her romantic fantasies.[19]

The famed courtesan Liane de Pougy was even more critical: 'she had a loud voice and a heavy manner, she lied, she dressed badly, she had no notion of shape or colour, and she walked mannishly.'[20] These criticisms, like those of Colette's, reveal that Mata Hari was never taken seriously by certain influential artists in Paris. The modernists might have praised Mata Hari as a *symbol* of the 'classical nude' but personally they found her 'a little vulgar'. Her triumphs in Monte Carlo and Milan, her well-tailored suits and prestigious but ageing lovers, were not enough for an entrée into the right circles.

Misia Sert, a wealthy 'intellectual hostess', was Diaghilev's closest friend and most enthusiastic patron in France. Her apartment on the Quai Voltaire in Paris was a pre-war meeting place for artists such as Picasso, Jean Cocteau, Colette and Diaghilev's dancers. But Sert was scathing about Mata Hari and recalled their first meeting on her yacht at Deauville, the fashionable resort in Normandy, where a friend persuaded her to meet this young(ish) dancer who wanted an introduction to Diaghilev. '[She was] of rather insignificant appearance [but] I very amiably told her she was ravishing,' remembered Sert. 'Before I had time to finish my sentence she was quite naked.' Mata Hari performed a few of her nude 'plastic' poses and Sert dismissed her as a 'sorry exhibition'. Sert's second recollection of meeting Mata Hari, however, reveals more about the hostess than the dancer:

> Many years passed; the war broke out, and one evening Boni de Castellane arrived at the [hotel] Meurice in his car to fetch Sert [Misia's husband] and myself to take us to a Hindoo dancer, of whom he had heard wonders, and who was to give us a little performance all to ourselves. The car took us for quite a long way before it stopped outside a sordid-looking house in the Paris suburbs. We were asked to go to the first floor, to a bedroom that reeked of poverty. Four little Hindoos in turbans were squatting on the floor, picking at guitars. At last, dressed in three triangles of jewel paste, the expected wonder appeared. To my astonishment, I immediately recognised my candidate for the Ballets Russes. Alas! She had made no progress. She was a trite night-club dancer, whose art consisted in showing her body. The musicians frantically twanged at their guitars. The whole thing was grim, miserable and rather nauseating.[21]

Where Misia Sert's memory failed, she invented. Mata Hari had left Paris by July 1914 and was never to perform in the city again, while the illustrious Inayat Khan – whose musicians played sitars rather than guitars – had married, moved to London and founded England's first Sufi Order.[22] But just as Mata Hari had aroused Colette's jealousy and spite, Sert conveniently transformed the celebrated dancer into her failed protégée ('*my candidate* for the Ballets Russes') performing with the pathetic Indian musicians. Sert emerges from the episode having dispensed her charity, after urging her husband to give the miserable creatures a handful of francs, and bolstered her superior social position. This petty-minded description, however, reveals that while Mata Hari could woo and often win the critics' approval, her success also made her enemies.

Sert's vicious and inaccurate attack on Mata Hari may have stemmed from her own bitterness about the French social acceptance of *les grandes horizontales*. Alfred Edward, owner of the Paris newspaper *Le Matin* and Misia Sert's second husband, had openly entertained his mistresses and his very public affair with the actress Ginette Lantelme, known on stage as Mademoiselle Léa, ended in scandal when she fell from from his yacht and drowned. Edward's second celebrated lover was the Italian diva, Lina Cavalieri, with whom Mata Hari had appeared on the same programme at Cécile Sorel's in 1905. Cavalieri not only took New York's Metropolitan Opera House by storm but 'was taken up with enthusiasm by a certain section of fashionable New York society', including Mrs Jacob Astor.[23] Mata Hari was categorized with those female performers who viewed their married lovers as patrons of the arts. But to Diaghilev's great friend, Misia Sert, Mata Hari hadn't enough talent to qualify as an artiste and so her criticism was unsparing.

While art critics looked hypocritically askance at Mata Hari's conduct, even greater approbation was reserved for her in more bourgeois quarters. Major Emile Massard, commander at the headquarters of the armies of Paris, would later claim that 'the supreme disorder' in Mata Hari's dance reflected the turmoil in her affairs. Félix Xavier Rousseau, a politician and financier, who met Mata Hari at a private engagement, was her 'last victim' before the war. Massard recounted how Rousseau was so bewitched by her dance he fell instantly in love, and neglected his wife and children for several months. Mata Hari allowed Rousseau to find and furnish the exquisite villa at 11 rue Windsor in Neuilly-sur-Seine which left him penniless; after they parted, he lived as a recluse for a decade.[24]

The reality, however, reveals that during 1910 Mata Hari lived at the Château de la Dorée, in Esvre, where Rousseau paid the rent but visited only at weekends. During the week, he returned to Paris where he lived with his wife and family, and ran his private bank at 41 rue Vivienne, near the Paris stock exchange. A friend of Rousseau's contacted the château's owner, the Countess de la Taille-Trétinville, and explained that it would be occupied by 'Madame Rousseau', the Dutch widow of Lord MacDonald, a former governor of India. Although Xavier and Mata Hari continued their arrangement for several months, by the end of 1911 Rousseau's bank began to collapse. He was forced to give up the lease on the château and with Mata Hari he moved back to Paris where they set up house at 11 rue Windsor. Before his fall, Xavier lavished gifts on his lover and bought her four thoroughbred horses for her to ride through the nearby woods. But under the strain of Rousseau's impending bankruptcy, they quarrelled and he left, probably hiding from his creditors in seclusion.[25] He ended his brilliant career as a humble seller of champagne.[26]

Emile Massard's argument that Rousseau was Mata Hari's *victim* was consistent with the prevailing belief that a woman's corrupt nature provoked adulterous male desires. The mistress bore sole responsibility for this moral crime and men like Rousseau or Alfred Edward were simply victims of 'tempting sirens and vampires'.[27] 'When a man has used up his fortune to satisfy the caprices of his mistress, when he has accumulated dishonour and despair,' biographer Charles Heymans wrote of Mata Hari, 'she coldly lets him fall.' Heymans repeated allegations made by the journalist and poet Paul Olivier that her stories about Rudolph MacLeod's brutality were invented to elicit sympathy from the press.

Mata Hari, said Olivier, had once told him that her husband was so violent, 'her body still carried the marks of his blows'.[28] According to another source, she always wore a cotton '*cache-sein*' (breast concealer) or bra which she stuffed with goose or duck down to conceal these 'wounds'. She always wore it, even in bed, and told enquiring lovers that it hid her breasts which were disfigured when, in a fit of rage, MacLeod had bitten off both nipples.[29] However, according to the testimony of Léon Bizard, the Saint-Lazare prison doctor who examined Mata Hari during her internment, 'The truth was much more simple; [she] had small breasts with highly discoloured overdeveloped nipples, and she was not interested at all in showing them.'[30] These could be the 'marks' that led Olivier to believe Mata Hari would say anything to attract attention. But the journalist was not always so bitter and had once written rapturous letters to this 'terrible man-eater'.[31] Following her appearance at the Université des Annales illustrating Olivier's lecture on Oriental temple festivals, he sent a letter of thanks. 'I put at your feet, dear Madame, my most fervent and grateful homage, and beg of you to consider me sufficiently worthy to accept the certitude of my profound and absolute devotion.'[32] They had been lovers before the war and were still corresponding in 1913, but if Olivier was among those whom Mata Hari had 'coldly let fall' this might explain his later disillusionment.[33]

But even if Mata Hari's breasts were still intact, there is strong evidence that MacLeod psychologically tormented his wife and often wished for her death. Even so, in a period when a husband had the right to control his wife, the abuse Madame MacLeod experienced was probably considered unexceptional.

The image of Mata Hari as a young woman tyrannized by an older man would, however, have contradicted her role as an exotic courtesan, temple dancer and socialite. While male audiences might vicariously thrill to her descriptions of young Indian temple dancers being whipped for disobedience, the success of this 'Oriental image' rested on its stark contrast with presumed European notions of domesticity, motherhood, marital relations and emotional dependency. Mata Hari's memories of a bitter marriage struck too close to home; the fantasy of an indomitable, bewitching, almost magical woman was infinitely more satisfying than her complex reality.

By 1913, however, Mata Hari was more concerned by Isadora Duncan's triumphal return to Paris after her blazing tour through Russia than by critics of her sexual behaviour. Mata Hari's Oriental dances paled in comparison to the 'divine Isadora', flushed with new ideas, and she was soon obliged to accept less prestigious engagements. After a warm reception in Paris, she appeared at a 'café-chantant-cinema' at the Trianon Palace in Palermo, Sicily, that autumn. A film projector rolled alongside Mata Hari as she danced, and the remaining nine acts on the programme included a performing dog.[34] After fulfilling her obligations, she returned to Paris and began working on new dances while Astruc continued his enquiries with agents in England and Germany.

The following summer, the London magazine *The Bystander* featured a graphic photo of 'Mata Stari [sic] in the very latest mode', dressed in a sleeveless white gown gathered at the hips and just below the knees. A flowered hat frames her profile and she holds a fan seductively to her face. Most striking of all is her hand that catches the bodice of her dress in a blatantly sexual gesture. 'The principal dancer of the Scala in Milan, the Grand Opera in Monte Carlo and the Berlin Metropol will be in the new production at that theatre,' the article announced. 'Altogether we feel that Madame Stari justifies her name.'[35]

Astruc had secured the German engagement which would start at the beginning of September. Mata Hari arrived at Berlin's Cumberland Hotel, armed with a ballet she had written entitled *Chimère ou Vision Profane* ('Wild Dream or Profane Vision') which she hoped to produce in Germany. Her part was vintage Mata Hari: a young priest is haunted by the vision of a goddess, 'a woman admirably beautiful, tall and slender'.[36] Mata Hari still projected herself as a feminine ideal that not even a priest with his vows of celibacy could resist.

Despite this new venture, she feared that her days as a goddess who could weave an 'ecstatic, a sacred dance' were numbered. She was approaching her tenth year as a performer and even highly celebrated dancers such as Saharet, who once inspired Otto Julius Bierbaum to date a letter from Munich 'in the month of Saharet', had to retire gracefully from the stage. It was also a dangerous age for a courtesan as Liane de Pougy discovered from the taunts of her lover, the playwright Henry Bernstein. ' "Soon you'll be forty, my girl. You'll be *forty years old* . . . No one will want you any more." '[37] A dancer could only hope her 'vogue' would span a decade and then, 'whether she was Australian, American or only German, people no longer cared'.[38] Combined with Mata Hari's fear of ageing was her insecurity, stemming from the knowledge that she was completely self-taught. Josephine Baker, another unschooled performer, once said, 'I had no talent when I started and I still have none . . . My personality was created by the press.'[39] Mata Hari had once made a similar confession to a friend; she was never any good at dancing, her audiences came to watch her strip. She too owed her success to gushing journalists.

But if Mata Hari realized that her future in the theatre was precarious, she could always broaden her horizons as a *grande horizontale*. After all, this was merely another form of performance which was indulged in by well-kept 'Stars of Dance' such as Cléo de Mérode, Caroline 'La Belle' Otero and the Folies Bergère's leading singer, Lina Cavalieri.

Mata Hari's on-stage ambitions were matched by her desire for lovers with the highest military rank, whom she pursued with equal devotion. General Messimy, who was the French minister of war in August 1914, discovered the truth of Mata Hari's conviction that, 'when I really want something I develop a stupefying power'.[40]

Monsieur Guimet, Messimy's compatriot from Lyons, had introduced the general to Mata Hari after her meteoric rise to fame in 1906. 'She danced marvellously,' Messimy recalled, 'she wasn't pretty; she had something else. She was a splendid creature of mystery.' He was then married, and divulges little about the specifics of their relationship, but admits they met riding through the Bois de Boulogne where Mata Hari 'would throw me engaging smiles'. But he sensed she was more attracted to his position than his personality. His friends warned that she was a *'mangeuse d'hommes terrible'* – a vicious man-eater – with a reputation for wreaking financial ruin. But then, virtually every woman of the demi-monde in early twentieth-century Paris had this reputation. As the famous courtesan, Léonide Leblanc, wrote in a fictional dialogue between Alice, a world-weary courtesan, and her protégée Lucie, their motto was, 'money and more money, always money'.[41] Mata Hari was a *femme galante* who sold herself to whomever she pleased, frequented the city's smartest quarters and displayed a degree of luxury indispensable to the maintenance of her rank.[42]

With men, Mata Hari was distinguished by her determination. She 'bombarded' Messimy with invitations and letters and even arrived on his doorstep to befriend his wife (whom he later divorced). He once tried to avoid an inopportune meeting with Mata Hari in Nice. But when they suddenly found themselves 'nose-to-nose' at a Monte Carlo casino, Messimy declined Mata Hari's suggestion for a walk in the moonlight by making the excuse that he was just leaving for Paris. Undeterred by the lie, Mata Hari comfortably installed herself in his train compartment – as if she were at home – where he found her the following day.[43]

Messimy had a vested interest in portraying this relationship as an almost entirely one-sided affair, subscribing to Massard's belief in blaming the woman. It was much easier for Messimy – whatever the reality of their affair – to make Mata Hari responsible for his adultery; she conveniently became the man-eater who swallowed up lovers and their fortunes. Whenever her own status in the theatre was jeopardized, her lovers grew in importance. If deprived of public adoration, these men privately satisfied her longings while providing all the necessary props for maintaining appearances: an apartment, jewels, furs and spending money. But her predilection for 'the most highly-placed personalities of the military, politics and diplomacy' would soon arouse suspicion.

During the summer of 1914, while Mata Hari waited for her six-month run at Berlin's Metropol to begin, she renewed her acquaintance with her former lover, Lieutenant Alfred Kiepert. A Berlin journalist noticed the couple, 'talking very animatedly and confidentially in a booth in one of the most fashionable restaurants in town'. Had she lost 'her several thousand [marks] which she had received from Mr K as a farewell present,' speculated the writer, 'or . . . was it love that brought her back to him?'[44] Whatever her motives, Mata Hari's affairs were public knowledge in Germany and therefore in France, while she remained oblivious to their consequences. Later, under interrogation by the French, she admitted that at the end of their affair Kiepert gave her 100,000 marks at the time and two drafts of 100,000 marks each postdated for the end of 1908 and 1909. Such transactions would later form the French prosecution's basis for their accusations that, even before the war, Mata Hari had been working for the Germans.[45]

Europe's fading star, like thousands of other travellers to Germany that summer, however, had at first been oblivious to signs of the impending turmoil. She would later describe her latent realization that the German public was intoxicated with the prospect of war:

> Towards the end of July 1914 [probably 28 July, the Austrian invasion of Serbia] I was dining one evening in a private restaurant room with one of my lovers, the chief of police Griebel, when we heard the noise of a disturbance. Griebel, who had not been informed about the meeting, took me along to the place where it was held. An enormous crowd was staging a completely mad demonstration in front of the Emperor's palace and screaming, 'Deutschland über Alles'.[46]

On 6 August 1914 Mata Hari sent her baggage on ahead and boarded a train for Paris via Switzerland. But new regulations now required travellers to show identification papers and Mata Hari was forced to return to Berlin the following day. She then travelled to Frankfurt am Main to request a travel permit from the Dutch consulate.[47] She began to worry that even if she could reach Paris, her villa in Neuilly-sur-Seine would be boarded up or confiscated by the French government because she was a foreigner. 'I can't go to France,' she wrote to Baron Fredi Lazarini, an Austrian cavalry officer and former lover, from the Grand Hotel on 25 August. 'I'm afraid I won't find my beautiful house there any more.' In a postscript, she added, 'Tomorrow I'll be going to Berlin – the Metropol is closed but I can't get away any more.'[48] On returning again to Berlin, she found her agent was holding her money; the costumier, fearing that he wouldn't be paid, kept her jewellery; and a fashion house had confiscated her furs. Her bank account was blocked because she was considered to be a French resident and all trading with the enemy had ceased. A Dutch compatriot at her hotel took pity on her and bought her a train ticket for Holland. A hastily scribbled line next to the advance notices of her Berlin performance in her photo album read simply, 'War – left Berlin – theatre closed.'[49]

As was the case with many foreigners trapped in Germany, the immediate consequences of the war provoked enormous shock. As Mata Hari later told her French interrogators, she was arrested several times 'accused of being [a] Russian [spy]' and noticed that 'the police treated all foreigners like animals'. But for Mata Hari, the rules that had guided her career were instantly inverted;

the exotic images that she had nurtured – Oriental dancer, cosmopolitan adventuress, mistress of high officials – were now considered distasteful and even dangerous. She could not insulate herself from the massive influence of propaganda and rumour that stoked a jingoistic fervour.

Throughout Europe female images – from whore to madonna – were re-invented to deliver messages about patriotism and the national struggle. Mari-anne, the bare-breasted figure of the French Republic featured in Delacroix's painting 'Liberty Guiding the People', reappeared as a goddess of war. In George Scott's 1917 poster for the Banque Nationale de Crédit, Marianne brandishes a sword in her right hand and a flag in her left; dressed in ancient Grecian robes, she fearlessly exposes her left breast in tribute to the Amazons of Greek mythology.[50] Mata Hari's 'nude of art' and the modernists' attempt to redefine the female body in aesthetic terms were immediately appropriated. Marianne's bared flesh became once again a desexualized symbol of national defiance rather than an invitation to erotic dreams. In other posters, she floated like a spirit above the battlefields or offered her breast to nurture the wounded soldier, dying for the fatherland's glory.

The propagandists' 'good woman', who was often an idealized mother-figure sacrificing her life to give succour to the troops or contentedly raising warriors, needed an antithesis. The dark foreigner, the manipulative courte-san who rejected her maternal duty to run a salon and play politics behind the scenes, became the perfect foil. Major James Edmonds, responsible for counter-intelligence and 'secret service' at the British War Office, lectured in 1907 that 'the use of *women* in procuring intelligence for the Germans is very considerable,' since they used 'professional *horizontales* [prostitutes]'.[51]

The spy-seductress would become an increasingly popular symbol for the sexual anxieties and tensions between the sexes that the circumstances of war provoked. Women 'manned' the industrial sector, managed their households without fathers or husbands and joined newly formed military services in Britain and America. In France Mata Hari's form of dancing, which was tolerated in the decadent *belle époque*, now threatened marital harmony. The mistress, who before the war signified a middle-class gentleman's conspicuous consumption, ran counter to the national mood of sacrifice and restraint. 'The man, in effect, wants the glory of possessing a woman of the world; star of the cinema, theatre, music-hall artist, dancer,' wrote Charles Heymans of the 'mistress phenomenon'. 'It matters little whether this woman has beauty or has any real talent.'[52] At the outbreak of war European armies organized prostitution for the troops, while the slogan for wives and daughters in Paris was gaiety – so that soldiers on leave could 'have their morale revived'.[53] Casual sexual relations may have proliferated between soldiers and women in the occupied zones, but the courtesans Heymans describes fled to neutral countries such as Switzerland and Spain. In popular fiction and in the public mind, the spoiled playmate of the bourgeois husband had become the 'enemy within', the heartless vamp who uses her sexuality to bleed men of vital military secrets as well as money.

Mata Hari fitted the bill perfectly and, bolstered by her own fantasy that she was irresistible to any audience, she blithely accepted the part. Even though she would live quietly in Holland until 1915, her detractors would later interpret her theatrical career as an excuse for treasonable deception. 'The false temple dancer, the false nautch-girl, the great cosmopolitan courtesan,' Alfred Morain wrote of her legend in 1930, 'all these roles masked the international spy, paid by the enemy to worm out military, political and diplomatic secrets – the last between France and her allies.'[54] Her carefully constructed masks which hid her frailties were interpreted as the perfect vehicle for political intrigue.

The spy-courtesan, however, had already become part of the national consciousness when Mata Hari decided to leave Berlin after war erupted. Any traveller in a foreign country might be suspect, but for the first time women were scrutinized on a mass scale and spy scares often focused on domestic scenes. In Britain, espionage writers had fuelled rumours that the Germans had trained nannies, nurses, schoolgirls and waitresses as spies to penetrate the country. British women were also vulnerable to entrapment in these nefarious schemes. Vernon Kell's notes on 'war delusions and spy scares' (he was the first head of MI5) mention an incident in 1915 when an English kitchen-maid claimed she had become enslaved to a German spy who forced her to make a plan of the Bristol Channel and to operate a Heath-Robinson type of signalling device called the 'Maxione'. Basil Thomson, head of Scotland Yard during the war, was amazed that a 'quite uneducated' sixteen-year-old girl could invent such an elaborate fraud. Spy plots in films, novels and comic books at the time were so popular, however, that even a 'simple, pleasant-faced country girl' could translate the fantasy into real life. Her confession not only brought her into contact with the highest police officials in the country, but gave her an unprecedented power over her employer; according to Thomson, the stories 'reduced her mistress to such distress that she did not dare leave the house'.[55] Like contemporary urban legends, the details of the spy stories were irrelevant and their meaning lay in the need to understand bizarre, frightening and potentially dangerous events that might have happened.[56]

Vernon Kell dismissed the 'Maxione' incident as 'the fantastic imaginings of a . . . girl's brain' but continued to monitor equally sensational reports of German governesses harbouring trunkloads of bombs and women hanging out their laundry in code – shorts and longs.[57] If Kell regarded such scares as a nuisance – and his office received an average of 300 cases of alleged spying a day during the war – they reflected widespread fears nourished in the vacuum that heavy censorship had created. Winifred Tower, a young woman with brothers in the Royal Navy who lived on the Isle of Wight, thought to be vulnerable to invasion, regarded all Germans with suspicion. She noted in her diary on 20 August 1914: 'There were two German servants living in a house near us who tried persistently to get into the Red Cross Hospital and were most abusive when refused. There were some very funny stories about them, they kept curious hours and we all felt sure they were spies.'[58] Another diarist noted on 13 August 1914 that Caterham residents now avoided Mrs Sekilling, an Englishwoman whose husband had become a naturalized Englishman several years before and was a manager of the Dresden bank; both were suspected of spying.[59] Even more insidious, however, were intelligence officers like Robert Baden-Powell, founder of the Boy Scout Movement, who fuelled the fantasy in his *Aids to Scouting for NCOs and Men* in 1914 with a warning that 'certain foreign governesses could tell you a great deal about our army'.[60]

In Germany officials and citizens were equally vigilant in looking out for potential agents, drawing on their own legends about Russian female agents. Felix Gross, a German secret service agent, claimed his office had an index of Russian spies that included: two grand duchesses, fourteen princesses, seventeen countesses, numerous members of the higher nobility as well as wives of ministers, ambassadors and scientists. These women, who were alleged to have operated mainly in diplomatic circles, were known as 'drawing-room geese', 'hotel bugs' or 'charity frogs'.[61]

However, as accounts of travellers from Allied countries stranded in Germany in August 1914 reveal, any foreign woman was suspect. Kitty and Rosie Neal of Hilgay, Norwich, members of the dance company 'Five Royal Brewsters', were scheduled to open a show in Hamburg at the beginning of August 1914. The first sign of trouble came when the landlady of their boarding house asked them to leave because 'she had heard the rumours of the war and wouldn't have us in her house as we were English.' That evening, their performance at the Hamburg theatre was cancelled and all boats to England were forced to remain in the port.

The only shipping offices still open were crowded with other foreigners fleeing the country and when the mail ships stopped arriving the women were stranded without money. As Rosie Neal noted, 'A terrible thing this, no ship to get to England, no work to do and no money to live on.' They couldn't leave because the British consul had stopped issuing passports and the German government restricted foreigners from leaving the country until the mobilization ended a fortnight later. There were ominous signs of impending violence; one night a man brandishing a stick chased Rosie Neal and Edie, another member of the Royal Brewsters, through the streets. A clergyman who tried to help the dancers arrange their passage home was arrested as a spy and an English 'lady' who caught the last boat to Grimsby was forced to return in a German cruiser and was held for thirty-six hours on espionage charges. 'We are nothing more or less than prisoners,' Rosie noted in her diary, 'true we are allowed to walk about the streets but we are not allowed to speak unless we speak German . . . people look at us as though we have done something terrible.'

Eventually the American consul authorized US passports for the women, making them temporary citizens while Rosie Neal thought bitterly about those 'ladies that had money' who had crossed the border long ago. En route to England, the women were questioned at the Dutch border where 'the trembling and cross-examining began, we lived in holy dread of being sent back and even worse than that, to prison.' Kitty Neal eventually persuaded a sceptical German guard that five Americans could travel on a single passport as she was their teacher and they were her pupils. Later that day, they were released.[62]

But not only dancers were suddenly suspected and hauled into local police stations for interrogation. Daisy Williams, an English schoolgirl studying music and German while living with her mother in Dresden, was arrested as a Russian spy on 4 August at Bielefeld. Since spies were so much a product of fiction, even the most outrageous and irrational stories were taken seriously. 'Rumours were rife of Russians trying to get over the frontier with gold, disguised as women – this particular tale had so caught hold of the popular imagination that people were hauled out of cars and shot without arguing,' Daisy Williams noted of their journey to Bielefeld from Dresden. Such episodes revealed the extent to which the normal rules of social behaviour were inverted. The ultimate role-reversal – men dressed as women in order to escape an enemy – which was traditionally associated with the contained chaos of Mardi Gras, reflected a fear of total disintegration. At the station leaving Dresden, Daisy, her mother and a group of English friends watched with horror as a German officer was arrested as a spy. But by the time they reached Magdeburg the following day, they had witnessed so many arrests that the incident at Dresden seemed insignificant.

In Hanover, Daisy Williams noted that the 'enthusiasm [for war] was to fever pitch' as mobilized soldiers at a café where she was sitting broke into *Deutschland über Alles*. The following day the windows in the railway carriages where Daisy and the English passengers sat were shut at every bridge guarded by armed sentries for fear of bombs being thrown. 'Where, if you hang a few hankies or gloves on a window sill to dry a watchful neighbour would report you to the police for making signs to the enemy,' wrote Daisy. As they had in Britain, innocent domestic items suddenly became metaphors for secret coded language that required everyone to search for enemy activity. These sinister gloves and hankies, sheets and pillowcases also signified how quickly the war had invaded every area of life. Even more disturbing, these sightings revealed a widespread willingness among ordinary citizens to involve themselves in this new kind of warfare. Just as anyone could be a spy, any good citizen could become a patriotic spy-catcher.

When Daisy Williams and her English compatriots pulled into Bielefeld, the station master flanked by his officials burst into their compartment. They were accused of being Russian spies and planting bombs in their luggage, and were marched to the police station by soldiers with fixed bayonets while the other passengers called out, 'Russian spies, Russian spies.' Several hours later, 'there was a clanking of swords and spurs in the passage and the head of police came in, very pompous and resplendent.' He looked over their passports, and told the official in charge that their arrest was 'a very stupid thing', but placed them under armed supervision at a nearby hotel for the following week. Daisy Williams and her mother returned to Dresden, eventually reaching England via the Dutch border just before the battle of the Marne.[63]

In Paris, Misia Sert recalled that 'in those first few months of the war . . . spy-mania had literally unhinged every brain'. Throughout the city, posters on windowpanes in shops, trams, the Underground and hoardings warned, 'Keep silent, beware of enemy ears listening to you' while in the country, farmers kept a constant watch.[64] Aviator Marthé Richard, who later worked as a double-agent for the French counterespionage bureau, described 'spy psychosis' as 'a serious form of mental derangement among hot-headed patriots' at the outbreak of war. While driving to Paris after a flying competition, Richard was accused of being a spy in a small village near Amiens. A crowd yelled as she drove past, '"Death to the spy!" . . . in a swelling volume of fury,' and forced her to stop. A local gendarme arrested her while the mob cried, 'Lynch her! Kill the spy!' Shaken with fear, Richard broke into tears at the local police station but was forced to spend two days in jail before a telegram from the authorities in Paris secured her release. But even on her return to Paris, hitching a lift on a French army transport truck she was reminded that the 'psychosis' was everywhere. A young officer Richard befriended jokingly told her that she looked like a spy since 'they are usually rather pretty like you and they are also sociable and rather enigmatical'. Richard put his flirtatious accusation down to reading too many thrillers and detective stories.[65]

As spy mania gripped the public imagination throughout Europe, the fictional link between espionage and entertainment became more firmly established. In Britain theatres were believed to harbour misfits, foreigners and people whose reputations might make them vulnerable to blackmail by enemy agents. Even in Holland, which remained neutral throughout the war, it became impossible to reproduce the demi-monde of Paris and Mata Hari never penetrated Dutch indifference to her work. Her appearance at The Hague's Royal Theatre, following Donizetti's opera *Lucia di Lammermoor* in December 1914, proved a moderate success. Her 'French Folies', an extract of a ballet about an eighteenth-century king with music by François Couperin, saw Mata Hari in a familiar mode, as she danced through 'eight moods': virginity, modesty, ardour, hope, faith, fidelity, change and flirtatiousness. But despite warm reviews, there was only a repeat performance in Arnhem that year.[66]

By August the following year, she had settled into a small house at 16 Nieuwe Uitleg in The Hague and tried to adjust to Dutch provincial life. But without a public and with only an elderly lover to feed her desire for adoration, she lapsed into misery. She would later write that in Holland, 'my cheerfulness is as if it were strangled'.[67] All her possessions were locked in her cherished villa at Neuilly, there were few trains to Paris, borders had closed and the city of her greatest triumphs was momentarily beyond reach. France was at war, the *belle époque* had ended as millions of men were mobilized and in this atmosphere a production by Mata Hari, famous for her nude 'Oriental' dancing and for courting powerful men, would have appeared obscene.

If Mata Hari had remained in Holland, she would have survived and perhaps even been able to return to Paris after the war. But life in The Hague had little to recommend it for a woman as accustomed to the excitement of the stage as Mata Hari was. Instead, she chose to return to France in 1915, travelling via England and Spain, in an attempt to resume her former life. But as she would soon learn, this was impossible. The shift in public mood had already banished her imitators from the Parisian stage. The role Frenchwomen were now expected to play is revealed in an article from the *Journal des Instituteurs*' 'review of reviews'. The greed for material acquisition had driven German women to support the barbarity of this war which had yet to tarnish French innocence.

> The *Petit Provincial* protests against those Gretchens whose letters were found on the German prisoners: they wrote asking their fiancés . . . to be sure to bring them back souvenirs . . . By souvenirs they meant valuable jewellery, gold watches, rings set with precious stones, fine linen, works of art . . . While the gentle French schoolgirl treasures the little wild flowers, or the prettily coloured engravings that remind her of a favourite girl friend . . . the Teuton female, coarse, thieving, dreams of showy expensive Nuremberg knick-knacks, then, being a girl, after all, of richly flowing gowns.[68]

As Mata Hari's accusers gathered evidence against her, as we shall see, her carefully constructed Orientalism could easily be translated into Teutonic characteristics. René Puaux's interview had already established that underneath Mata Hari's glittering gowns beat a German, and therefore an enemy's, heart. She was no longer the unknown, half-glimpsed foreigner, but the Germans' own spy-courtesan.

CHAPTER THREE

FINAL PERFORMANCES

> Such is the real significance of the Secret War, whose importance
> and whose perils are consequently ignored that it is represented in
> the symbolic guise of a dancer with golden slippers, who seeks to
> pluck from the lips of a chance lover, the secret of the exact location
> of an army corps.
>
> MAJOR GEORGES LADOUX (1932)[1]

I N EARLY DECEMBER 1915, bored with her life in The Hague, Mata Hari
made her first wartime trip to Paris. She had reached a comfortable financial
arrangement with her current lover, the Baron Edouard van der Capellen, a colonel in the Dutch cavalry, who paid her rent and provided a generous allowance.
They were old friends and had been reintroduced two months after Mata Hari's
return to Holland. Now the married Baron visited her whenever he was on leave
from the front, allowing his mistress a degree of independence. But Paris was
on her mind and on 27 November she collected her new Dutch passport and
bought her ticket for France. She had obtained an English visa on her French
passport from the British consulate in Rotterdam several months earlier, which
she would need for the journey. Since the war, the only way to reach France
from Holland was to travel to England, or through Switzerland or Spain. On
this trip, Mata Hari planned to collect her silverware, linen and furniture from
her villa at Neuilly which she now required in The Hague.[2]

Her return to the city where she had been reborn as Mata Hari, adored
by audiences and praised by critics, must have been painful. As she wrote
wistfully to a friend the following year, 'since we cannot live in Paris, we will
talk about it and that is something at least.'[3] From her room at the Grand
Hotel at 12 Boulevard des Capucines, she organized the task of collecting her
household goods from a storage firm named Maple.[4] She packed ten cases and
sold everything else from Neuilly, including the four thoroughbred horses that
were a gift from her former lover, Félix Rousseau. A story went round the city
that rather than sell her favourite horse Vichnou to a new master, she plunged
a golden dagger into his heart.[5] The absurdity of the claim reveals how strongly
she still represented a figure whose passion bordered on wild excess. But her
ties to Paris were strong; on this trip she renewed her intimate relationship
with her mentor Henry de Marguérie who was now the second secretary of
the French legation in The Hague.[6] Marguérie had helped Margaretha Zelle
MacLeod launch her career in 1904, and he was a man to whom she could
turn in a crisis or for reassurance that she was still desirable. Neither expected
a deeper commitment and Mata Hari had soon become involved with another
hotel guest, the Marquis de Beaufort, a Belgian officer.

Mata Hari, although ostensibly in Paris to settle her business affairs, wrote
to her agent Gabriel Astruc to ask if Serge Diaghilev might like to see 'some new

and rather strange dances' she had created. The Baron was generous so she didn't need money, she wrote, but she longed to work again.[7] Misia Sert confirms that during the war Mata Hari pursued Diaghilev's interest as a way to relaunch her career. When war was declared the Russian impresario and his ballet company were stuck in Madrid where they had difficulty in obtaining French visas for their return. Finally, Misia's husband went to Spain to rescue the troupe. A few minutes before crossing the Spanish border into France, Sert asked Diaghilev to check if he was carrying any papers that might be considered suspicious. After Diaghilev hotly denied that he had anything remotely incriminating, 'he pulled from his pockets a pile of papers on the top of which was a letter from Mata Hari!'[8]

Whatever reputation Mata Hari was evolving, she remained oblivious of the Allies' mounting suspicion against her. According to a Metropolitan Police file released in 1992, Madame Margaretha Zelle, aged thirty-nine, arrived at Folkestone Port by the Dieppe boat train on 3 December 1915. The Police Alien and Military Authorities interviewed her and noted that she gave conflicting versions of the reasons for her journey to France. During her first interview, she claimed she was en route to Paris to sell her effects and sign professional contracts, possibly for performances in South America. But during a second interrogation, she told Captain Dillon of MO5 (the forerunner of MI5) that she was planning to sell her home in Neuilly and establish a permanent residence in The Hague since the Baron van der Capellen was mobilized and could only visit her there. She said nothing about South America. Madame Zelle's luggage was searched and although nothing incriminating was found, she was deemed to be 'not above suspicion and her subsequent movements should be watched'. She left by the SS *Arundel* for Dieppe at 2.30 p.m. The following day a notice was circulated to all British authorities, including the ports, warning that Madame Zelle 'appeared most unsatisfactory and should be refused permission to return to the UK'.[9]

Perhaps Mata Hari assumed that such interrogations were routine since she never mentioned this first confrontation with the British authorities. However, when she applied for a visa from the British consul in Rotterdam the following spring, she was inexplicably refused. On 27 April 1916 a telegram signed by the Dutch Foreign Minister Jonkheer Loudon was dispatched to DeMarees van Swinderen, the Netherlands ambassador in London, enquiring about the matter. 'Well-known dancing artist Mata Hari Netherland subject whose real name is MacLeod Zelle wants to go for personal affairs to Paris where she has lived before war,' he wrote. 'British consul Rotterdam declines to put visa to passport though French consul has done so, please beg British government to give orders consul Rotterdam.'[10] The embassy replied that the British denied the 'well-known Dutch artist Mata Hari' a visa because 'authorities have reasons why admission of lady mentioned your 74 [telegram] is undesirable.'[11] The December 1915 warning about Madame Zelle was clearly in effect.

To put the British suspicion in perspective, however, it must be remembered that during the war MI5 supervised an 'alien population' in Britain of more than 200,000 and detained, arrested and temporarily interned 30,000 'alien enemies and dangerous persons'. From 1910 onwards, MI5's first head, Captain (later Major General Sir) Vernon Kell, was responsible for 'building up a secret registration of all the potentially dangerous aliens of certain selected nationalities' that were numbered in the thousands.[12] Given the scale of operations, there were several possible reasons why Mata Hari might be considered undesirable: she was the citizen of a neutral country, she had been in the company of a German police officer in Berlin at the outbreak of war and she had a reputation as a courtesan and nude dancer. The criterion used by espionage agencies was often so vague that any woman travelling independently might be considered dangerous. Lady Kell noted in an unpublished biography documenting her husband's intelligence work that 'women were occasionally used by the Germans as agents if they were possessed of a ready wit and adept at using it when in a tight corner'.[13] A self-fulfilling prophecy therefore doomed the female suspect; if she eloquently defended herself against accusations of spying, she was displaying the characteristics of a shrewd Hun agent. If she remained passive, her acquiescence was construed as guilt.

Mata Hari's determination to control every situation would surely have roused Sir Vernon Kell's nose for intrigue. On 24 May 1916 Mata Hari boarded the *Zeelandia* which sailed from Amsterdam along the Iberian route on her second journey to France. She later told Captain Pierre Bouchardon, her principal interrogator during the Council of War's investigation in 1917, that a 'Jew of Dutch nationality called Hodenmaker [sic]' had harassed her on the journey. Other passengers had told Mata Hari that Hoedemaker, who claimed to work for the British secret service, had boasted of searching her room and baggage. Incensed at the invasion of privacy, Mata Hari decided to challenge this ham-fisted spy. She gathered the other passengers on deck at teatime as witnesses and accused Hoedemaker of spying. He denied the charges but Mata Hari insisted on an apology. When he refused, to the passengers' delight she slapped Hoedemaker 'so violently that blood flowed from his mouth'.[14]

By the time the ship arrived in Spain, Hoedemaker was still threatening trouble and followed Mata Hari to the Continental Hotel in Vigo. She quickly lost him, however, by recruiting two of the ship's male passengers to escort her to her room.[15] Mata Hari reported her arrival to the Dutch consulate in Vigo on 12 June and two days later was in Madrid en route for Paris. Albert F. Calvert, an English writer, claimed he was also staying at the Ritz Hotel during this period where he spoke with Mata Hari about the difficulties of travelling during wartime. She allegedly told Calvert that although she was always carefully searched at English ports, since she committed everything to memory, there was nothing for the authorities to find. 'From Madrid I warned the authorities about her departure and the nature of her business,' Calvert wrote in a letter to *The Observer* on 29 July 1917. '[I] was afterwards surprised to hear that there were many women engaged in the same business and others were even travelling on the same boat.' Calvert may have added to the suspicion that was already mounting against Mata Hari.

She was, in fact, refused entry at Hendaye, just across the French border from San Sebastian, without explanation and immediately wrote an indignant letter to Mr van Royen, the Dutch consul in Madrid. She must have explained her plan to write about the matter to her old friend Jules Cambon who was then the secretary-general of the French Ministry for Foreign Affairs. Van Royen made enquiries and on 17 June the French ambassador in Madrid explained that, 'it seems that Mrs MacLeod is on the list of English suspects and that is really why her entry into France was refused.' The ambassador also passed on confidential information that the French considered her relations in The Hague suspicious and that she was mysteriously 'mixed up with a seller of wheat'.[16] Van Royen instructed his assistant, J. Higby, to reply to Mata Hari and on 18 June, after she had already left Spain, he wrote, '[Mr van Royen] has done everything in his power to get permission for you to enter France. But not even the intervention of the Minister could avail anything; neither the declarations that your sympathies are pro-Ally.'[17] However, Mata Hari had solved the problem herself; although the letter to Cambon was never sent, its threat convinced the Hendaye border guards to let her pass.[18]

By the time Mata Hari arrived at the Grand Hotel in Paris on 16 June, she was being followed. The Deuxième Bureau had assigned two inspectors, Tarlet and Monier, to keep close tabs on the suspicious Dutch dancer. The inspectors reported to Captain Georges Ladoux, who had been appointed to head the espionage bureau in August 1914 because of his unique experience as a military officer and journalist. Ladoux graduated from Saint-Cyr, the country's most prestigious military academy, in 1898 as a protégé of General Joffre, who was now commander of the French forces. However, Ladoux's rise through the ranks was less than meteoric. He was made captain in 1908 when he returned to Saint-Cyr as an instructor, taking on the 103rd infantry of Alençon. In May 1914 Ladoux left the military to become a defence correspondent for the Paris *Radical* where he was soon appointed editor.[19] General Joffre appointed Ladoux to head the Press Censorship bureau at the outbreak of war and then promoted him to the Deuxième Bureau – the French office of military espionage and counterespionage – the following year.[20]

Ladoux's inspectors filed regular reports from 18 June 1916 to 13 January 1917, which recorded Mata Hari's visitors, telephone calls, letters, shopping trips and outings. Although her trial was conducted in camera and the inspector's findings were never made public, their observations formed a central tenet in Ladoux's theory about his new suspect. He saw Mata Hari first and foremost as a *femme galante* – who was less than a mistress but more than a prostitute.[21] And if she could extract valuable information during her liaisons, this made her exceptionally dangerous. Like La Castiglione, a 'fine political agent' who seduced Napoleon III for the Italian leader, Cavour, and Georges Clemenceau's courtesan Léonide Leblanc who urged him to entrust her with state secrets, the connection between sex and espionage had a long tradition in France.[22] Ladoux regarded Mata Hari as a natural in this game; if her seductive powers were channelled in the right direction, she might make an excellent agent. However, Ladoux was not entirely satisfied that she was working for the Allies and after the British notified him that she was on their list of suspects, he had her trailed.

The inspectors, who followed Mata Hari day and night throughout the summer of 1916, built up a portrait of a cosmopolitan woman with a suspicious number of male visitors, mostly officers. When the Marquis de Beaufort arrived at the Grand Hotel from the Yser valley on 11 July, Mata Hari had reserved a room adjoining hers for the duration of his leave. But after his departure on 19 July, for the following two evenings Mata Hari was seen dining with Antoine

Bernard, a distiller from Martres de Veyre in the Puy-de-Dôme region. On 30 July she dined with Nicholas Yovilchevilch, a thirty-four-year-old Montenegrin officer, and on 4 August with an Italian captain of the military police. Throughout August, her guests included: a 'French lieutenant about thirty', wearing an infantry uniform; the Baron 'Robert' [Henry] de Marguérie; two Irish officers, James Plunkett and Edwin Cecil O'Brien, a twenty-year-old Scottish officer, James Stewart Fernie, a Belgian General Baumgarten and a British captain.[23]

But when Mata Hari fell in love, she resolved to earn enough money to retire from the *maison de rendezvous*, where she often took her casual lovers. In late July 1916 she visited the home of a retired actress and friend Mrs Dangeville who ran a salon that entertained officers. That evening, she was introduced to a man she had already noticed at the Grand Hotel.[24] As she would later write, he would become the lover for whom 'I would have gone through fire'. He was Vladimir de Masloff, a twenty-one-year-old captain in the First Russian Special Imperial regiment, who was on leave from the front near Champagne. They spent the night together and Mata Hari saw 'Vadime' again on 3 August in Paris while he was on convalescent leave after mustard gas had burned his throat and destroyed the sight of his left eye.

Mata Hari saw him off at the Gare de l'Est, and afterwards tried to obtain a traveller's pass for Vittel, a French spa town at the foot of the Vosges mountains famous for its aquatic treatments. Since Vadime was stationed close by, she could use the excuse of needing to take the cure while making a rendezvous with her lover. But since the town was in the military zone, non-residents needed police permission to visit it.[25] On 31 July she stopped at the police station on the rue Taitbout and asked for permits to stay at Vittel for three weeks and for safe conduct to Calais. When both were refused, she went to see Henri Maunoury at the Prefecture of Police on the Boulevard du Palais three days later to see if he could overrule the rue Taitbout's decision. However, Maunoury was no more co-operative. She next solicited the help of an old friend, Jean Hallaure, a cavalry lieutenant posted to a desk job with the Ministry of War after being wounded at the front. Hallaure suggested she ask the advice of Georges Ladoux at the Military Bureau for Foreigners on the Boulevard Saint-Germain.

In Ladoux's memoirs, he vividly recalls their first meeting in August 1916. With hindsight, he claimed to have suspected Mata Hari was a German agent from the start and hiring her as a double-agent was an effective trap. By this time British MI5 had notified Ladoux that they believed Mata Hari was a German operative with the code number AF44 – AF for Antwerp, where the mysterious Dr Schragmuller was alleged to have run a spy school.[26] But according to Mata Hari, this initial discussion with Ladoux about working for the French was entirely unexpected.

On that day in August 1916, she opened a door at 282 Boulevard Saint-Germain, which was also the headquarters for the Deuxième Bureau, and confronted 'a fat man with a very black beard and very black hair and spectacles with . . . a little cigarette between his lips'.[27] Ladoux thought he had finally found the perfect spy-courtesan: vulgar, hard-bitten and manipulative.

I can still see her, as though it were yesterday, despite the summer weather, in a suit of dark cloth, and a straw hat with a wide brim and a floating grey feather.

She strode into my office with that easy gait which actors have, being used to walking on stage . . . When I did not hasten to offer her a seat, she took a chair, brought it over to my desk and sat down familiarly, as though she were part of the establishment.

'What do you want of me?' she said in perfect French, only slightly marred by a guttural inflection that went quite well with her oriental type.

I said that I knew she wanted to go to Vittel and was ready to give her a pass to do so.

'In that case,' she pursued, 'do me a favour and tell those cops [Tarlet and Monier] downstairs who stick to me like my own shadow, that since it's very hot, you give them permission to have a drink to my health in that *bistro* across the street.'

I made believe that I did not know what she was talking about.

'I'm followed wherever I go . . . they even take advantage of my being out of the hotel to search my luggage . . . When I return, everything is upside down . . . and you know that I don't have the means to give extra tips to the chambermaid.'

I asked myself, seeing her tranquil self-assurance and control . . . *if British Intelligence which swamped me with notes about Mata Hari for over a year now*, was not wrong in affirming, without any proof moreover, that she must be a German spy, a fact which she seemed quite aware of and spoke about freely.[28]

Aside from attributing 'Oriental' characteristics to the Dutch Madame MacLeod, Ladoux may also have exaggerated MI5's interest in the case. Notes in the Public Record Office files show that British intelligence had circulated two MI5E notices about her: the first on 9 December 1915 and the second on 22 February 1916. Moreover, as the testimony of Marthé Richard, the French double-agent who in 1915 became the mistress of the German naval attaché Baron von Krohn in Madrid, would later reveal, Ladoux had a great propensity for fictionalizing the events of his intelligence career.

Ladoux said he found Mata Hari very frank about her involvement with the German secret service. 'Now this idiotic game has to end,' she allegedly told him. 'Either I am dangerous, and in that case, you must expel me from France, or I am just a nice little woman who, having danced all winter, would like . . . some peace of mind.'[29] Ladoux suggested she could perform a 'great service' for France, would she consider it?

'I've never thought about it,' she replied.

'You must be very expensive,' he countered.

'That's for sure!'

'What do you think such work is worth?'

'A lot or nothing.'

'Think about it,' suggested Ladoux. 'See if you can't do something for us. I will give you your card for Vittel. Only promise me that you won't seduce any French officers . . . Whatever it is, when you have made a decision on what I have said to you, come back and see me.'[30] At the end of this first interview, Ladoux signed her passport and sent her back to Maunoury to collect the necessary pass for Vittel.[31]

She finally received her *carnet* on 28 August and immediately made preparations for the trip. She was reunited with Vadime in Vittel and spent a few glorious days with her lover who proposed, and she agreed to marry him as soon as possible.[32] Upon her return to Paris, she saw Ladoux for a second interview on 17 September. This time she poured out her longing to marry Masloff (whom Ladoux calls Malzov), but his noble family would disapprove and she needed substantial funds. Ladoux claimed she told him simply, 'I want to be rich enough not to have to deceive Vadime with others.'[33] She suggested an ambitious plan: to secure an introduction to General Moritz Ferdinand von Bissing, the German officer commanding the Belgian occupation, and through him to seduce the Crown Prince. For a million francs she could carry out this seduction since 'I've already been his mistress and it's only up to me to see him again.' Then she elaborated. 'The Germans adored me and treated me like a queen whereas to you I'm nothing but a whore . . . Ah, if you had seen our orgies in Berlin! . . . When they were lying on the floor, fawning over my naked feet . . . and I unleashed their animal desires.'[34]

As the 'marvellous artist' stood there 'trembling with emotion' at these memories, Ladoux felt his 'love for France and the passion for my work' was being manipulated. He fought back by challenging her that no one could get to see the Kronprinz at Stenay. But Mata Hari replied that she could; a lover named Kroemer (the honorary German consul in Amsterdam) would help her. Although Ladoux was certain she was a German agent he warned that espionage was a game involving luck and betting against the odds. Was she willing to take the risk? 'I'm a gambler, it's true,' she replied, 'but I'm also superstitious.' She had spent the night gambling and this morning she had gone to the Jardin d'Acclimatation to watch the snakes rise at her bidding. They were her birth sign but this time they didn't stir – an omen that risks were worth taking. She would accept the assignment knowing that if she betrayed Ladoux's trust, the military tribunal would spare her no mercy.[35] But in this version of their conversation, Ladoux insists that the idea of combining espionage with seduction came from Mata Hari herself. As the interview drew to a close, Ladoux suggested she travel to Belgium via Holland but Mata Hari rejected the idea and they finally agreed that she would return to The Hague via Spain and England. Once back in the Netherlands, she would wait for further contact from a French agent.

Police superintendent Faux-Pas Bidet, who served with Ladoux during the war, commented that his chief 'was endowed with an overflowing imagination that, if he had allowed it, often untangled the threads of a complicated intrigue'.[36] Fifteen years after Ladoux's first encounter with Mata Hari, his memory appears to have become entwined with his fantasies. His descriptions are riddled with inaccuracies, including the fact that she had never met the German Kronprinz, let alone slept with him. Mata Hari had never danced with snakes, and mocked those music-hall dancers who did. But these exaggerations all help to build the portrait of a lascivious dancer, whose penchant for orgies reflected a moral weakness and a willingness to do anything for money. From wherever Ladoux drew these lurid scenes, he believed that the enemy's vulnerability to this type of female company should be exploited. Mata Hari, therefore, was the perfect lure.

To complete the picture of the immoral *femme galante*, the bureau's detectives were rapidly gathering evidence of Mata Hari's relationships with a variety of Allied officers. However, Ladoux would never accept that, despite her financial arrangements with her casual lovers, she was completely enamoured of Vadime. Her affair with the handsome Russian officer was the inverse of the courtesan's relationship with an older, wealthy client. Perhaps Vadime's damaged eye and lungs, which made him dependent on her, were a reminder that she had once been a mother of adoring children. But if this blissful union was to work, Mata Hari needed the equivalent of a dowry and her options for making money were limited. Diaghilev had not replied to her letters and the prospects of mounting a new production looked bleak. Ladoux's tantalizing offer of a million francs came like a godsend. It would save her from the *maison de rendezvous* where, at the best establishments, a woman could demand a minimum fee from clients of between sixty and a hundred francs a night. Before the war they had been 'the recourse of widows in financial straits or dowerless daughters who hoped to obtain the necessary principal to make a marriage to which their rank in society would permit them'.[37]

If this was Mata Hari's sole means of financing her marriage to Vadime, she would have been in respectable company; even bored aristocratic wives conducted their illicit affairs or charged for their company behind such discreet doors in fashionable districts. Many of the city's most honoured female performers supplemented their wages through this practice. Even the illustrious Sarah Bernhardt, who once declared, 'I have been among the great lovers of my time,' was the daughter of a *cocotte*.[38]

Ladoux's offer would also help Mata Hari pay off numerous small debts and therefore restore her reputation with several upmarket restaurants and hotels. Her funds often ran low and, though the Baron was generous, he was often difficult to contact. All communication was conducted through Mata Hari's maid, Anna Lintjens, to avoid upsetting the Baron's marital relations. Her trail of debts included a nasty confrontation with the manager of the Hotel Meurice, who on 14 October 1916 used a court order to seize Mata Hari's luggage in payment for a bill of 1,300 francs outstanding from 1913. She paid 200 francs immediately and another 300 before her property was returned.[39] But once one difficulty had been settled, her appetite for acquisition grew again. In October, she signed a lease on an apartment at 33 Avenue Henri Matin in a fashionable district near the Bois de Boulogne. She was soon writing to a friend in The Hague to ask Anna Lintjens to contact the Baron since, 'I have spent a bit too much here and Anna must send me 6,000 francs. Tell her it is very urgent.'[40] However, the Baron did not wire the funds to the Comptoir National d'Escompte de Paris until 4 November.

Whenever there were these difficult periods, Mata Hari resorted to soliciting. During the 1917 investigation prior to her trial, at least one witness testified to paying for her services. A man named in the transcripts as 'Henri Rapférer [probably Henri Raphérer, a famous *aéronaute*], who is described as a 46-year-old engineer and reserve lieutenant, met Mata Hari at a pre-war reception of the Stella Aeroclub at the Palais d'Orsay. Since Raphérer had lived in Java and

Sumatra, he expressed an interest in her 'Oriental' dancing and then accepted an invitation to her villa in Neuilly that evening. They dined, went to bed and after Raphérer left, he sent Mata Hari 200 francs which was 'the price of her evening'.[41] If Tarlet and Monier's report is any indication, she ranked among the city's *femmes galantes*, many of whom were educated but without an honourable profession. They included victims of scandal, divorcées, aspiring actresses, widows, women without class and wealthy foreigners.[42] However many men Mata Hari slept with, it was Captain Georges Ladoux who first suggested she combine this career with espionage.

But Ladoux may have begun to doubt his decision to hire Mata Hari soon after their second interview on 17 September to discuss her services for the bureau. With marvellous indiscretion, two days later Mata Hari sent Ladoux a letter through the post asking for an advance to buy dresses she would need to lure von Bissing.[43] When Ladoux did not reply, she phoned his office where he refused her calls. At their next meeting on 20 September Ladoux claimed to have stressed to Mata Hari that she was merely a freelance agent. However, he had offered her the use of secret ink which she declined and gave her names to contact in Belgium – both indications of an agent's trusted status.[44] He told her to return to Holland and wait for further instructions. However, Ladoux was to hear of his agent eight days later.

While Mata Hari was returning to The Hague via Spain and England, aboard the *Hollandia*, she ran into trouble when the ship docked at Falmouth. George Reid Grant, a Scotland Yard official, became convinced she was Clara Benedix, a German agent from Hamburg known to MI5 and the Director of the Naval Intelligence Division (DID). He thought Mata Hari might be Benedix, who was living in Spain, pretending to be Spanish and working as a flamenco dancer, and now travelling under an assumed name with a false passport.[45] 'An officer checked my identity, looked at me closely and pulled from his pocket an amateur photograph of a woman in a Spanish dress with a white mantilla, carrying a fan in her right hand and with her hand on her left hip,' she told the French interrogators in 1917. 'The woman resembled me slightly but she was shorter and plumper than I.'

Grant's confusion probably stemmed from MI5's list of suspects. The report wrongly gave her height as 5 ft 5 in. (she was actually five inches taller), and described her as 'medium stout', a 'handsome, bold type', who was 'well and fashionably dressed; brown costume, racoon fur trimming; hat to match'. She was listed as speaking French, English, Italian, Dutch and probably German, although Mata Hari spoke neither English nor Italian.[46] But according to Grant's report, the photographic coincidence and several contradictory statements in 'Madame MacLeod's' story about her journey to The Hague resulted in her detention. Mata Hari admitted to having once met Clara Benedix in a dining car where she sat at her table with an English and German consul while travelling by train from Madrid to Lisbon. 'As Madame MacLeod's story seems altogether very strange,' Grant reported to his superiors, 'it was decided to remove her and send her to London.'[47]

However, MI5's competence in this case was highly dubious, since neither Grant nor anyone else would mention Mata Hari's first interrogation in Britain at Folkestone in 1915. The MI5E notice of 22 February 1916 stated bluntly,

'This woman is now in Holland. If she comes to this country she should be arrested and sent to Scotland Yard.'[48]

She spent the night of 12 November aboard the *Hollandia* which docked at Falmouth. Early the next morning George Grant's wife Janet, a policewoman hired to search female suspects, 'stripped Mata Hari and searched her thoroughly' while the suffragettes, who volunteered for such work, went through her belongings and the ship's carpenters unscrewed the cabin mirrors.[49] The Grants ignored the pleas of the Dutch captain who claimed Mata Hari was the ship's most popular passenger and took her to their home. They allowed her to bathe but she refused food, 'cried a lot' and 'drank an awful lot of coffee'. The couple escorted Mata Hari on an overnight train to London where they fulfilled their promise to let her bathe and change her clothes again before taking her to Scotland Yard.[50]

Mata Hari, now appearing as Madame MacLeod despite her divorce, faced Sir Basil Thomson, then assistant metropolitan police commissioner at Scotland Yard and head of the Special Branch. The suspect was considered sufficiently important for DID Captain Reginald 'Blinker' Hall to attend along with his assistant Lord Herschell, who ran a substantial agent network in Spain from Gibraltar.[51] Thomson was prepared for La Scala's former *grande dame* to create a dramatic scene refuting the charges brought against her. Her reputation of beauty preceded her but Thomson was disappointed on both accounts. 'I expected to see a lady who would bring the whole battery of her charms to bear upon the officers who were to question her,' he wrote in 1922. 'There walked into the room a severely practical person who was prepared to answer any question with a kind of reserved courtesy, who felt so sure of herself and of her innocence that all that remained in her was a desire to help her interrogators.'[52]

The subject was seated in a comfortable chair in the full light while Sir Basil sat on a high stool slightly in the shadows.[53] In a gentle voice, he asked Mata Hari to state her real name and place of birth, then with a flourish produced a photograph of the suspected German spy, Clara Benedix. Was this not proof that she and the elusive Hamburg agent were one and the same, just as Grant had said?

ACC [Thomson] – That is your photograph?
MZM [Mata Hari aka Margaretha Zelle MacLeod] – No, it is not my photograph.
ACC – I put it to you that your real name is Clara Benedix.
MZM - I swear to you that it is a mistake.
ACC – I put it to you that that passport is a false passport on which somebody has written the upper part.
MZM - Send it over to Holland and you will see that it is right.
ACC – Are you ready to account for the fact that that seal does not meet?
MZM - I did nothing with my passport, Sir.
ACC – Can you account in any way for that seal not meeting? Do you wish to say anything about the writing coming under the photograph?
MZM - That is my passport.
ACC – You wish to say nothing?
MZM - Nothing.[54]

Throughout this first interview Thomson attempted to catch his subject offguard by veering from details about her childhood to her marriage and then suddenly to her career. The interview was conducted in French since Mata Hari did not speak English and the translator stumbled over spellings in the recorded transcript. But Mata Hari's answers were equally inconsistent, confusing dates or tailoring her responses to establish her innocence. Despite the intimidating circumstances, she at first treated her interrogators as if they were journalists probing for sensational revelations.

Although Mata Hari vehemently denied that she was Clara Benedix and by implication a German spy, she blurred the facts of her history. (This was also consistent with her interview in Folkestone in December 1915 when she insisted she was in Milan at the outbreak of war.) She claimed she was in Italy, dancing at La Scala, when the war broke out and since her engagement at Berlin's Metropol was cancelled, she returned to Holland; she also claimed that her son Norman had died in India rather than in Java. To Mata Hari these were inconsequential details which lent legitimacy to her *invented* history. After all, La Scala was the site of her greatest triumph and a none-too-subtle reminder to her questioners that she was once a 'Star of Dance'. Shifting Norman's death from Java, the Dutch East Indies, to India was another allusion to her role as nautch temple dancer turned officer's wife. It was effective enough for Thomson, seven years after their meeting, to remember her as a part-Javanese woman who was 'an exponent of a voluptuous oriental dancing'.[55]

Thomson also recalled Mata Hari's intelligence, wit and vivacious manner and seemed to enjoy their two long interviews. His dramatic technique of interrogation, and his obvious appreciation of his subject, may have given her the impression that this was only a game. Thomson focused on small details and seemingly petty similarities between Mata Hari and her presumed *doppelgänger* Clara Benedix. Both women, the detective noticed, had a slight droop in the left eyelid, 'a very rare thing'. When Mata Hari dismissed this as mere coincidence, he suggested with irony that she was 'a victim of circumstance'. No reference was made to the 1915 interrogation which initially placed her on the suspects' list, until Mata Hari requested a permit to travel from Whitehall. But the first interview ended with a twist for 'Madame MacLeod', who was stunned to learn that she would be kept in custody on suspicion of espionage and on the charge of possessing a forged passport. That evening she was sent to Cannon Row police station, supplied with pen and paper and instructed to write a list of witnesses to be called from Holland in case of a trial.

However, Mata Hari's answers during the interview reveal how completely she had severed her ties with Holland since living in Paris. Her father had died in 1913, but she wasn't sure in which month and had not seen him since her divorce from MacLeod in 1907. She had last met her daughter, who was now sixteen years old, ten years ago because 'she does not want to see me' even though Non was attending a teacher's college in The Hague.[56] As she would state the following day, 'I have no family . . . I am quite alone.' That night at Cannon Row Mata Hari appreciated that this game might prove to be deadly serious. Basil Thomson warned that while she was free to contact the Dutch legation, he would write that 'we have grave doubts as to your passport [and] I shall also tell him that I believe you to be Clara Benedix, a German.'[57]

Mata Hari immediately wrote to Count van Limburg Styrum at the Dutch legation in Paris: 'please send someone from the embassy to London immediately for identification or come yourself. I am at Scotland Yard in despair.' To Amsterdam's police commissioner she pleaded simply, 'help me . . .' and to the Netherlands Minister in London DeMarees van Swinderen she pleaded:

> Can I ask your excellency politely but urgently to do everything in your power to help me? A great misfortune has overcome me . . . I am travelling from Spain to Holland, with my *very own* passport. The English police assert it is not genuine and that I am not Mrs Zelle MacLeod. I'm at the end of my tether. I'm imprisoned here at Scotland Yard since this morning. I pray to you come and help me . . . I'm totally on my own here, and I swear *that everything is totally in order*. It is a misunderstanding but I beseech you, help me.[58] [emphasis in original]

Mata Hari peppered her list of witnesses with prestigious friends and those best disposed to vouch for her character. Baron van der Capellen topped the list and among others she named Albert Keyzer, the Belgian correspondent for the *Daily Mail*, the artist Henri Rudeaux residing at the Savoy Hotel, her lover the Marquis de Beaufort of the Belgian army's Fourth Lancers, Monsieur Guimet, Monsieur Maunoury, Chef de Police in Paris, Dr van Dieren in Amsterdam who attended her first confirmation and Captain Georges Ladoux of the French secret service.[59] The last would prove extremely significant when Mata Hari returned to Scotland Yard the following day.

On 16 November, Major Reginald Drake of MI5 joined Thomson, Hall and Herschell at Scotland Yard for the second interview with the suspect. This time, however, Mata Hari offered an explanation for the confusion with Clara Benedix who had been cited by a second secret service official in Liverpool. 'Madame MacLeod' had once been confused with an English Mrs MacLeod at the Grand Hotel in Paris and had even received the other woman's love letters which were intended for the Grand Hotel, London. Thomson soon dropped this line of enquiry and returned to questions about Mata Hari's past to establish her real identity. At the mention of Adam Zelle's 1906 book, *The Life of Mata Hari – the Biography of my Daughter and Grievances against her former Husband*, Madame MacLeod grew indignant:

> MZM – Sir, that is a dirty story . . . My father left my mother twelve years ago. He went to Amsterdam and lived with a woman, one of the common class. I married to become happier. He was twenty-two years older than I. Then my father married this woman. I always sent my father money, and then, as I left McCleod [sic], I went to Paris and became a great dancer. Two writers went to my father, and asked him if he would give his name, and she [Zelle's wife] wrote the book and my father gave my photographs. I have been very unhappy through this horrible book. She wrote this book, and my father gave the name and one day 60,000 books went to India where I am known very well . . . It was the greatest unhappiness of my life.[60]

Again Mata Hari added details to her history to reinforce her public personae; she had never travelled to India and there is no evidence that she was 'known very well' there in any circles. But her irritation at the mention of the biography had not satisfied Thomson who once more pursued his enquiry about Clara Benedix.

PLATE 1 *An early portrait of Margaretha Zelle MacLead, a.k.a. Mata Hari,*
in 'Oriental' costume, c. 1905. (ULLSTEIN BILDERDIENST, BERLIN)

PLATE 2 *English music-hall comedian Phyllis Dare with child 'Salome's' at the Queen's Theatre, London, June 1908, in a parody of Maud Allan's provocative dance, the 'Vision of Salome'. Dare's scene with the 'tiny Maud Allan's' led to an investigation by outraged members of the Society for the Protection of Children.* (MANDER AND MITCHENSON THEATRE COLLECTION, LONDON)

PLATE 3 *The American dancer Maud Allan as 'Salome', which led to accusations of 'Salomania' spreading through London. Note the breast-plates and head-dress which became Mata Hari's hallmarks.* (MANDER AND MITCHENSON THEATRE COLLECTION, LONDON)

PLATE 4 *Ruth St Denis, an 'Oriental' dancer who rivalled Maud Allan in 1908.* (MANDER AND MITCHENSON THEATRE COLLECTION, LONDON)

PLATE 5 *Mata Hari, who 'personifies all the poetry of India', in classic costume.* (*ULLSTEIN BILDERDIENST, BERLIN*)

PLATE 6 *Mata Hari in Spanish costume for her performance in 'la revue en chemise' at the Folies Bergère, Paris, 28 June 1913.*
(COLLECTION ROGER-VIOLLET, PARIS)

PLATE 7 'Lady MacLeod', November 1911, at the 'Steeple Militaire' in Paris.
(ULLSTEIN BILDERDIENST, BERLIN)

PLATE 8 Mata Hari just after her final performance as a dancer, in Holland, March 1915. (ULLSTEIN BILDERDIENST, BERLIN)

A telegram from Holland, he claimed, had now confirmed that 'Madame Zelle is a German agent, and Mata Hari is truly a German agent, and so is Clara Benedix.'[61]

Suddenly Mata Hari announced that she had something important to say. She was a spy, yes, but for the French, not the Germans. She had had two interviews with Captain Georges Ladoux, Thomson's counterpart in Paris, so there was no need for this interrogation. As a rule, agents did not divulge their identity, even to the Allies, but since Mata Hari faced such serious charges she gambled that the truth would set her free. She had hesitated in telling her interrogators before because, she said, 'I thought it was too big a secret'. Mata Hari explained she had met Ladoux when enquiring about permission for a *carnet* to travel to Vittel.

> MZM – I saw Captain Ladoux on the second floor. He was very polite. He said, 'I know you very well. I have seen you dancing' . . . One day the Captain said to me, 'You can do so many things for us if you like', and he looked me in the eyes. I understood. I thought a long time. I said 'I can.' He said, 'Would you.' I said 'I would.' 'Would you ask much money?' he said. I said, 'Yes, I would.' 'What would you ask?' I said, 'If I give you plenty of satisfaction I ask you 1,000,000.' He said, 'Go to Holland, and you will receive my instructions.' 'If it is for Germany I do not like to go.' 'No,' he said, 'it is for Belgium.' So I awaited his instructions in my home.[62]

Thomson's scepticism went undetected as Mata Hari 'plunged into a sea of reminiscence' about her adventures as a spy for the French.[63] But the official transcript shows that her only further revelation was her promise to the French consul from the Dutch legation to gather information about the Austrian forces on the Eastern Front since she 'loved a Russian officer'. She ignored Thomson's caustic comment that 'it would be awkward to have a levee of all the belligerent countries in your room', and insisted she was an Allied agent.[64]

Although Mata Hari later recalled meeting Martial Cazeaux, a Frenchman who worked as a clerk at the honorary Dutch consulate in Vigo, in December 1916, it must have been earlier. As the interview transcript reveals, by this time Mata Hari had already met a 'French consul from the Dutch legation' – Cazeaux – who knew about her relationship with Masloff.[65] She told Thomson that this man offered her money to supply information to the Russians. 'You would give [Vadime Masloff] the pleasure of sending a telegram to see if he is wounded and work a little with me. Will you do something for the Russians?' I did not tell him about the French. He said 'Can you go to Austria?' He said he wanted to know what Reserves they had to fight.'[66] Mata Hari later elaborated the story, claiming that Cazeaux had offered a huge reward if she could get into Austria. A Russian, said Cazeaux, would call at her hotel in Madrid, carrying the other half of Cazeaux's calling card as a form of identification.[67] However, Mata Hari must have confused the sequence of events since she stopped in Vigo in November 1916 only long enough to catch the *Hollandia* for Falmouth.

Thomson paid little attention to Mata Hari's claims to be working for a string of Allied intelligence networks and ended the interview announcing his intention to send for someone from Spain who knew Clara Benedix. He would also follow up her references.[68] Although the British had no evidence that she intended to commit an act of espionage in their country, Thomson was convinced she was 'acting for the Germans' and had memorized valuable information. The official transcript also contradicts his claim to have warned Mata Hari against continuing as a spy. He may have spoken with Mata Hari in a private aside but, given the inaccuracy of his memory, it seems doubtful. According to Thomson, he chided her in an avuncular tone, 'we are going to send you back to Spain, and if you will take the advice of someone nearly twice your age [he was actually fifteen years her senior], give up what you have been doing.' Mata Hari allegedly replied, confirming her guilt: 'Sir, I thank you from my heart. I shall not forget your advice. What I have been doing I will do no more. You may trust me implicitly.' But this, Thomson claimed, was another ruse and within a month she had returned to Spain and 'was at it again'.[69]

Mata Hari was executed five years before Basil Thomson's account of his wartime experiences at Scotland Yard was published. But since official sources about her case remained sealed at the time, Thomson's presumption of her guilt contributed to the legend of Mata Hari, the espionage agent *par excellence*. The British in 1916 had no evidence that she was guilty of spying but as the Clara Benedix confusion illustrates, little was needed. Nowhere does Thomson mention the initial suspicion about Benedix that led to Mata Hari's interrogation; who and what Clara Benedix was even now remains a mystery. But where Thomson's memory of Mata Hari had faded, the mythology had firmly lodged in its place so that the two became indistinguishable. Just as Mata Hari was guilty of imaginatively altering the events of her life to suit an audience, so too were her interrogators.

Basil Thomson decided to 'make inquiries by cable' after the second interview and contacted Captain Ladoux to confirm whether Mata Hari was working for the Deuxième Bureau. Thomson must have wondered why Ladoux would engage a woman whom MI5 had earlier warned him about. His telegram from Paris, however, denied any connection with 'Madame MacLeod'; 'Understand nothing,' Ladoux wrote. 'Send Mata Hari back to Spain.' If she returned to Madrid, she might finally reveal her connection with the Germans and thus confirm his suspicion. The message to Thomson, however, neatly avoided mentioning that she really had been hired by Ladoux for French counterespionage work.[70]

Earlier that year, MI5 had warned American military intelligence that Mata Hari was 'most unsatisfactory; if come across to be arrested and sent to Scotland Yard'. The report, dated 11 July 1916, further reveals that MI5 had been following her movements for several months. However, they wrongly recorded that she had been in Milan at La Scala when the war broke out and returned to Holland via Switzerland and Germany. Her first wartime trip to France via Spain and England had been recorded and the War Office claimed to have a photograph and copy of her handwriting. They also stated that she 'hopes for engagement on her return, in London and English theatres', which was also information based on the 1915 interview.[71] However, her interview with Basil Thomson appears to have compounded the suspicion the British already harboured rather than proving her innocence.

Meanwhile, Thomson had been checking her Dutch references and the case had come to the attention of van Swinderen, the Dutch legate in London.[72] Thomson had also contacted the Dutch consul in Paris, whom Ladoux told he had never assigned Mata Hari to a mission. If she said she was returning to Holland for intelligence work, it must be for the Germans, Ladoux suggested, and therefore she should return to Spain. By 26 November van Swinderen reported back to The Hague that Mata Hari was 'returning to Spain of her own free will'.[73] On 12 December 1916 the Minister of Foreign Affairs in The Hague wrote to warn Mr van Royen, the Dutch envoy in Madrid, that Mata Hari might turn up at the legation. He enclosed a copy of van Swinderen's report on the whole episode sent on 1 December:

> This compatriot had originally been stopped because [some]one thought her passport was a fake and it was suspected her real nationality was German and she was a certain Clara Benedix from Hamburg. However, these suspicions were soon proven unfounded but official messages from Paris gave reason to believe that Mrs MacLeod had indeed been carrying out activities in ways that the [French] police look on unfavourably. . . . She said that the allies in Paris had trusted her to convey messages and she had to do this in Holland. The police were suspicious about these communications and this was confirmed from information gained from Paris from which it became clear that the orders had not gone out from the allies but the enemy . . . She declared she was willing to return to Spain of her own free will . . . I detect she wants to avoid anything which could spread rumours about this 'adventure' (I quote) of hers.[74]

This letter reveals that Ladoux had done more than just send a telegram to Thomson about Mata Hari. He not only denied to the Dutch legation in Paris that he had hired her as an agent but encouraged suspicions about her working for the Germans. Mata Hari from now on would be regarded as an enemy agent and nothing more; the plan to have her seduce von Bissing was off.

Meanwhile, Mata Hari had been released and sought solace at the Savoy Hotel. From there, she soon visited the Permit Office in Whitehall, which recorded her destination as The Hague and the object of her journey to 'marry Captain Vadince [sic] de Masloff'. The office rang Thomson who only then confirmed that Mata Hari was the 'person mentioned' in the MI5 circulars and advised against issuing the permit.

She was, said Thomson, believed to be 'an agent of the Deutsche Bank. Must not be given a visa or permit for Holland. No objection to a permit for Spain.' Thomson told Mata Hari the British government forbade Dutch citizens to return home and she must continue to Spain instead.[75] On 25 November she pleaded with Thomson for permission to catch the *New Amsterdam* leaving Falmouth for Rotterdam in five days' time. However, Thomson replied three days later that 'it was decided that you cannot be allowed to go anywhere from here except to Spain, whence you came.'[76] On 1 December she left London from Euston station with her ten pieces of luggage to embark from Liverpool on the SS *Arguaya* en route for Vigo, Spain.[77]

When Mata Hari arrived in Vigo the following week, she knew nothing of Ladoux's change of mind and proceeded as if she were still working for the French. She left for Madrid on 11 December where she telegraphed van der Capellen, repeating an earlier request for funds and explaining that she was stranded in Spain. She also wrote to Ladoux describing her interrogations at Falmouth and at Scotland Yard and asking for instructions. When he did not reply, Mata Hari plotted a course of action and contacted the German envoy in Madrid – Major Arnold Kalle. If Ladoux wanted information which might yield a large financial reward, Mata Hari could begin here, extracting what she could from the Germans and proving her worth.

Mata Hari's method was simple; she looked through the diplomatic register at the Ritz Hotel in Madrid, found Kalle's name listed as army attaché and wrote for an appointment, stating only that she would like to meet him. She arrived at Kalle's home later that day, and asked him why she had been confused with Clara Benedix at Falmouth. After Kalle referred her to a Baron de Roland in Madrid, they chatted and, according to Mata Hari, 'I did what a woman does in such circumstances when she wants to make a conquest of a gentleman, and I soon realized that von [sic] Kalle was mine.'[78] They went to bed and soon afterwards she returned to the Ritz.

During this first meeting Mata Hari would later claim that she told Kalle she was working for the Germans to win his trust and gather whatever she could for Ladoux. As they talked, she repeated gossip current in France that the Greek princess Marie Bonaparte had been urging the French prime minister Aristide Briand to replace the neutral King Constantine with her pro-German husband, Prince George, on the Greek throne at the end of the war, and that the French resented British military tactics and believed an offensive would be launched in the spring. In exchange, Kalle let slip the news that submarines would land a few German and Turkish officers onto the Morocco coast, a French military zone.[79]

Before retiring at the hotel, Mata Hari proudly wrote to Ladoux that she had 'renewed acquaintance' with a German in the Madrid embassy and passed on Kalle's story about the submarine landing which was intended to provoke a revolution against the French. Mata Hari would later reveal under interrogation that she wrote to Ladoux, 'I await your instructions; I can do what I want with my informer.'[80] Her letter, as usual, was sent through the regular post and Ladoux did not reply. He regarded this trip as another opportunity to gather proof that Mata Hari was a German agent, even though her previous visits had yielded nothing. This time, however, he claimed to have 'received evidence concerning her activities – the secret radiograms exchanged between Berlin and Madrid which the cipher service of the [War] Ministry had succeeded in intercepting and deciphering'.[81]

Mata Hari thought her initial meeting with Kalle had successfully established her as double-agent for the French; the Germans thought she was working for them while Ladoux knew she was on the Allies' side. The following day, she met two Dutch consuls at her hotel who introduced her to Colonel Joseph Denvignes, the French military attaché responsible for French espionage in Madrid. During a 'gala' at the Ritz the next evening, Denvignes told Mata Hari how delightful he found her company and generally 'behaved like a smitten sub-lieutenant'.[82] Discomfited by his inappropriately open display of affection, she diverted their conversation to her encounter with Kalle and the following morning Denvignes asked for further details about the submarine landings in Morocco. But at their next meeting Kalle was more circumspect and only discussed which route Mata

Hari would take in returning to Paris. She met Denvignes on several occasions before he accompanied the war minister General Lyautey back to Paris on 20 December. His infatuation with Mata Hari overshadowed his interest in her espionage activities; he suggested that when she return to the capital they might find an apartment together. As a souvenir, he pulled a ribbon from her bodice to tie a violet he had taken from the bunch nestled in her bosom. If she discovered anything important from Kalle, she must write to him at the war ministry and he would speak about her work with Ladoux, who had still not replied to her letters.[83]

When Mata Hari met Kalle the next time, he knew that she had been seen in the company of Denvignes, the French military attaché. He claimed to be furious and complained that, because the Germans had learned the key to the French radio cipher, he knew she had passed on the information about the submarine landings in Morocco. Mata Hari should have immediately detected a lie since no military attaché would volunteer such information. After Kalle appeared to recover from his irritation, they made love and he then gave her several items of 'intoxification' – stale or even false news – which Mata Hari took at face value. She naïvely thought Kalle was simply being indiscreet rather than using her to see how much information would get back to the French. He said the Germans knew the French pilot who dropped spies behind their lines in France and that German spies carried crystals under their fingernails that could be turned into invisible ink. In return, Mata Hari reported rumours that had circulated in Paris or were printed in the city's newspapers: food shortages were growing and morale in the trenches was low. To seal this exchange, Kalle gave this *agent-double* a payment of 3,500 pesetas which Mata Hari understood was payment for her 'caresses'.[84] She stayed in Madrid for another week, then on 2 January headed for Paris where she expected a lucrative award.

Meanwhile, Ladoux's most successful double-agent in Spain was milking Kalle's much more important colleague, the naval attaché Korvettenkapitän Krohn, for vital information. Marthé Richard had arrived in Madrid in June 1916 and crossed paths with Mata Hari at the Ritz, where they were both staying. If Mata Hari had been an important German agent, it seems unlikely that Richard would have learned that 'Lady MacLeod' was at the hotel from a chambermaid – also in the pay of the Germans – who inaccurately described the guest as an 'English artist'. Ironically, as Richard would later write, although Ladoux had assigned the women to similar missions, 'I got the Legion of Honour and [she] got the firing squad.'[85] What separated the two women was Ladoux's perception of their worth; as he wrote in 1932, 'they were as different as a highly bred pedigree French race-horse and a Dutch half-breed. Several classes intervened between them, as would be said in the language of the track.'[86]

The legacy that would surround the spy-courtesan stemmed directly from events in Spain which would be used not only to condemn her but to construct her legend. To her opponents, Mata Hari embodied the values of the demi-monde which many in France now believed had led to a moral weakness. While the Germans thrived on sexual debauchery, the Allies battled valiantly to preserve the virtues of the state, the family and the church. Mata Hari's arrest as an enemy agent seemed almost inevitable. In the struggle for control over her natural instincts and her 'Orientalism', she had lost; she had rejected marriage, motherhood and family to pursue a licentious life of pleasure which she had turned into the art of betrayal. Nor had she poured her energies into the war effort but had foolishly ventured into the male sphere of espionage and political intrigue. Ladoux even intimated that Mata Hari desired punishment when she allegedly told him she risked arrest to return to Paris in early 1917 because 'the gallows attracted her'.[87] But any woman like Mata Hari, whether she was a courtesan, prostitute or mistress, who chose to exploit her lovers, was equally betraying her country. In a neat reversal of roles, Mata Hari's biographer Major Coulson describes how dangerous the prostitute had become in wartime Paris where espionage had given her new powers:

> Throughout the war Paris was the Mecca of many a sorry pilgrimage for those who had faced the inferno of the advanced posts, with its horror of death and mutilation ... its monastic deprivations from the soft and endearing charms of gentle companions. It is futile to blame these men, whose eyes still carried the reflection of death, for their excesses ... In the feeling of unbounded relief which Paris leave afforded, many a decent and healthy-minded man sought gratification in the smiles and enchantments of Montmartre's mocking, laughing cherubim of hell ... And no one credits him with achieving great happiness through his solution.[88]

As a former British intelligence officer, Coulson's experience of the brothels was presumably based on experience. His stark contrast between the hellish women and the 'healthy-minded' men who desperately seek solace in such treacherous quarters easily suggests parallels with the spy-courtesan. By drawing these two female figures together – the evil foreigner, intent on betraying the Allies, and the slovenly whore – spy writers and propagandists had created a powerful icon. Mata Hari's opponents found her a potent and immediately recognizable symbol. As Ladoux wrote of his investigation, 'I must confess that the personality of this woman preoccupied me, attracting me and disquieting me at the same time.'[89] By early 1917, it was merely a matter of fleshing out the evidence against her.

CHAPTER FOUR

SHADOW PLAYS

When piety and maternal sentiment are wanting, and in their place are strong passions and intensely erotic tendencies, much muscular strength and a superior intelligence for the conception and execution of evil, it is clear that the innocuous semi-criminal present in the normal woman must be transformed into a born criminal more terrible than any man.

LOMBROSO AND FERRERO, *The Female Offender* (1899)[1]

WHILE MATA HARI WAS PREPARED TO CONTINUE enjoying the company of the two eminent Spanish politicians who had joined her in Madrid, she was perturbed that Georges Ladoux had not replied to her letters. Impatient for the substantial reward she expected for the startling news she had passed on to the enigmatic head of French counterespionage, she resolved to deliver it again in person. After all, she believed that in less than a week she had engineered a coup for Ladoux's secret service through her amorous meetings with the German military attaché, Kalle. Armed with this information, she left Madrid on 2 January 1917. At the border, she flashed a visiting card from Colonel Denvignes, the French military attaché, and was promptly issued a visa to cross the border back into France.[2]

When she arrived in Paris by train on 3 January 1917, two of Ladoux's inspectors were waiting. They followed her cab from the Gare d'Orsay to the Hotel d'Iéna, then the Hotel du Palais, and finally to the Plaza Athénée Hotel where, after negotiating a reduction in the price of the room, she registered.[3] Even before she left Madrid, Don Emilio Junoy, a Spanish senator and one of the two politicians with whom she had enjoyed a brief affair, had written from Barcelona to warn that a secret agent for the French had visited them. Junoy and Mata Hari's other lover, Monsieur de Léon, had been seen in her company and the agent wanted to know what business they had with a person 'known as hostile to the Entente' (Britain and France).[4] The Spaniards had responded that they knew only of the charms, intellectual and spiritual, that Madame Zelle possessed; they had discussed nothing to do with politics at all. Yet the letter was an ominous warning.

Mata Hari had indeed returned to a country of the gallows. That spring, after almost three years of heavy losses, soldiers would begin to mutiny, provoking more than 250 cases of 'collective insubordination' among combat troops on the Western Front. Spies were blamed for the mounting 'crisis of morale'. Strikes in Paris became visible demonstrations against the miserable conditions the war had imposed. Four days after Mata Hari's return, the female clothing workers at Agnès in the rue Aubert and Bernard in the rue de l'Opéra poured into the streets to demand higher wages. Although a settlement was quickly reached, discontent festered and throughout the city building workers, public officials and transport workers protested against conditions and inflationary prices. Conversations overheard in trains made it clear to everyone in France that 'the *weariness* of [French] soldiers has reached an altogether unexpected level'.[5] The government was ineffectual, weakened by a series of short-term leaders; Briand, who became premier on 29 October 1915, was replaced in March 1917 by the septuagenarian Alexandre Ribat who lasted until 12 September when he was succeeded by Paul Painlevé. Only two months later Georges Clemenceau, who had often railed against the 'rot' in French life that prevented the organization of an effective political system, came to power.[6]

The public mood, however, was never a particular concern of Mata Hari's. After arriving in Paris, she went to Captain Ladoux's office and when she was told he wasn't in, she asked for Colonel Denvignes. After traversing the city by cab, she eventually tracked down Denvignes at the Gare d'Austerlitz where he sat aboard the Madrid Express, waiting to leave. He had passed on Mata Hari's information to Ladoux and spoken with his superior, Colonel Antoine Goubet, about her. As she later recounted to Bouchardon, Denvignes said Goubet was interested in the information about the Moroccan landings, thought she must be very intelligent, but questioned who she was dealing with. Although she had given Denvignes detailed accounts of her meetings with Kalle, he kept this from Goubet. Mata Hari was furious that he had belittled her achievement and cast suspicion on her source.[7] 'Why did you lie?' she cried but the colonel would only sigh and, as the train whistle blew, he crooned as if to placate her, 'My child! My child!'[8]

Meanwhile, Ladoux still refused to see her. When they finally met on 7 January he was distant and immediately reproached Mata Hari for openly visiting the French embassy in Madrid. Denvignes had passed on nothing from her. Worse still, when she recounted the information Kalle had given her – the Germans had broken the French code, they knew about the French aviator who dropped agents behind their lines and German agents carried secret ink crystals under their fingernails – Ladoux was unimpressed. He responded that the Germans couldn't possibly have broken the French code and, furthermore, he would pay her nothing until he had checked her story with Denvignes.

She had fallen into a trap. She had no money to return to Holland and, anyway, could not leave without official permission from the French. There had been no word from her young Russian lover, Captain Vladimir de Masloff, and her plan to make a fortune from espionage had failed. The following night the hotel staff had noticed her weeping in the dining room over dinner. She was listless, spending her days visiting her dentist and her fortune-teller, writing long, urgent letters to Vadime and waiting.[9] They finally met in late January when Vadime was given leave to visit the capital but the reunion was later marred by the alarming news he received upon his return. The Russian embassy in Paris had warned Vadime's commanding officer to tell Masloff that he was dealing with 'an adventuress'. Mata Hari could not relinquish her dream of marrying this handsome man, young enough to be her son, but in reality the affair was over. It was the last time she would ever see him.[10]

Mata Hari grew increasingly desperate to leave France for The Hague. She needed to placate her lover, the Baron van der Capellen, and made three separate requests for exit papers to Switzerland. When her funds ran low, she economized by moving to the Elysée Palace Hotel in the Champs Elysées. She stopped paying bills and put off her creditors whenever she could. Ladoux remained elusive and the assignment to Belgium, with its promise of a million francs, was fading fast. She described her current difficulties in a letter probably written to her friend, Count van Limburg Styrum:[11]

> Since November 20, I have hoped to return to my home and now I am in Paris. I have spent two weeks in England [12 November to 1 December] and returned by way of Spain and France. Trips are impossible and I would really like to take no more of these journeys in time of war. You warned me, but I had such a desire to return to Paris and my friends, and I thought one would find it possible to overcome the difficulties and even enjoy them a little.
>
> I have written Anna [Lintjens, her maid] to give you my regards. We are neighbours in a small town where we usually see each other day by day, so I have promised I would send news frequently.
>
> The Baron is furious that I have not returned. Evidently, I have failed him. Also, old Anna is not so pleased.[12]

The letter reveals that Mata Hari feared she might lose the Baron which also meant losing her only stable source of income and her house in The Hague. As usual, she was accumulating debts rapidly; according to later police estimates, she was spending 1,000 francs a week when, for example, her hotel bill was only thirty francs a night.[13] Since Ladoux had become so evasive, and she had no idea when she might see Vadime again, she was anxious to return to The Hague.

Ladoux, meanwhile, was playing for time. After his inspectors reported that Mata Hari had checked into the Plaza Athénée on 4 January, he passed this information to Captain Pierre Bouchardon, who would act as the chief investigating officer of the military tribunal (the Third Council of War). Ladoux explained to Bouchardon that Margaretha Zelle, aka Mata Hari, was the woman Scotland Yard suspected of being AF44. At 9 o'clock on 13 February 1917 inspectors Mercadier, Curnier, Des Logères, Quentin and Pinson entered room 131 at the Elysée Palace Hotel. Behind them stood the police commissioner, André Priolet, who informed Mata Hari they had orders for her arrest.

> The woman Zelle, Margaretha, known as Mata Hari, living at the Palace Hotel, of Protestant religion, foreigner, born in Holland on 7 August, 1876, one metre 75 centimetres tall, being able to read and write, is accused of espionage, complicity and intelligence with the enemy, in an effort to assist them in their operations.[14]

Contrary to the later rumours that would insist Mata Hari had brashly leapt from her bed naked, and dressed shamelessly before the police, Priolet reported she was eating breakfast and in ill-health.[15] He also claimed she gave him a cap with red and blue ribbons and a bunch of wild violets as a souvenir of their peculiar meeting.[16] She was taken directly to Bouchardon's diminutive office in the Palais de Justice on the Quai de l'Horloge where she would endure fourteen separate interrogations conducted over more than four months.

Bouchardon himself would prove one of her greatest obstacles to a just hearing. In later interviews, he would openly admit his contempt for Mata Hari; she was, he said, 'hideous, heavy-lipped, copper-coloured' and 'a born spy, who clearly showed that she was one'.[17] Neither would Bouchardon hide his antagonism towards her lawyer, the seventy-four-year-old Edouard Clunet who was a sentimental but inappropriate choice. Although an expert in international corporate law, he was not a criminal lawyer and was ill-prepared for an espionage trial. Lieutenant Jean Hallaure explained to Bouchardon that Mata Hari had 'the most frank attachment to Monsieur Clunet' and believed 'he was the most honest lawyer in the world and the only truly international one'. On one occasion, said Hallaure, she had even sent him flowers. However Mata Hari might have felt about the matter, Clunet was actually chosen for her by Henri Robert, the solicitor-general and president of the Corporation of Barristers.[18] Bouchardon in a letter to the chief military prosecutor, Major Jullien, dismissed Clunet as:

> an old and somewhat naïve admirer of the dancer that Madame Zelle used to be. He brings to the defence of his client the ardour of a neophyte and shows her such kind attention that I have difficulty in understanding since he knows that on the eve of the war the accused was, in Berlin itself, the mistress of two officers and the chief of police. It is Madame Zelle who has said this.[19]

Bouchardon always portrayed Clunet as an old fool. He recalled Mata Hari and her lawyer in Clunet's 'austere apartment on the rue de Rome' caressing one another – 'it was a little ridiculous.'[20]

Mata Hari's other problem was Ladoux, who would distort the evidence against her to strengthen his case that she was an agent for Germany. While he came under increasing pressure to justify his department, he had to rationalize the assignment of two detectives to follow a suspect for six months without yielding anything whatsoever. Ladoux was adroit at shaping the evidence to fit the crime. His account of Mata Hari's November 1916 trip to Spain, for example, was riddled with factual errors. He described her interviewing several people in the entourage of the German ambassador, whom he incorrectly named as Prince Radolin (the name was actually Ratibor), while Ladoux's detectives reported nothing suspicious about Mata Hari on this trip. He claimed the British Admiralty intercepted the *Hollandia* and forced Mata Hari onto their man-of-war, the *Marvellous*, which sailed for Liverpool where she was questioned. In reality, she was interrogated after the *Hollandia* docked at Falmouth. Neither is there evidence for Ladoux's enticing claim that 'she had received information from well-informed sources that the *Marvellous* stood twenty-four chances in a hundred of being torpedoed in the Gulf of Gascogne'. Nor could he prove that she left France 'several times to give recitals' in Hamburg and Berlin during the war.[21] When asked in later years about the Mata Hari trial, Lieutenant André Mornet, the trial counsel, commented, 'Oh, you know, in the Mata Hari case there was not enough evidence to whip a cat.'[22] But if specific proof of her recruitment and experience as an agent for Germany was thin, Ladoux supplied it from his 'overflowing imagination'.

For several months, a listening post on the Eiffel Tower had been intercepting German messages in Morse code between Germany and Spain. A cryptographer

Edmond Locard revealed that in 1916 he and his colleagues had broken the Germans' current code which the Allies kept secret. Ladoux, however, made several contradictory statements regarding this crucial evidence. In his memoirs, he claimed that secret coded messages had been intercepted between Madrid and Berlin *before* Mata Hari's first meeting with Kalle in 1916, although he offers no evidence of this.[23] More importantly, however, Ladoux contradicted himself and other witnesses over what the messages actually contained. The first that mentioned an agent 'H21' (the gender in German and French was unspecified), sent from Kalle in Madrid to Berlin, was deciphered on 13 December 1916. According to Ladoux it read:

> Agent H21 has just arrived in Madrid. She has succeeded in being engaged by the French Secret Service, but has been sent back here by the British. She asks for instructions and money. She has given me the following information [there followed the positions of a certain number of French regiments at the front, which were not at all exact] and the news that a certain French statesman X [(the name has been deleted but it can be presumed it was Aristide Briand)] has close relations with a foreign princess . . .[24]

The reply from Berlin forty-eight hours later read, 'Tell agent H21 to go back to France and to continue her mission there. She will receive a cheque of 5,000 francs from [the German consul in Amsterdam] Craemer [sic] on his account.'[25]

Police Commissioner Maunoury, who heard Ladoux read the 13 December message just as it was deciphered, remembered the text quite differently. He thought that it had read, 'H21, an excellent agent before the war, has given us nothing since the war . . . (Tell H21 to go back to France . . . etc).' This seems unlikely since Mata Hari, caught in Berlin at the outbreak of war, was treated as *French* because she had lived for so long in Paris. Neither was there any evidence that the Germans had recruited her before the war and this suggestion may simply have been 'intoxification' – false information intended to mislead its readers. The gossip about Aristide Briand and the princess and the position of French regiments at the front, Maunoury thought had come from a postcard Mata Hari sent from Spain. He did not recall hearing it in the original radio message. However, he agreed with Ladoux that Kalle's communiqué to Berlin had made critical comments about H21's abilities which suggested she was their agent.[26]

Ladoux would later claim he believed that, since Mata Hari worked for the Germans, when she arrived in Madrid she went immediately to Kalle for instructions. Colonel Cartier, head of the cryptographic unit at the French war ministry, claimed the radio messages confirmed this and revealed that Mata Hari's controller was the mysterious Dr Elisabeth Schragmuller, who ran the alleged German spy school in Antwerp. However, Ladoux, in this version of events, gave yet another twist to the tale. The messages intercepted between Madrid and Berlin, he said, revealed that agent H21's mission had been 'frustrated by an English cruiser [a reference to her detention at Falmouth in 1916] and [s/he] was demanding instructions and money'. Since the British secret service insisted on arresting Mata Hari, Ladoux had set a trap; he had Lieutenant Hallaure suggest she visit the Deuxième Bureau so that Ladoux could offer her a mission. In Madrid, Kalle had sent a radio message to Berlin for advice about her next move. This time, Ladoux's recollection almost matched Maunoury's; the text read, 'a good agent before the war. We have been given nothing since the war. All the same, pay her/him 15,000 pesetas.' Cartier, however, said he had never seen this text in the dossier and believed Mata Hari could not have been convicted on the evidence of the decoded messages alone. 'I think,' he said, 'there were other charges against her.'[27]

Ironically, Ladoux's memoirs considered the possibility that the whole set of radio messages about agent H21 – all sent in a broken code – was a set-up. However, he failed to give his readers this critical clue and in answer to an agent P's suggestion that the Germans knew their code would be intercepted and the messages were intended to ruin Mata Hari, Ladoux replied: 'Fact and personages were mentioned there which our enemies had the greatest interest in not unmasking.'[28] His rather obtuse comment was preceded by an invitation to agent P to 'decipher the remainder of the message', implying that Mata Hari had imparted more than local gossip to Kalle. The rumours about the French regiments, the British dominating the military campaign, and Aristide Briand and Marie Bonaparte, Princess George of Greece, hardly constituted a political secret. But, in effect, Ladoux greatly exaggerated Mata Hari's importance as an agent to justify his actions and elevate his own status.

The discrepancy between all the different texts and interpretation of the messages supports the argument that Ladoux had doctored them to strengthen his case. There is, however, yet another version of Kalle's first message to Berlin. In the French military archives, the communication deciphered on 13 December reads:

> H21 informs us: Princess George of Greece, Marie Bonaparte, is using her 'intimate relations' with Briand to get French support for her husband's access to the Greek throne. S/he says Briand's enemies would welcome further defeats in the war to overthrow him. Britain has political and military control of France. French are afraid to speak up. General offensive planned for the spring.[29]

Kalle sent messages about agent H21 to Berlin on 20 and 22 December. By Christmas Eve the radiogram carried a complaint that Kalle had received no reply to his earlier messages and instructed that H21 should be given 3,000 francs and told that: 1) the results obtained were unsatisfactory; 2) the French could not develop the ink H21 was given if the correspondence paper was treated according to instructions; 3) if H21 does not want to use ink s/he should come to Switzerland and from there, contact 'A'. It remained unclear whether 'A' referred to Antwerp – the German centre for espionage operations in Francophone countries and home of Dr Schragmuller's school – or the name of an agent known to the French.[30]

On 26 December Kalle sent another message saying that since he had received no instructions, he had given H21 3,500 pesetas. This agent would request an additional sum by sending a telegram via the Dutch consul in Paris to 'domestic servants' (sic) in Holland and asked that the German consul in Amsterdam (whose name was actually spelt Cramer), Kroemer (sic) be advised. Berlin replied two days later and Kalle immediately sent a message back that

H21 would arrive in Paris tomorrow and through Anna Lintjens would ask that 5,000 francs be sent to the Comptoir National d'Escompte de Paris and handed to the Dutch consul Otto Bunge. On 29 December Kalle confirmed that H21 had left Madrid and on 5 January Berlin asked for details about the information concerning the princess and the French statesman. The radio messages, however, were wrong on two counts; Mata Hari arrived in Paris not in late December but on 3 January, and although she received 5,000 francs through the Dutch consul Bunge, this was not until 15 January. Mata Hari thought the 3,500 pesetas that Kalle had given her on 16 December was a 'gift' from a lover rather than payment for information.[31]

However, when Bouchardon admitted Mata Hari to his office in the Palais de Justice on 13 February 1917, he had yet to receive this evidence – in any form – from Ladoux. Since Bouchardon had so little to go on, Mata Hari's statements would be crucial to the prosecution. The only other witness to these sessions was Sergeant-clerk Emmanuel Baudouin, who sat silently at a small table transcribing in shorthand. After Bouchardon explained that their conversation was being recorded and verified that she had read the warrant for her arrest, she signed a statement protesting her innocence. 'Someone is playing with me – French counterespionage, since I am in its service and I have only acted on its instructions.'[32] Bouchardon described his impressions at the end of the first interview. 'I saw a tall woman with thick lips, dark skin and imitation pearls in her ears, who somewhat resembled a savage . . .'[33] His distaste for what he perceived to be Mata Hari's profession – a courtesan and therefore a 'savage' – was revealed throughout the interrogation. When Bouchardon informed her she would be taken to Saint-Lazare prison for women, she burst into tears. 'She turned to me, a haggard look in her eyes, dumb with fear, bits of dyed hair sticking to her temples.'[34] His loaded descriptions of her suggest that it was impossible for him to be dispassionate in assessing her case. As Colonel Cartier commented, there were other, unstated crimes with which she was charged.

Saint-Lazare had been established as a prison-hospital in the nineteenth century to treat prostitutes – most often for venereal diseases – from brothels throughout Paris. The prison's infirmary was so infamous that it became an emblem for the evils of prostitution in literature on the subject during the Third Republic.[35] Only recently had the prison been used for the internment of female spies. Its reputation was an added humiliation for Mata Hari who would be forced to live among women who had worked full-time in the 'trade', an uncomfortable reminder of what she might become. Neither were her surroundings reassuring. She spent the first night at the now demolished Faubourg Saint-Denis section of the prison; it was entirely padded (a precaution against suicides) and furnished with only a straw pallet on the floor. There was no window and only a weak light entered from a barred opening high in the brick wall outside of which was a weak gas jet. A small peephole in the door of the cell allowed the guards to watch the inmate, making privacy impossible.[36]

The conditions at Saint-Lazare, run by the Sisters of Marie-Joseph, were so harsh that until the First World War their female prisoners regularly staged mutinies. The rooms were rarely heated, the food, which was served at 8.45 a.m. and 3 p.m., consisted of bread, boiled vegetables and a weekly slice of beef. The women received a clean chemise only once a week, even during their periods, and were forced to work eleven hours a day stitching mailbags under the supervision of a nun. All correspondence was opened and those who were allowed visitors could speak to them only through a heavy metal grille. Since the prison housed so many prostitutes, either for the treatment of venereal disease or for crimes related to their profession, it was nicknamed the *campagne* (the country). A visit, however, was the antithesis of 'going to the country' for a break.[37]

Léon Bizard, the prison doctor, paid the new inmate Mata Hari a routine visit that first night. He recommended she be moved to a better cell and asked if she needed anything. 'Yes,' she replied with astonishing naïvety, 'a telephone and a bath.'[38] Both were impossible in the circumstances. Yet in prison she was a celebrity whose reputation as a *grande dame* preceded her. A prisoner who acted as Mata Hari's nurse under Dr Bizard exclaimed when she saw her, 'What a great mare! She has a restless air! A woman fatal to men and not to be trusted.'[39]

After Mata Hari's second interview with Bouchardon on 15 February, however, she was transferred to a marginally better section of the prison known as the *Ménagerie* – the animal house – where rats rushed along the stone corridors.[40] This was an ordinary cell, with two wooden beds with straw mattresses and coarse brown blankets, a brick floor, whitewashed walls and a skirting board of tar. She spent the days by herself but in the evenings another woman slept in the room with her.[41] During the first few days she remained constantly indoors but was later allowed a fifteen-minute daily walk around the courtyard. She resented having to pay for the abysmal meals she received in her cell. Dr Bizard found her an accommodating prisoner who made few demands, although she was moody, easily bored and longed for conversation.[42]

On 15 February Mata Hari was brought before Bouchardon for her first interrogation. The thin-faced, bearded attorney began by asking his subject to tell her life history while he waited, watched and chewed his fingernails. At the age of forty-six, with considerable experience as a prosecuting attorney in Rouen and Paris, Bouchardon had perfected his dramatic technique of jumping from his chair while talking to the accused. He would pace the room and then stop in front of a window, tapping his fingers on the glass, all to exasperate his subject.[43] But for the moment, he sat patiently while Mata Hari talked.

As she had with Sir Basil Thomson, during her interview in London, she confused dates and rearranged events to create a more favourable impression. She stressed, for example, that before the war she had twice sent information to the French authorities from Germany. During her final meeting with her former lover Alfred Kiepert in Berlin, April 1914, they had discussed a reunion in Paris. When Mata Hari told Kiepert she would not return to the French capital for six months, he replied, 'You'll be in Paris before then and so will I.' She had immediately written to the French Minister of War, Colonel Messimy, another former lover, relating this astonishing conversation and suggesting he investigate in Berlin. Messimy replied that it was impossible since he could not cross the border.[44] She had once written a similar letter to Henry Raphérer, the French aviator, after another of her lovers, the German naval chief of a 'Hydro Aeroplane' station at Putsig, also predicted that his country would invade France.[45]

She recounted her brief affair with the police officer Griebel in Berlin with whom she had dined the day war broke out, her trouble in leaving Germany and her reunion with Baron van der Capellen in The Hague after her return to Holland in 1914. She described her first wartime visit to Paris, confusing the date as *May* 1915 instead of December, when she collected her ten packing cases and became the mistress of the Marquis de Beaufort. Taking the advice of the Dutch consul, she had returned to Holland via Spain. There the interview ended and Bouchardon showed a glimmer of grudging respect for his subject's intelligence. 'She had taken hold of herself again,' he wrote of her performance, 'and put up a good fight.'[46]

Mata Hari returned to Saint-Lazare without knowing when she would next be questioned. She was allowed no visitors other than Clunet who came regularly. She was forbidden to send letters to friends or relatives since nothing could appear about her case in the press until after the trial had begun. Instead, she wrote copious letters to Bouchardon to complain of the prison conditions and, presuming that she would eventually be released, to make domestic arrangements. She saw herself as superior to the other women prisoners and, as she wrote to Lieutenant Mornet, 'you must realize that I am different from those around me and yet I am treated like them.'[47] Many of her concerns were practical: she asked for clean sheets and nightshirts, she wanted her laundry collected from the hotel and small bills paid. But by railing against the prison system, she also attempted to gain control over a terrifying situation. As long as she could deal with the minutiae of her life – even a life in limbo – she would not have to confront the prospect of endless incarceration or death.

Much was denied her. In an undated letter she reproached Lieutenant Mornet for 'refusing to send me my clean shirts from my laundry that I asked him for *twice*, two weeks ago. Why force me to live in dirt; what use is it?'[48] She also requested that a pair of blue leather slippers, her brass Portuguese earrings and her toiletries be collected from the Palace Hotel. Also, Madame Daludier Madiste at 16 rue Duphot must be paid fifteen francs for her white feather boa. However, what concerned Mata Hari most was another chance to visit her beloved Vadime Masloff. Although on their last visit Vadime had warned that his relationship with her might have endangered his position, she still dreamed of their future together. As she wrote to Bouchardon, 'what I would appreciate most in my heart is the permission to go to see my fiancé, Captain de Masloff.' She added plaintively, 'I have never, never done any harm towards you. Let me go free.' These requests were all impossible to grant. The question of bail had yet to be decided but the French would never have allowed a suspected spy to visit an officer at the front. Her arrest was a state secret and even the Dutch legation would not be 'semi-officially' informed of her arrest until 23 April.[49]

During the following week Mata Hari met Bouchardon on 21, 23, 24 and 28 February. During these interviews the prosecutor framed his questions to prove that Mata Hari had offered to work for the French under orders from the German secret service. If this was true, he then argued, the money from Holland had come not from the Baron van der Capellen, as she claimed, but from Cramer, the German consul, as payment for information. At Mata Hari's 1 March interrogation she insisted the 5,000 francs she received in Paris through the Dutch consul was her allowance from the Baron and was accompanied by a note saying that he threatened to give up the house in The Hague if she did not return soon.[50] A letter from Anna Lintjens, mentioning that the Baron had sent the money as requested, corroborated Mata Hari's statements. Anna had also sent a telegram, which arrived in Paris after Mata Hari's arrest, asking if the funds had reached her yet.[51]

But her defence fell on deaf ears. Bouchardon was convinced from the outset that he was dealing with a woman who had primarily supported herself through exploiting her intimate relations with men and therefore did not deserve his trust. It was a short leap, in his eyes, from sleeping with a man for money to milking him for information which could be profitably sold to the enemy. His biographical report on Mata Hari emphasized her time as a courtesan and dismissed her phenomenal dancing career in a few lines, touching only on her appearances at the Musée Guimet, private salons and the Folies Bergère. Meanwhile, she was asked to give details about the customers she took to the *maisons de rendezvous* at 5 rue de Galilée, 86 avenue Kléber and 14 rue Lord Byron.[52] In another report, he described the 'delicate situation' with Clunet, who enjoyed 'a place of honour among those closest to [Margaretha] Zelle, [Mata Hari]'. He suggested that Clunet had so confused his feelings towards his client with his role as attorney that he would overlook vital evidence. Even such a learned man was vulnerable to her once-blinding charms.[53] Bouchardon's description of his investigation pivoted round his desire to see this dissolute woman, who dragged a horde of well-bred admirers in her wake, get the punishment she deserved.

On 6 and 8 March two further radio messages concerning agent H21 which passed between the German embassy in Madrid and Berlin in the broken code were deciphered at the Eiffel Tower. Kalle was now asking if H21 should use invisible ink and return to Holland via Switzerland (and therefore Germany) and the reply from Berlin asked whether the agent had left Spain. If agent H21 was so important, why didn't Kalle know that she had left Madrid two months before? The exchange, like the other set of intercepted messages sent in the old code, differed from all the other traffic and suggested either that the Germans were weighing the case against Mata Hari or giving the impression they were so incompetent they couldn't keep track of her.[54] Yet Ladoux withheld this information from Bouchardon as the investigation continued.

Meanwhile, Mata Hari vented her frustration through writing to Bouchardon. 'You have made me suffer too much,' she wrote during a week when Dr Bizard noted how nervous she was, 'crying all the time'. 'I am completely mad. I beg of you, put an end to this. I am a woman. I cannot support [myself] above my strength.'[55] Her mental state deteriorated and on 9 March she stayed in bed rather than continue the interrogation with Bouchardon. During the week, she had coughed up blood during the night. 'I cried with fear and nobody could hear me. Show a bit of humanity for me,' she wrote. 'The shock has upset me so much that I no longer feel myself. I think I am going mad. I beg you not to leave me locked up in this cell.'[56] Bouchardon would later claim that he thought Mata Hari was suffering from VD but it seems extremely unlikely that an inmate in a prison-hospital specializing in its treatment would go undiagnosed. The military physician Dr Socquet, who examined her, found she was so healthy that he refused Clunet's suggestion of hospitalization.[57]

Every letter revealed her increasing desperation to leave prison, even if it was for the relatively cleaner environment of a locked hospital ward. But Bouchardon remained unmoved by her campaign and on 12 March called her back for another session.

A month later, on 12 April, Mata Hari was asked to describe the contents of her travel bag which were being tested for possible use as invisible ink solutions. Among her perfumes, face creams, lipsticks, rouges and powders, two items were taken away for further investigation. One was a lotion Mata Hari had on prescription from her physician Dr Vergne, which was found on file at the Pharmacie Roberts in Paris. Chemical analysis revealed it was a spermicide commonly used by French prostitutes and courtesans.[58] The other was a product which contained oxycyanide of mercury – also a contraceptive. As Mata Hari explained patiently to Bouchardon, 'It is nothing but a product one puts into injections to prevent the birth of children after each coition.' A doctor in Madrid had given it to her the previous December.[59] Both substances were believed to make excellent solutions for secret writing. However, testing for invisible inks was conducted on an absurd variety of solutions during the war and anything from urine to milk to lemon juice was considered ideal. MI5's General Sir Walter Kirke, stationed on the Western Front, was once given a report that 'the best *invisible ink* is *semen*'.[60] Being found in possession of any of these substances, however, was clearly no proof of guilt.

Once the investigators had cleared Mata Hari's belongings of any incriminating evidence, she hoped finally to convince Bouchardon of her innocence. On 12 April she ended the interrogation by pleading, 'I beg of you, stop making me suffer in this prison . . . I have not done any espionage in France and there is nothing bad in my luggage, in my bottles or my strongbox.'[61] She also requested that since 'you were able to see that I own nothing suspicious', her toiletries and travelling bag should be returned. Her letter-writing campaign continued and, aside from the unhygienic and degrading conditions of prison life, her deepest fear was facing Vadime across the courtroom. While she would be 'delighted' to have her former lovers such as General Messimy called as witnesses – since she believed they would support her claim of innocence – she begged that Captain Masloff be exempt.

> I have thought hard about it and the mere idea of seeing him again in these circumstances has already made me cry so much that I foresee that in front of the council of war when I see him again it will be even worse.
>
> I know myself well. As long as I don't cry, it will be alright, but once I start there would be little anyone could do with me. You would be forced to rearrange the interview.
>
> Since he is the man I love the most in all the world, he is also the only one that I don't have the strength to see . . . Since it has already been understood in a report where he stated that I had never asked him one question about the war, that will be enough.[62]

In an interview on 19 May, Captain Louis Pineau, commander of the gendarmerie at Rennes, interviewed Vadime who was then a patient at the city's military hospital. The Russian officer remembered that Mata Hari had only once asked him questions about where he was stationed and then it was merely so that she could follow his regiment's movements in the newspaper.[63] He was 'very astonished', when he rushed to see her at the Elysée Palace Hotel on March, to discover that she had gone.

By the time Bouchardon called Mata Hari for the ninth interrogation on 1 May, he had received Ladoux's version of the intercepted messages between Berlin and Madrid. On 21 April Lieutenant General Dubail, the military governor of Paris, was given fourteen messages in deciphered code from Ladoux. Bouchardon was offered this vital evidence in the form of a memo – an amended version of the radio messages – that conveniently justified Ladoux's decision to hire Mata Hari for a mission in Brussels. Ladoux argued that since he had only a few examples of Mata Hari's 'indiscreet curiosity', her suggestion to seduce the German governor of Belgium, General Moritz Ferdinand von Bissing, would finally establish that she was working for the Germans all along. Now there was evidence which proved Ladoux's suspicions were correct. However, there were only *nine* messages in the memo Bouchardon received and they differed significantly from those originally decoded at the Eiffel Tower.[64] Neither did Ladoux inform either Dubail or Bouchardon that every message concerning 'agent H21' was sent in the broken code. Bouchardon would later describe how vital this memo from Ladoux was: 'I brought [Mata Hari] back time and again to the one document which constituted her condemnation.'[65]

The door to Bouchardon's tiny office in the Palais de Justice remained closed that day as he shut himself up with his clerk Baudouin and Mata Hari 'inside a sort of cave'.[66] He would confidently compare this crucial interrogation to a skilfully executed game of cards. 'You are agent H21 of the intelligence section of Cologne sent for the second time to France in May 1916 . . . You pretended to accept Captain Ladoux's offers and to accomplish a journey in Belgium on behalf of his service.' But in November 1916, he continued, she had received 5,000 francs in Paris for supplying the German military attaché in Madrid with political, diplomatic and military information. Mata Hari was unmoved by Bouchardon's latest list of her crimes. But this time, the prosecuting attorney claimed he had proof and read a selection from the intercepted messages. She rose hotly to her defence; how did Bouchardon know that she was an enemy agent? Spain was full of spies and the Germans could have got the personal information mentioned in the decoded messages from her letters posted in Madrid. 'Captain Ladoux claimed to have proof and the English confused her with Clara Benedix, but they were both obliged to face facts,' she replied.[67]

For Bouchardon 'it was an emotional duel' but this time he believed Mata Hari was weakening. However, her prosecutor was so convinced of her guilt that her logical arguments could have no effect. Bouchardon even mocked her suggestion that Kalle had been paying staff at Madrid's Hotel Ritz to inspect her mail and report who she was corresponding with. Yet the French double-agent Marthé Richard, who was staying at the Ritz at the same time as Mata Hari, had told Ladoux that the Germans had precisely this arrangement with the hotel staff.[68] In the face of Bouchardon's contempt, Mata Hari 'used every trick in the book', he would later write; 'cries, tears, smiles, indignation, invective.' She shouted back at him, 'How can you be so without pity . . . to torture a poor woman like that and ask her such vile questions?'[69]

Despite the emotional response that Bouchardon describes, the records reveal that she continued to press her case with a cool logic. 'In any case,' she told him, 'I am not agent H21, von Kalle [sic] never gave me a penny and the 5,000 francs that I received in November and another 5,000 francs that I received in January of this year came from my lover, the Baron van der Capellen.' Moreover, she reminded her prosecutor that contrary to his claim that she had volunteered for the Deuxième Bureau (implying that she was under German orders) it was Ladoux who suggested she join the French espionage service. 'I am not an expert on spying,' she said. 'I never thought of that before Captain Ladoux spoke of it to me.'[70]

But if her arguments made sense, Bouchardon had another basis on which he could attack. In his memoirs, he cruelly describes her as a once-celebrated dancer who could no longer rely on her physical charms. 'Had she been pretty? Without a doubt from her passport photo. But this woman . . . in my office . . . had suffered many affronts from time,' he wrote. Her bloodshot eyes were 'as big as eggs', she had 'a bulbous nose, chapped skin, a mouth that touched the ears, the swollen lips of a negress, teeth as big as plates . . . greying hair no longer covered by dye.' His earlier reference to Mata Hari as a 'savage' and now a 'negress' suggests that in her degraded state she represented the underside of the racist 'Oriental' fantasy. An ageing exotic had no value but became a grotesque, syphilitic parody of the desirable. Deprived of physical and mental comfort, intellectual stimulation and friendship, Mata Hari had been worn down by prison life. Bouchardon concluded smugly, 'she hardly resembled the dancer who had bewitched so many men.'[71]

How could Mata Hari defend herself against accusations that the prosecutors did not even realize they were making? Why were they so intent on finding her guilty? Ladoux's motives were more straightforward; he needed to justify the expense of assigning two detectives to follow a suspect for six months without discovering anything. He had also to regain his reputation with the British secret service after the embarrassment of hiring a woman they had warned him about several months earlier. But Bouchardon's memoirs reveal that his interrogations involved more than accumulating evidence against an accused spy. His inaccurate references to Mata Hari's venereal disease, his grotesque physical descriptions and his references to game-playing suggest a desire to punish the courtesan who has transgressed the rules of marriage, motherhood and the family. By now Mata Hari's case had taken on a symbolic importance and she was to represent the 'rot' in French society. Spies – a vague and all-encompassing category of traitors – were being blamed for the mutinies erupting along the Western Front. The war was dragging on and any demonstration that the political forces and individuals responsible had been brought to justice had a potent effect. Mata Hari's capture was a sensation and to place her before the firing squad was to symbolize a cleansing of the ills that plagued the nation.[72]

While the investigation dragged inexorably forward, Mata Hari continued to plead for bail, for the right to have Clunet with her during the hearings and to contact the Dutch legation. On 4 April her former lover Jules Cambon, the current secretary-general of the Ministry for Foreign Affairs, wrote to the war minister concerning her case: 'I reckon it is not possible to prevent the accused from addressing an appeal to a representative of her country. We would [otherwise] expose ourselves, when the situation of the Dutchwoman is finally known, to the claims of the legation of the Netherlands and from the Dutch government.' But it was not until early May that Mata Hari was finally allowed to write directly to the Dutch foreign minister whom Clunet was forbidden to contact on her behalf.[73]

Meanwhile, the Baron van der Capellen had begun to worry about his 'little kitten' and wrote to the Dutch foreign minister, Loudon, on 11 April. Loudon sent a telegram to Otto David Eduard Bunge, the head of the Dutch legation in Paris, asking for information: 'Please communicate by telegram the present address of Margaretha Zelle, alias Mata Hari, last known address Plaza Hotel, 25 rue Montaigne, Paris and ask if she intends to return soon.'[74] After a delay of almost two weeks, the Paris legation replied to The Hague that the minister in charge had been 'semi-officially' informed by the French government that Margaretha Zelle aka Mata Hari was in Saint-Lazare prison, charged with espionage.[75]

Once the Dutch legation knew about the investigation, Mata Hari received permission to contact her friends through their offices. She was most concerned that Anna Lintjens and the Baron should know where she was. Her letters, however, reveal that she was either trying to protect her friends by diminishing the gravity of her situation or that she could not accept its reality. 'For the last six weeks I have been imprisoned in Saint-Lazare, accused of espionage, which I have not done,' she wrote to the Dutch consulate in Paris on 16 April. 'If you can advise my maid without mentioning my arrest, but only in telling her that I am having difficulties in leaving France and that above all, she should not worry, then please do write this letter for me . . . I assure you that I am half crazy with grief.'[76] She also asked Count Styrum to reassure Anna, and, as usual, to make domestic arrangements.

> I am having many difficulties right now . . . since I have to look after my interests . . . I beg you to be good enough to call on old Anna and tell her not to worry, that she must take good care of my house and that she must not permit anyone to enter . . . there are no bills to pay except my dressmaker, Kuhne, and if she has the least difficulty, let her write at once to my lawyer.[77]

Both Anna Lintjens and the Baron could have supported Mata Hari's most important claim that the 5,000 francs she was paid in Paris on 4 November 1916 had come from van der Capellen and not Cramer, the German consul. But because the case was meant to be confidential, the defence counsel could not call civilian witnesses. The given reason was that since Mata Hari's arrest was still a confidential matter, German intelligence might be alerted if any civilians were told about the case. However, as Bouchardon mentions in his memoirs, although the story was kept from the press, journalists followed him throughout Mata Hari's investigation. At the trial, only one civilian witness was actually cleared to read the prosecution's confidential documents, and to give evidence.[78]

Since Mata Hari's arrest in February when she temporarily waived the right to have her lawyer present, Clunet had been unable to attend her interrogations at the Palais de Justice. On 4 May he wrote to Bouchardon about this who, in turn, asked the opinion of Major Jullien, the chief military prosecutor. Bouchardon argued that if Clunet was allowed to attend the interrogations, he would also be entitled to read Ladoux's dossier of intercepted messages and would learn that French intelligence had broken the German code. 'In the present affair there exists an urgent reason to hold firm to the strict legal prescriptions [that would presumably bar Clunet],' wrote Bouchardon. 'In the face of the messages from Madame Zelle, our counterespionage finds it necessary to provide documents of an ultra-confidential nature.' Furthermore, he said, 'the least indiscretion would have major consequences ... in assigning the documents to the file, the Minister of War under his own signature has attracted the attention of the governor concerning the grave disadvantages of a divulgence.' However, since Bouchardon was never told that the radio messages sent between Madrid and Berlin were in a *broken* code, his fears about leaking vital information were completely unfounded.

Since Clunet had once been Mata Hari's lover, Bouchardon simply didn't trust him. As he wrote to Jullien, 'I must add that at the moment when this woman, clearly sent by the German consul to Paris, introduced herself to our military attaché [Colonel Denvignes, in Madrid] she gave Clunet as a kind of reference.' Did this not suggest that Clunet, a specialist in international corporate law with contacts throughout Europe, was somehow involved in Mata Hari's operations? Bouchardon even cast doubt on Clunet's ability to give any relevant legal opinion on the case. 'His keen attachment for his client has still not permitted him, I perceive, to see the gravity of the affair. With the best faith in the world he would not be able to maintain the reserve which I must impose.' Despite his arguments, however, Bouchardon was really only playing for time since Clunet would have to see the dossier containing the messages to prepare his case before the trial.[79] However, Jullien supported Bouchardon and, as was required by French law, Clunet was only allowed to attend the final interrogation.

Meanwhile, the police inspectors were having difficulty gathering the evidence the prosecution required. Inspector Priolet's report failed to find whether Mata Hari had any source of money other than the 5,000 francs she had received via the Dutch legation from the Baron. Instead, they discovered that she had accumulated debts at restaurants and hotels all over the city. The Hotel Meurice's manager had even obtained a court order forcing Mata Hari to pay at least part of an outstanding bill. Neither could the prosecution prove that she had seduced officers into divulging military information. Interviews with most of the individuals listed on fifty-three calling cards found in Mata Hari's possession – many of whom were former lovers – unanimously agreed that she only asked questions about the war to establish how her beloved Captain Masloff was faring.[80] The investigation, as Bouchardon would later recall, had ground to a halt.

It was Mata Hari who eventually gave away her best chance for survival. During an interrogation on 21 May where Ladoux was present, Mata Hari played her trump card. 'Today I want to tell you the truth,' she announced. 'If I have not said everything completely until now, it is because I had certain doubts which I will explain.' One evening a year before, she had received a visitor at her home in The Hague. It was Karl Cramer, a businessman who had been made an honorary German consul in Amsterdam. When he heard that Mata Hari had applied for a visa for France, he thought he might ask 'whether you would render us a service'. If she agreed to gather certain useful information on her trip, Cramer was instructed to pay her 20,000 francs. When she objected that the price was too low, he promised there would be more once she proved herself. She asked to consider the proposal and Cramer left.

The 20,000 francs, Mata Hari then reasoned, would adequately compensate her for the furs that were seized in Germany in 1914 and never returned. After she wrote to Cramer agreeing to his suggestion, he immediately called again and handed her the money in French bills. He also gave her three bottles of secret ink and showed her how to moisten a piece of paper in the first solution, to write with the second and clean it with the third. Cramer told her always to sign her letters, H [for Holland] 21. He could be reached through the Hotel de l'Europe in Amsterdam where he kept a suite. But after she 'bowed Monsieur Cramer politely out of the front door', she resolved that she would not help him. She never wrote to the hotel and dropped the three incriminating bottles over the side of the *Zeelandia* into a canal leading to the North Sea.

Mata Hari had seen no reason to tell Ladoux before. Since he insisted that she must prove her worth before he would pay her, why should she reveal her greatest secret for free? However, she assured her interrogators that she had done nothing for the Germans. As proof, she pointed out that when Ladoux asked whether she wanted to return to Holland through Spain or Switzerland, she had chosen the latter to avoid travelling through Germany. She feared the Germans might question her since she had done nothing for her 20,000 francs.[81] This payment was far higher than most of their agents ever received; Ottillie Voss, a German woman whom the French caught in February 1915, confessed that she had been paid 160 marks for travelling through Nice, Montpelier, Marseilles and Lyons and 500 francs for expenses.[82] As Mata Hari told her interrogators:

> Once in Madrid the circumstances required that I act along the lines you know by now. Captain Ladoux had not paid me anything. He had abused my confidence, and I had only a few hundred pesetas left . . . I received not a word from Paris, and my hotel bill kept going up and up. It was then that I went to see von Kalle [sic], who knew nothing about me.[83]

She had hoped the military attaché would be able to safeguard her trip through Germany but first she had to gain his confidence. She told him the French had tried to recruit her into their secret service and to sound convincing she 'made up some information for him which I got partly from old newspapers and partly composed from memory'. Kalle sent a message to Berlin asking if he could pay her but her price of 10,000 francs was refused. After committing 'intimate acts' with Kalle in his office, he gave her the 3,500 pesetas as a lover's gesture.[84]

The two payments of 5,000 francs sent via the Dutch consulate in November 1916 might have come from Cramer, she wasn't sure. A month earlier she had sent a message to Anna asking her to contact the Baron but, if this was impossible, to ask Cramer at the Hotel de l'Europe. Bouchardon then asked why Mata Hari had told Kalle about working for the French but refused to tell Ladoux about meeting Cramer, the secret ink and the number H21. 'Whom did you betray?' he demanded. 'France or Germany? It seems to us that the answer is simple.'

Mata Hari struck back. 'If my attitude towards the Germans and French was different, then it was because I wanted to harm the former – a plan that I succeeded in – and help the latter, a plan which was equally successful.' She was forced to convince the Germans she was on their side although, in reality, 'the French were leading the game.' Once Kalle had given her something useful, she had rushed back to Paris and went to Ladoux's office three times before she was allowed to see him. Bouchardon was unconvinced and offered his explanation: Mata Hari knew it was impossible to visit Kalle without alerting Ladoux's agents so she claimed she was going to the German attaché for the French. However, Mata Hari replied that spying was something she had never considered until Ladoux had suggested she might carry out an important mission in Belgium. It was also his idea that she work as a double-agent for the Germans, just as Marthé Richard was then doing in Spain.

Naïvely Mata Hari believed that this confession would strengthen her case. She thought she had just proved that she had never spied at all, but now Bouchardon was claiming that every officer she had ever loved provided her with 'an overall knowledge that would have been interesting to the Germans'. But to Mata Hari, officers were simply great lovers; 'they went happily away, without ever having spoken to me of the war and without my asking anything indiscreet of them. The only one I held onto was Masloff because I adored him.' Bouchardon regarded this as another evasion and, before the interrogation ended, asked for clarification of her earlier statements. His subject had provided the final evidence he needed to complete his case.

Much worse was to come for Mata Hari. In a letter on 31 May Ladoux explained that unless she now gave her interrogators the names of her accomplices in the German secret service, she would be shot. In desperation, she replied to Bouchardon:

> I swear to you ... that I have never had any accomplices, and that I am not a coward enough to invent names under the threat of death ...
>
> Captain Ladoux and I will never understand each other. Because of my travels, my foreign acquaintances, my life and situation, I have a grand view of events, and grand methods. With him, it's quite the contrary. He sees everything small; petty ... He never knew how to use me. That is his fault and not mine.
>
> As for myself, I have been sincere. My love and my self-interest are the guarantees of that. Today, around me, everything is collapsing, everyone turns his back, even he for whom I would have gone through fire. Never would I have believed in so much human cowardice. Well, so be it. I am alone. I will defend myself and if I must fall it will be with a smile of profound contempt.[85]

As 'everything collapsed', her desire to escape grew stronger as her hold on reality began to slip. The following day she offered to find the details of the German intelligence system in France in exchange for her immediate liberty. But she warned, 'you can threaten me and make me suffer but I cannot tell you what I do not know.'[86]

A few days later she wrote again to Bouchardon, this time to explain that when she was in Berlin at the outbreak of war the Germans treated her as a French resident and, therefore, an enemy; her bank account was frozen, her luggage, jewellery and furs were seized. She even had to hire the Amsterdam lawyer Eduard Phillips to retrieve her property but the furs were never returned. She insisted that she took Cramer's money as payment for this loss. 'I defend myself when I am attacked. I take when someone has taken from me,' she wrote. 'But I beg you to believe me; I have never done an act of espionage against France.'[87] After considering the evidence, she sent another letter on 8 June, begging Bouchardon 'not to play into [German] hands'; Kalle's messages were intended to put French intelligence 'on a false track, to permit some true woman agent to be left unbothered'.[88] However, although Ladoux and Goubet knew the Germans had deliberately sent messages in a broken code intended to be read by the French, Bouchardon never knew this. In his mind there was irrefutable evidence of Mata Hari's guilt so that no matter how logical her arguments were, she would never change his mind. Since she knew nothing about the falsified radio messages, she had no way of knowing exactly what charges she was defending herself against.

The final 'interrogatory and confrontation' was held on 21 June and Clunet was legally required to attend. The confident Bouchardon turned to Mata Hari and said simply, 'To sum it all up it's . . . a case of *en flagrant délit*.'[89] Since he had caught her 'in the act', the trial was a mere formality and the military tribunal would act on Mornet's judgement. Ironically, Bouchardon's chosen phrase – *en flagrant délit* or *in flagrante delicto* – is also used to describe a couple caught in the act of love-making – another instance where his concepts of espionage and sexuality were so intertwined they became virtually indistinguishable.

In reality, the case against Mata Hari rested entirely with the doctored telegrams that Ladoux had passed on to Bouchardon. Her defence was also handicapped by Clunet's inability to call upon crucial witnesses or to see the *original* radio messages sent between Berlin and Madrid. The elderly attorney tried to comfort his client by shaking his head and crooning. 'No, no, Poincaré [the current president of the Republic] will never allow your body, formed by the hand of the Graces, to return to clay.'[90] If the statement is true, it seems sad that even Clunet could not evaluate the case in terms of its justice. Rather he relied on a mystical and naïve notion that a woman might be respected, revered and spared an awful punishment if she possessed a beautiful body.

But Mata Hari had not given up her fight and on 27 June she wrote another angry letter to Mornet in her strong, looped handwriting. She requested permission to correspond with Mr Hijmans, her lawyer in The Hague, to inform him of her situation and to receive letters through the Dutch legation in Paris. Both requests were denied. She must have been thinking of Vadime for the following day she asked Clunet to try to persuade Bouchardon 'to give me just one photograph of my lover Captain de Massloff [sic] – . . . all of mine were taken from me.'[91] Neither had she accepted Mornet's decision against her communicating with the outside world. She responded on 2 July, demanding to know how he could possibly justify his position. Furthermore, she complained of a guard who 'offends me as much as he can' and described the appalling conditions in which she lived and challenged him to 'imagine this Saint-Lazare prison in its depraved, dirty and humiliating state'.

Four days later, she wrote to the Dutch legation in Paris asking them to forward a letter about her case to her Mr Hijmans. Another letter must be sent to Anna Lintjens, she said, who could produce receipts of payments made to the Amsterdam lawyer, Eduard Phillips, who had gone to Berlin in January 1915 to argue Mata Hari's case for collecting the jewels and money which had been confiscated in 1914. 'This will prove that my relations with Germany are *far* from being good,' she wrote.[92] The same day she wrote to Mornet, demanding that something be done about her filthy cell, the dismal food and her deteriorating emotional state; she was 'suffering enormously', losing weight, her bed was full of vermin and she was too weak even to protest like the other inmates. 'Why, my Lieutenant, am I being made to suffer this, the greatest misery?'

On 10 July she wrote to Mornet, again complaining about his refusal to forward her letters to Anna Lintjens. She argued that since she was a foreigner and did not have money 'in my pocket', her only means of raising funds to pay Clunet's fee was through Anna. If this wasn't possible, she suggested Mornet take her gold cigarette case which was worth 'at least 400 francs'. But, she added, 'leave me my lawyer and don't prevent me from defending myself.' In another letter written that day, she told Mornet indignantly that they were forcing her to ask Vadime Masloff for the 3,000 francs she had lent him on 16 January 1917 to settle a 'debt of honour'. A memo from Bouchardon to Mornet commented, 'there is something repugnant about seeing a soldier receiving money from Mata Hari.'[93]

Nearly a fortnight was to pass before Mata Hari had any reply from the authorities. On 19 July it came in the form of a parcel of clothes from her hotel. It contained a pair of buttoned ankle-high boots, a pair of pantaloons, two corsets, a tailored skirt and jacket and two blouses which she was allowed in preparation for her appearance at the trial.[94] The trial, which was to be held in camera and would be described by Bouchardon as a mere formality, was due to open at the Palais de Justice five days later. There was nothing for Mata Hari to do but wait in her freezing cell while she listened to the other inmates crying out, the rats scurrying along the corridor and a nun reading from a book for lost souls.

CHAPTER FIVE

TRIAL AND ERRORS

The evil that this woman has done is unbelievable. This is perhaps
the greatest woman spy of the century.[1]

LIEUTENANT ANDRÉ MORNET, PROSECUTOR (1917)

THROUGHOUT THE LONG WEEKS OF INTERROGATION with Captain Pierre
Bouchardon, Mata Hari was convinced that she would be rescued. The
Dutch consul in Paris, her lawyer Edouard Clunet or a French benefactor
would step forward with proof of her innocence. She reasoned that since
she had committed no crime, the prosecutors would eventually realize their
mistake. However, even her own government's attempts to intervene met with
indifference. Mr Hannema, secretary-general of the Dutch Foreign Ministry, sent
a telegram from The Hague on 30 June 1917 to Clunet asking to be 'kept closely
informed' about the case. He noted that several Dutch newspapers had 'published
articles about the arrest of the aforementioned lady'. Hannema, however, would
wait more than three weeks for a reply.

When Clunet finally answered on 24 July, he revealed only that the legation's two communications had been added to his client's file and that at 1
p.m. that day she would appear before the Third Military Tribunal at the
Palais de Justice where the proceedings would last only two days. Since the
tribunal was set to rubber-stamp Bouchardon's accusations, there was little the
Dutch government could do.[2] Four days before the trial began, Mata Hari was
moved from Saint-Lazare to the Conciergerie to be near the hall reserved for
court martials at the Palais de Justice. Sister Léonide was in attendance while
Sister Claudia shared the cell with the prisoner at night.

During the long weeks before the trial, Dr Bizard noticed that Mata Hari
had increasingly turned to her fantasy 'Orient' for comfort. Her final escape –
like the confection she had created as an Indian princess, a temple goddess, a
Salome – was a mythical world of sensual delights. 'When people speak to me
of their native countries,' she once told Dr Jean Bralez, Bizard's intern assistant,
'my spirit yearns towards a distant land, where a golden pagoda is reflected in
a winding river. There is a secret about my origin, in my blood.'[3] But neither
Mata Hari's identification with this imaginary 'Orient' nor her tireless campaign
against Bouchardon's charges could have any effect. She had become the victim
of her success. So convincing and potent was this high priestess of 'love and faith',
who had once displayed her body like a charm before the most cultured Parisians,
that the mask became the reality. The unwritten charges that stemmed from her
reputation as an 'international woman' had no defence.

'Neither the type, nor the character, nor her culture, nor her coloured
skin, nor her mentality – nothing of her belongs to our latitudes,' commented
Inspector Alfred Morain, the Metropolitan Police Commissioner of Paris. 'She
had something of the primitive savage about her and at the same time something

refined – sacerdotal.'[4] Morain, like the prosecutor Bouchardon, was oblivious to the contradictions in his description of Mata Hari. While he insisted she was a 'savage', whose skin colour, thoughts and character were completely alien, he also knew that the Dutch-born Margaretha Zelle had invented her 'Oriental' history as a useful stage device in 1904. Bouchardon had heard every detail of Madame Zelle's aka Mata Hari's life history but chose to equate her deteriorating appearance with an inferior Eastern 'race'; he noted how the grey showed through her dyed black hair, her skin had coarsened and without her rouge, lipstick and powders she had aged rapidly. Even Dr Bizard couched his description of Mata Hari, a woman whom he respected as 'proud and wayward . . . [who] had determined to please and had succeeded', in racist terms:

> The features of Mata Hari, especially when looked at full face, gave no impression of beauty. She was of an Asiatic type, with plenty of long hair, black and sleek. She had a low forehead, prominent cheek bones, a big mouth with lascivious lips, large ears, with a large nose with wide nostrils. But her black eyes fringed with long lashes lit up in a singular manner her very mobile features, which were, all the same, without fineness and not at all feminine. Mata Hari, in profile, was not much better looking. A being without physical charm, something of a savage, it was certainly through hard work before her mirror and by strength of will that this woman had succeeded in cultivating beauty, by gracious expert expression and by putting her body into the most pleasing attitudes.[5]

Instead of acknowledging that Mata Hari, the temple goddess, was just a useful disguise, they believed her exoticism camouflaged an 'Asiatic' savage, a 'negress' without charm, culture or even character. Mata Hari had become more real to her prosecutors than Margaretha Zelle, the middle-class Dutch divorcée, the runaway wife, who had turned to dancing to support her independence during the *belle époque*. It was this deceptive Other, who they believed had lured so many men into deceitful operations with Germany, that deserved the brutal punishment she would soon receive.

Just before 1 p.m. on 24 July, Mata Hari walked through the courtyards and climbed the spiral staircase to the second floor of the central building in the Palais de Justice. The trial would soon begin in the Court of Assizes room and would continue until seven o'clock that evening and then adjourn until the following morning at 8.30. Félix Belle, from the Paris newspaper *Le Gaulois*, caught a glimpse of Mata Hari before the military tribunal decided the trial should be held in camera and the courtroom cleared. '[She was] very elegant in her large, dark blue coat that hung loosely over a generously cut blouse . . . she passed with her supple dancer's walk, the head high and her lips smiling, the last smile to her last public!'[6] Major Emile Massard, the chief of military staff in Paris who represented General Dubail, the military governor of Paris, and was the only officer allowed to attend the trial, thought Mata Hari's appearance was calculated to flatter the jurors. The tricornered hat she sported was 'coquettishly military', and her dress was 'very low-cut'. But Massard commented smugly, 'she hadn't forgotten her elegance but she was totally without grace . . . she was really German in form and in heart.'[7]

Mata Hari faced the president of the tribunal, the fifty-four-year-old Colonel

Albert Ernest Somprou who commanded the Garde Républicaine, trial counsel, Lieutenant Mornet, and the clerk, Sergeant Major Rivière. The judges sat on a raised dais in full dress uniform; including Somprou, there were seven officers on the jury bench, all members of the Third Permanent Council of War of the military government in Paris and appointed by the military governor.[8] Sworn in were: Major Fernand Joubert, Lieutenant Henri Deguesseau, Captain Lionel de Cayla; Gendarmerie Captain Jean Chatin; Second-Lieutenant Joseph de Mercier de Malval and Sergeant Major Berthommé.[9] It was hardly a jury of Mata Hari's peers. The trial was, at first, open to the public who watched as the accused entered the courtroom and sat just above and behind Clunet. Lieutenant Mornet requested that the proceedings be held in camera and press reports banned; after a short deliberation, the judges agreed and the audience was ushered out.[10] The court sentries were instructed not to allow anyone to approach within ten paces.[11]

Somprou began by asking Mata Hari why she had ridden in an official car of Berlin's Metropolitan Police Commissioner (the *préfet*) through the city's streets on the day war was declared. Even Somprou repeated the confusion about Griebel's title; he was not the *préfet* – in French, a chief commissioner of police – but a mere officer. Massard claimed that Mata Hari also spoke of Griebel as a *préfet* although, in reality, Traugott von Jagow was Berlin's Metropolitan Police Commissioner who would have dealt with espionage matters.[12] Mata Hari's lover was clearly not a spy master; they had met at the Metropol Theatre when Griebel had been sent to inspect the dancer's costumes to ensure they were not 'too nude'.

Following this meeting with Griebel, Somprou asked Mata Hari if she then became an agent of the German espionage service and was given a mission to France [for 20,000 francs] and the number, CA42. According to Massard, Mata Hari told the court this was all true except that the payment was not for information but the current 'price of my favours'. However, Massard had confused both her *nom de baptême* (code name), which was H21, and her relations with German officers. In reality, she had received a generous parting gift from her wealthy lover Herr Kiepert, but although he was a German officer he wasn't a chief of espionage. Somprou went on to ask why Mata Hari had come to France in 1915 and stayed for seven months under the pretext that she was attached to an ambulance unit at Vittel. Mata Hari had never been a nurse and her only attachment to Vittel, as she was quoted as stating, was 'to a poor Russian captain Marow [sic] who had been wounded . . . he was the only man that I ever loved.'[13]

Somprou then called upon Mornet to give the prosecution's evidence on behalf of the government. He opened by asking Mata Hari about her relations with Allied officers:

> You have been under surveillance since June 1916. Our reports show that you were always accompanied by military men. Exclusively military men. The wealthy men who frequented the Grand Hotel at that time did not interest you. You had to have uniforms. The rank, the branch, the nationality, did not matter. What you wanted were soldiers. Is that usual for a courtesan who is not interested in military secrets?[14]

Officers, Mata Hari explained, had always attracted her; they were a 'sort of artist' who lived grandly and under their uniforms were always seductive. Yes, she had enjoyed a number of lovers but it was the brave soldiers, always ready to fight, always friendly and gallant, whom she cherished above all. 'To me, the officer forms a race apart . . . I never noticed whether they were German, Italian or French.'[15]

This was simply another ploy, calculated to impress the jurors, claimed Massard. But Mata Hari had told Bouchardon the same thing and had cultivated officers throughout her courtesan's career. Now Mornet turned to a much more sinister accusation: she had told Captain Ladoux she wanted to visit Vittel to take the waters but had written to the Baron van der Capellen that she was in perfect health. Had she not spent her time at Vittel with officers – Captain Masloff wasn't mentioned – and aviators from the Contrexéville airfield? She had continued to correspond with Amsterdam, said Mornet, and when she became suspicious that she was being followed, she returned to Paris.

No, said Mata Hari, she told Captain Ladoux she was ill as an excuse to see Masloff. She could hardly explain this to the Baron and besides, 'men who pay . . . want women who are merry, always ready for feasts and pleasure, scantily dressed in lace, not wrapped in flannel and wool blankets.'[16] At first, she took no notice of Ladoux's detectives because 'a woman of the theatre, such as myself, expects to be followed, it's only natural.' Mornet persisted; in Paris she knew she was going to be arrested and, to protect herself, she sought out Captain Ladoux and falsely offered her services for France. She had then left for Holland and returned to Spain via England. During this period, messages between Madrid and Berlin had been intercepted showing that Mata Hari was agent H21 (or CA42, according to Massard) and the German military attaché had asked that she be paid 15,000 francs from Amsterdam through the Dutch consul in Paris. This evidence had led the war minister General Lyautey to order the military government of Paris to arrest her. The telegrams – presumably the messages which Ladoux had altered – were read out.

But Mata Hari protested. Major Kalle had paid her, not for information, but for 'my caresses' and found it more convenient to use the government's money than his own. Marthé Richard, the French double-agent who was the lover of Baron von Krohn, the German naval attaché in Madrid at the time, confirmed that this was the usual arrangement for paying a mistress. Moreover, when Richard read in the Paris newspapers the erroneous report that Mata Hari had been the lover of Krohn (rather than Kalle), she challenged the Baron to disprove it. He took out his file on agents operating in Spain, packed with documents and appended photographs. 'It would have been very easy for me to pick out Mata Hari's photograph,' wrote Richard, 'but it was not there.'[17] It was on this charge of Mata Hari's relationship with Kalle, however, that Morain claims 'the prosecution thought itself justified in believing her responsible for the torpedoing of several ships that were chartered as transports to carry Allied troops to Morocco'.[18]

From the witness box Mata Hari also challenged Mornet's accusation that her 'beautiful relationships' with officers were a means to extract information for the Germans. Although she had many lovers, she said, she was always short of money so she had offered to be useful to France. Yes, the prosecutor countered, you did this because the Germans were unable to send you funds at that moment but Cramer, the German consul in Amsterdam, later sent 20,000 francs through the Dutch legation.

'That was the money from my friend,' interrupted Mata Hari.

'From your friend, the chief of espionage,' retorted Mornet, who then asked her to prove what she had done as a spy for France.

'I gave information to the chief of the Deuxième Bureau on the points about the Moroccan coast where the German submarines were off-loading their soldiers, very important and useful information . . .'

'Ah! And from where did you get hold of this information? If it was correct, you had direct relations with the enemy. If it was false, then you have triumphed over us.'

Massard claimed that Mata Hari reeled at this accusation and stammered, 'After all, I did what I was able to do for France. My information was good. I am not French and I have never done anything to you . . . You look for a way to confuse me. I am only a poor woman and for an officer, you are not gallant.' General Wattine, chief legal counsel of the French army, then reportedly shouted, 'We are defending our country, Madame, excuse us!'[19]

During the summer of 1917, a 'crisis of morale' was mounting in France and Mornet's exhortations to punish a woman indirectly responsible for the slaughter of French troops struck a bitter chord. 'What makes me certain of her guilt are proofs that have passed through my hands and the very confessions of this shameless spy,' the judge, Police Captain Jean Chatin, would later comment. '[She] has caused the death perhaps of 50,000 of our men, without counting those who perished at sea through her information.' Mata Hari was thus guilty of 'collective assassination'.[20] Throughout France, postal censors reported that complaints about the shortage of coal, food and supplies were contrasted with those making 'colossal' fortunes. Some believed this acute deprivation could even lead to revolution.[21] Mornet depicted Mata Hari as the perfect example of a female war profiteer. She was an 'international woman' who fed like a parasite on the moral rot of French society and whose decadent demand for luxury was in obscene contrast to the nation's deprivation.

Mata Hari might have hoped that her influential friends called as witnesses would break through Mornet's convoluted evidence. The prosecution's witnesses, however, were called: Inspector Monier, who gave evidence about his six months' surveillance of Mata Hari, Commissioner André Priolet who detailed her arrest, Colonel Goubet and Captain Ladoux who described their investigation which attested to the truth of Mornet's account; and Albert Ramillay, a furrier who said she had asked him to cash three post-dated cheques from her lover, Herr Alfred Kiepert, in 1908.[22]

General Adolphe-Pierre Messimy, who was unable to attend the trial, testified in a letter that Mata Hari had never profited from her relations with him by asking for military or diplomatic information.[23] According to Massard, among the many letters from officers, pilots and notable Parisians found in her hotel room after her arrest, was a missive from a minister of war that spoke of current events and 'very intimate things'. When Mornet began to read this letter during the trial, Mata Hari stopped him, 'because the author is married and I don't want to be the cause of a drama in an honest family. Please don't say his name.' Somprou and the other judges were, however, allowed to read the signature on the letter, which produced 'profound stupefaction and, to be exact, a number of smiles'. As Massard commented, 'Discretion is, in effect, a quality of the professional *filles galantes*. It doesn't pay to compromise a friend at any price – even if it's a friend for a day or a night – never disclose the identity of a client, never betray their cover, and especially one who visits often and is head of the French army.'

Although a transcript of Clunet's defence has not survived, it seems he never challenged such obvious contradictions. If the prosecution's case against Mata Hari was built around portraying her as a traitor to France, how could they explain her remarkable discretion when it was clearly not in her interest? Despite Mornet's insistence that she had systematically seduced officers and pumped them for information, not a single testimony supported this claim. Messimy would later reveal that during the first days of the war Mata Hari had even written with a vague offer to work for France. She thought her international relations and knowledge of foreign languages might make her a suitable espionage agent. Although this contradicts her statement to Bouchardon that she had never thought of espionage until Captain Ladoux suggested it, Messimy may have been referring to her letter about Kiepert's comments on a German invasion of France. As Messimy testified:

> In a letter addressed to the President of the Council of War, I said that in response to your call, I declare very clearly that to my knowledge, nothing led me to think that she was able to be a spy, and that she had not extracted or searched to extract a single piece of information. M. de Margerie [Henry de Marguérie] made, I think, the same declaration.[24]

The judge's decision not to disclose Messimy's name as Mata Hari's lover caused political ructions that would reverberate for years.[25] However, in later years, Messimy would claim that his relationship with the Dutch dancer was entirely innocent. He had found her charming, even seductive, but he had always suspected her motives for pursuing him.[26]

Mata Hari's old friend and long-time lover, Henry de Marguérie, who was, ironically, an expert in deciphering codes for the Ministry for Foreign Affairs, did not disappoint her. Marguérie testified that they had been occasional lovers and constant friends since 1904 and concurred with Mata Hari's statement that he was the 'first friend I had after my divorce'. During their three days together at the Grand Hotel during her first wartime visit to Paris in 1915, he stated that 'Madame didn't ask me a single question' about politics or military matters that would have compromised him. 'You well know that she is not a spy!' he told Mornet. 'If she had wanted to collect valuable information she would not have showed her hand.'

Mornet was stunned by Marguérie's testimony. 'Are you asking us to accept, sir, that you spent three days always in each other's company and you didn't speak with her about the subject which obsesses us all – the war?'

'We spoke of art,' replied the witness, 'Indian art.' He added that since the war was his work, to talk of other things with Mata Hari was an extremely pleasant relief. His final word was simply that 'nothing has ever spoiled the good opinion I have of this lady'.[27] Jules Cambon, who was then the secretary-general of the

Ministry for Foreign Affairs, also supported Mata Hari's defence that she had never discussed the war with her lovers.[28]

The court was adjourned at 7 p.m. and resumed the following day at 8.30 a.m. Depositions were read from the absent witnesses Lieutenant Hallaure and Captain Vladimir de Masloff, both attesting that she had never extracted military or political information from them. Mornet then gave a summary of the evidence:

> The Zelle lady appeared to us as one of those international women – the word is her own – who have become so dangerous since the hostilities. The ease with which she expresses herself in several languages, especially French, her numerous relations, her subtle ways, her aplomb, her remarkable intelligence, her immorality, congenital or acquired, all contributed to make her a suspect.

Moreover, Mornet saw that Mata Hari had given herself to these officers 'as a sort of Messalina, dragging a horde of admirers behind her chariot'. His language perfectly crystallized the unstated accusations against her: her independence, her intelligence, and her unwillingness to conform to the war's new moral order.

The prosecutor thundered on. The 'Zelle lady' had given Kalle, the German military attaché in Madrid, information about: the intentions of Princess George of Greece, politics in Paris, opposition to Briand's government, French fears of English domination and the anxiety this inspired. She discussed with Kalle the Allies' possible spring offensive, the spies that French aviator Védrine had dropped behind enemy lines, travel limitations imposed on officers and the French knowledge of German secret inks. A spy chief in German intelligence named Griebel was her lover and controller. 'On two occasions, in December 1915 and June 1916, she penetrated the place of war of Paris with a mission to collect documents and information in the enemy's interests,' Mornet alleged. '[She] had maintained intelligence with Germany in the person of Consul Kramer [sic] and the military attaché von Kalle [sic].' The payment of 20,000 francs received in Amsterdam, the two payments of 5,000 francs [from the Baron van der Capellen] and the 3,500 pesetas from Kalle, were proof that she was a spy.[29]

Mornet ended with an emotional flourish. 'The evil that this woman has done is unbelievable. This is perhaps the greatest woman spy of the century.'[30]

During the recess, Massard approached Clunet and asked his opinion of the trial. 'He had confidence,' wrote Massard. 'Always, he had confidence. Even before opening his dossier he affirmed the innocence of Mata Hari.' Clunet alone appeared to presume Mata Hari was innocent until proven guilty. During the elderly attorney's speech for the defence, Massard described how Mata Hari sat composed as an actress before a performance, 'a siren of strange charm'. She had ceased to be the accused but had become a woman and an artist, flashing the judges a stunning smile. Colonel Somprou asked if she had anything to say in her defence.

'My defence,' she replied, 'is to speak the truth. I am not French. I have the right to have friends in other countries, even those at war with France. I have remained neutral. I count on the good hearts of the French officers.'

Somprou announced the hearings closed. The judges then retired to deliberate on the charges against Mata Hari and pronounce their verdict on the following eight questions:

1. The aforementioned Zelle (Margaretha Geertruida), divorced wife of Mac Léod [sic], called Mata Hari, is she guilty of having entered the entrenched camp of Paris in December 1915 to procure information or documents in the interests of Germany, an enemy power?
2. The same, is she guilty, while in Holland during the first six months of 1916 or in any case within the period of the statute of limitations, of having delivered to Germany, an enemy power, and notably to the person Consul Kramer [sic], documents and information susceptible to damaging the operations of the army?
3. The same, is she guilty, in Holland in May 1916, of having maintained intelligence with the agents of Germany, an enemy power, in the person of the aforementioned Kramer, to favour the enterprises of the enemy?
4. The same, is she guilty of having entered the entrenched camp of Paris in June 1916, or in any case within the period of the statute of limitations, to obtain documents or information in the interests of Germany, an enemy power?
5. The same, is she guilty, in Paris since May 1916 or in any case within the period of the statute of limitations, of having maintained intelligence with Germany, an enemy power, in order to favour the projected task of said enemy?
6. The same, is she guilty, in Madrid in December 1916 or in any case within the period of the statute of limitations, of having maintained intelligence with Germany, an enemy power, in the person of the military attaché von [sic] Kalle, in order to facilitate the task of the enemy?
7. The same, is she guilty, under the same circumstances of time and place, of having delivered to Germany, an enemy power, in the person of said von Kalle, documents or information susceptible of damaging the operations of the army, or to endanger the safety of places, posts, or other military establishments, said documents or information dealing in particular with interior politics, the spring offensive, the discovery by the French of a secret of a German invisible ink, and the disclosure of the name of an agent in the service of England?
8. The same, is she guilty, in Paris in January 1917 or in any case within the period of the statute of limitations, of having maintained intelligence with Germany, an enemy power, in order to facilitate the projected task of said enemy?[31]

On the first question, the prosecution would have to prove that on Mata Hari's December 1915 trip to Paris, she had extracted useful information and relayed it to the Germans. There was no evidence for this. On the second, the accused was charged with handing over military documents and information to Cramer, the German consul in Amsterdam. However, as Mata Hari testified, she had never given him anything but had only accepted the 20,000 francs as compensation for her property confiscated in 1914. Moreover, this may explain Kalle's determination to set up Mata Hari by sending messages from Madrid to Berlin in a code the French had already broken. It may also have been, as Mata Hari once suggested, a clever way for the Germans to distract the Allies' attention from a much more valuable agent operating in Spain.

On the third charge, the prosecution had only to prove that Mata Hari had intended to deliver information to Cramer when she accepted the 20,000 francs. This would constitute 'maintaining intelligence' even if no such action was ever carried out. The fourth charge also refers to Mata Hari's intentions while the fifth refers to whether she had actually obtained information for the Germans during the summer of 1916. However, Ladoux's inspectors who followed Mata Hari during this period produced no evidence that she had communicated with the enemy or procured documents. The sixth and seventh charges refer to her meetings with Kalle and asked the jurors to evaluate whether the information she offered – which she claimed was culled from newspapers and Parisian gossip – constituted actual 'intelligence'. The final charge should have been disproved by Ladoux's agents who had begun following Mata Hari upon her return to Paris during this period. Again, there was nothing to support this charge.

While the judges were out of the courtroom, Massard claimed he overheard a Commander C. say with emotion, 'It is awful to send to her death a creature so seductive and of real intelligence . . . But she has caused such disasters that I would condemn her a dozen times if I could!' After a mere forty-five minutes the judges' verdict was read before the grand assembly. Mata Hari, pale and stiff, sat next to Clunet.

'Sentence,' cried the clerk of the court. 'In the name of the French people . . .'

'Present arms,' commanded the adjutant.[32]

The jury unanimously agreed that Mata Hari had been in the places mentioned in the list of accusations. However, one member of the jury gave a negative answer to the second, fifth and seventh charges, thus belying the numerous reports that the verdict against Mata Hari was unanimous. But this juror had given in to the final charge and his dissent had no influence on the final outcome.[33] The sentence was read: 'The Council unanimously condemns the named person Zelle, Margaretha Geertruida, as mentioned above, to the punishment of death, for espionage and intelligence with the enemy for the end of assisting their enterprises.' The accused was ordered to pay for the cost of the trial.[34] Clunet began to weep while Mata Hari sat next to him murmuring, 'It's impossible! It's impossible!'[35]

The following morning, the prisoner was returned to Saint-Lazare. Sister Léonide and Sister Marie were waiting to guide Mata Hari down a long corridor lit weakly by flickering gas lamps, across a small bridge and into the infamous cell number 12 reserved for the condemned. It contained three iron beds placed side by side which Mata Hari would share with two prisoners, both prostitutes, chosen for their good character.

Perhaps Mata Hari realized that now she would gain the immortality which she had so long sought through her performances. The dank cell 12 had housed, along with the tragic women condemned for killing their husbands and children, those who had become entangled in French politics. It was a temporary home for Madame Henriette Caillaux, the wife of former prime minister Joseph Caillaux, who on 16 March 1914 shot the editor of *Le Figaro*, Gaston Calmette, for his tireless campaigns against her husband.[36] The courtesan Meg Steinheil had languished here for being unlucky enough to have president Félix Faure die *in flagrante delicto*, 'clutching [her] curly head to his groin'.[37] Even now, Mata Hari's incarceration was prompting Paris journalists to compare her with Madame de Stael, the eighteenth-century writer and literary critic who had attempted to defend herself before Napoleon III's death sentence. In answer to the emperor's question about when women had been permitted to have civil rights, she answered, 'when they have been permitted to die for their ideas.'[38]

Cell 12, however, had its small compensations. The food that Sister Aurea brought had improved, Mata Hari enjoyed wine with her meals and had permission to smoke and read. Although she had never been fond of cigarettes, she requested a Buddhist gospel and received frequent visits from Pastor Jules Arboux, the prison chaplain, and Abbé Doumergue, a Catholic priest. Sister Léonide, who swore like a sailor, stayed with her throughout the day. The new regime, however, denied Mata Hari the pleasure of a few minutes' walk through the prison courtyard and she complained of this in a letter to Dr Bizard. 'I can't stand it any longer,' she wrote. 'I need some air and exercise. This will not prevent them from killing me if they absolutely want to, but it is useless to make me suffer, closed in the way I am. It is too much to bear.'[39]

Dr Bizard, who saw Mata Hari frequently, denied the rumours that she was deluged with flowers and chocolates during her final days. Neither is there any evidence for Massard's story that she asked the prison director, at a time when food shortages in Paris were desperately acute, if she could continue her daily custom of bathing in milk. Massard compared the pinched, white faces of 'our little children' with this monstrous vanity.[40] Aside from Clunet, there were no visitors – it had become dangerous to be a friend of Mata Hari's. Dr van Tienhoven, a Dutch Red Cross doctor, was detained in England for six weeks after Scotland Yard officials searched his luggage and found a picture of him standing next to the infamous dancer taken at a Paris hospital.[41]

Since the verdict of Mata Hari's trial was announced, the European press had reported that she had 'confessed' to espionage charges or had been found guilty on irrefutable evidence.[42] Maurice de Waleffe described her in *Le Journal* as 'a sinister Salome, who played with the heads of our soldiers in front of the German Herod'. Like Delilah with Samson, this 'Javanese dancer', famous in the demi-monde, was an expert in convincing young men to surrender their secrets. 'The moral of the story,' concluded de Waleffe, 'is that, after the war, we should be able to close our frontiers to these exotic adventuresses.'[43] On 1 August the *Daily Sketch* followed a similar theme, juxtaposing photographs of the fateful 'woman spy' with an angelic Canadian nurse. In a full-length photograph, 'Margaretha Zelle, the Dutch dancer', wears a straw hat while clutching a fox fur round her face and revealing a chic dress, adorned with ribbons, beneath a full-length, open coat. Next to this ran a shot of 'young Hun prisoners on the way to a field hospital' and further down the page was Sister McAdam, a Canadian nurse at the Ontario military hospital in Kent, who would represent 38,000 soldiers in the Ontario parliament. If Mata Hari was a coquettish Delilah – a captured enemy equal to the young 'Huns' – the nursing sister in her spotless white uniform, ministering to ailing tommies, was her antidote.[44]

News of Mata Hari's arrest had also reached Holland. On 12 September she was allowed to receive a letter from A.J. Kooij, who described himself as a 'publisher, printer, binder and maker of packing paper'. While Kooij reserved judgement on Mata Hari's crimes, he wanted permission to publish the memoirs she was rumoured to be writing. He was confident that the French government would grant her grace and he hoped she would agree to his proposal. However, there is no indication that Mata Hari gave permission for the publication of her life story to Kooij or anyone else. However, she was still prevented from sending letters to Anna Lintjens and from communicating directly with Mr E. Hijmans, her lawyer in The Hague.

Meanwhile, the Dutch Foreign Ministry had become increasingly concerned about the case. On 28 July the Dutch ambassador in Paris was requested to attempt to have the sentence reduced to a prison term in case the Council for Revision – which would hear an appeal on the Third Tribunal's decision – found the trial legal.[45] On 17 August, the Appeal Court reviewed the legal process of Mata Hari's trial, and decided there were no grounds for a retrial since it had been properly conducted. Clunet immediately relayed the decision to the Dutch legation although, since he was not authorized to present a case before this court, it had been deputized to a Maître Bailby.[46]

However, even though Mata Hari was incarcerated in Saint-Lazare, General Dubail and Major Jullien feared that she might attempt to leak information either to the enemy or the public. The officers debated whether Monsieur Milhaud, the solicitor appointed to look after her affairs, should communicate directly with her. It was decided that Milhaud's letters to Mata Hari would be opened at the prison but her responses would remain confidential. The solicitor was also given permission to visit his client. Her request to receive her dentist Monsieur Charavet in prison in the presence of Dr Bizard was also granted soon afterwards. However, although she was given these liberties, three of her letters to the Dutch legation in Paris and to Anna Lintjens were returned to her. The grounds for refusing her the right to send these letters were 'the disagreeable terms which she has used with regard to French justice'.[47]

The Dutch Foreign Minister Loudon, however, had not given up on the case and on 31 August sent an urgent telegram from The Hague: 'If judgement Mata Hari is maintained, please take steps to have request for pardon presented before execution.'[48] Mata Hari made a final attempt to seize control of the situation and wrote a lengthy letter to the Dutch legate, Ridder van Stuers, on 22 September.

> I beg your Excellency to please intervene for me with the French government.
> The Third War Council has condemned me to death and it is nothing but a grave error. [There are] *some outward appearances* [this passage is underlined], but no acts, and all my international connections are necessarily the result of my profession as a dancer, and nothing else. At this moment everything is wrongly explained and the most natural things are greatly exaggerated.
> I have asked for the revision of the case and have appealed against the judgement, but inasmuch as they would have to discover juridical errors, I do not think I shall get satisfaction.
> After that only the request for pardon from the President of the Republic remains. Since I truly have not done any espionage in France, it is really terrible that I cannot defend myself.
> Jealousy – vengeance – there are so many things that crop up in the life of a woman like me, once people know that she finds herself in a difficult position.[49]

She ended by informing the Dutch ambassador that Count van Limburg Styrum could provide information about her history. The letter, however, reveals that Clunet had not informed his client that almost three weeks earlier the Council had reviewed the case and refused a retrial.

The following week another legal option was exhausted when the Supreme Court of Appeals [*la chambre criminelle de la cour suprême*], after a fifteen-minute discussion, denied Mata Hari's case.[50] As the solicitor-general Peysonnié stated, the court had only to decide whether the Third Council was competent to try crimes of espionage and intelligence with the enemy in wartime. Clunet was unable to represent his client in this court and his deputy, Maître Bailby, who was unable to attend at the last moment, sent a Maître Reynal who 'yielded to the wisdom of the court'.[51]

The next day van Stuers rang Clunet to discuss the matter but was persuaded that urgent action was not required and 'there was still plenty of time to talk about the case'.[52] Yet Clunet reconsidered this and on 29 September sent a letter to the Dutch envoy, urging that the only hope now was a presidential pardon. The Hague was informed and the Foreign Minister, Jonkheer Loudon, immediately sent a cable asking van Stuers to appeal to President Poincaré for clemency. On 1 October the envoy wrote to the French Foreign Minister pleading with him to forward this request from The Hague to the president, 'for reasons of humanity, to ask for the pardon of Madame Zelle MacLeod known as Mata Hari'.

However, Poincaré refused all such appeals on principle, affirming every death verdict he was asked to consider. Given the president's reputation, in certain cases the courts were compelled to withhold recommendations of a death sentence if the judges felt the proof of guilt was not overwhelming.[53] Poincaré made no exception in Mata Hari's case, and sent his rejection of the Dutch government's plea to Clunet's office on 13 October. The same day, the Foreign Office in The Hague cabled Paris stating that six Dutch newspapers had already reported Mata Hari's execution and the government wanted an answer to 'prevent further comment'.[54] The British envoy in The Hague, Sir W. Townley, had also noticed these reports in the press and sent the following telegram to Whitehall on 14 October:

> *Nieuwe Courant* [The Hague edition] states that it has been reproached with not having devoted indignant comment on execution of Mata Hari as coolness with which report of her sentence was received is unfavourably compared with indignation at Miss Cavell's case. Paper considers reproach unfair. It admits knowing very little Mata Hary [sic] case but presumes Netherlands government had taken steps ascertain she had fair trial though French government has done nothing in Holland to convince the public of her guilt.[55]

Mata Hari's brother in Rotterdam, J.H. Zelle, who had been trying for several weeks to make contact with his sister through the intervention of her lawyer in The Hague, was shocked by these reports. 'As soon as the sentence was announced, I asked our Foreign Affairs Minister to send me a copy of the accusations against her, and to let me know the nature of the sentence,' Zelle told Paul Allard in 1934. It was impossible even for the Foreign Minister to obtain such a document and Zelle would have to wait until 15 February 1918 to receive official confirmation that van Stuers' efforts in Paris had been unsuccessful.[56]

By the time Clunet delivered Poincaré's rejection of the plea for clemency, it was too late. Rather than disturb the Dutch envoy during the weekend, Clunet had waited until the morning of 15 October, and by the time the envoy's office opened Mata Hari had been dead for several hours.

There were only a few witnesses to her execution, which took place on an unseasonably cold autumn morning. By then, even Mata Hari's most hardened prosecutors were moved to respect and sympathy at her calm acceptance of death. They believed the woman they had vilified as a traitor and assassin was at the final moment redeemed by her dignity before the firing squad. Only when she could no longer defend herself, it seemed, could they see her as human rather than as a pastiche of theatrical clichés. Yet the insight was short-lived and Bouchardon, Mornet and Massard would need to continue to defend the justice of her case.

On the Sunday morning of 14 October Dr Bizard learned that Mata Hari's execution was fixed for the following day. He spoke with Sister Léonide and that evening they paid their usual visit to the 'spy's' cell. 'Our features betraying no emotion, we reassured her to the point of imagining she would be pardoned,' Bizard would write later. 'After asking after her health, we exchanged commonplaces and I turned the conversation to the subject of dancing. "Show us", said Sister Léonide in encouraging tones, "how you dance." Mata Hari rose, smiling, loosened her dress a little and began to dance.'[57] After her performance, Dr Bizard slipped a double dose of the sedative, chloral, into his patient's drinking water and bade her good night.

The following morning at 3 a.m. Massard, the representative of the military governor of Paris, was woken by a phone call announcing that Margaretha Geertruida Zelle, known as Mata Hari, would be shot at 5.45 that morning. The Deuxième Bureau had been informed, then the Elysée Palace, who ordered the military parade and the firing squad at Vincennes to be prepared. Then Massard drove through the dark, empty streets to Saint-Lazare prison to join Dr Bizard and his assistant Bralez, the prison director Jean Estachy, Captain Bouchardon, André Mornet, Colonel Somprou, Captain Thibaud, the chief military court clerk, Major Jullien, the chief military prosecutor, Dr Socquet, General Wattine, Pastor Arboux and, finally, Edouard Clunet.

Massard arrived at 4.45 as the night still lingered. There were a dozen cars waiting outside the prison, journalists who had already heard the news. 'Devils!' Massard cursed to himself. Who had warned them? He was furious that news of the execution had already leaked out but since he was late, he hurried into the office of prison director Jean Estachy. When Massard appeared, Clunet turned to Somprou and asked to speak about an important matter. 'Mata Hari is not able to be executed this morning,' announced the elderly attorney. 'I formally oppose it and invoke ... article 27 [of the penal code] which states, "if a woman condemned to death declares and is able to verify that she is pregnant, she cannot be subjected to death until after the birth."'[58]

The crowd of men looked at Clunet with amazement. 'It's impossible,' said Estachy. 'No man has entered her cell, you know that.'

'Yes, there was one . . . me,' he replied and Dr Socquet was ordered to examine the prisoner to verify the claim.

'Let us go,' commanded Estachy. The officers followed the director down the cavernous corridors with walls so filthy that visitors were allegedly warned not to touch them for fear of contamination. The group arrived in a gloomy passage lit by flickering gas jets. Massard's heart pounded wildly as he reminded himself the prisoner was 'the greatest spy of the century' and the door to cell 12 was opened.[59] Three women were asleep side by side in the iron beds. 'Which one?' asked Bouchardon. 'The one in the middle,' said Sister Léonide, directing the other two prisoners, who were now awake and sobbing, to the refectory.

Mata Hari was still groggy from the chloral and opened her eyes slowly. 'The hour of justice has arrived. Your request for clemency has been rejected by the President of the Republic. You must wake up,' said Bouchardon. 'Zelle, have courage.'

She began to moan softly, 'It's not possible! . . . It's not possible!' She noticed Clunet, who had deceived her again by refusing to give her the bad news, standing among the group of men. Massard recalled that Clunet then stammered, 'Margaretha, if you wish . . . your pregnancy . . . the penal code says that . . . it is article 27 . . . Margaretha, I implore you.' But when Dr Socquet approached, she angrily flung back the covers and said, 'No! No! I don't want to resort to this subterfuge . . . No! It is useless . . . I am going to get up.'[60]

Bizard recalled that she turned to comfort Sister Léonide who had begun to weep. 'Don't fear, Sister. I know how to die without weakness. You shall see a good end!' The men, except for Dr Bizard, then left while Mata Hari dressed.

She asked if she could wear a corset. Bizard agreed. She sat on her bed and dressed herself with care: stockings, a pearl-grey dress, long buttoned gloves, her ankle-boots and her tricornered felt hat. She rejected the smelling salts that the doctor offered. She asked to see Pastor Arboux who had tried to comfort her the day before. ' "Do you think I am for it?" she had asked him. "In that case I must make a will." I told her I knew nothing . . . she was living in the hope that she would not be executed and made an object of exchange.' Clunet had told Mata Hari that since she was condemned as a spy for the Germans, the Kaiser might be willing to exchange her for the French prisoner, General Marchard.[61] 'She thought there would be questions about this last affair at the Elysée the next day . . . She dreamed from one day to the next.'[62] Another desperate measure by Clunet had failed. Now the only comfort Arboux could offer was a blessing with water from her prison mug.

The officers and Clunet returned to the cell. Captain Thibaud approached with a pencil and notebook in his hand. 'Do you have any revelations to make?'

'Me?' asked Mata Hari. 'I have nothing to say but if I had . . . it wouldn't be to you.' She shrugged her shoulders and looked disdainfully at the officers.

She thanked Dr Bizard for his help and when Sister Marie began to cry, she tried to comfort her. 'Don't cry. Be cheerful like me.' She patted the Sister's cheek and smiled. 'How little she is, Sister Marie. It would take two Sisters to make one Mata Hari! Don't cry.' But the nun shook with sobs. 'Imagine that I am going on a long journey, that I will return and we will find each other again. Besides, you are going to come a little way with me aren't you? You are going to accompany me.' The women embraced.

She asked the director for time to write two or three letters which she gave to Arboux. One was to her daughter Non and another two were for 'people who were members of her close circle of friends', probably Vadime Masloff and Henry de Marguérie.[63] There was no will and none of the letters ever arrived at their destination. In seven or eight minutes she had finished her letters, arranged her hair, adjusted her hat and thrown a bright blue coat over her shoulders and announced, 'I am ready, gentlemen.' The judges left, followed by Mata Hari, Clunet, the pastor and the nuns. When a warder reached for her arm, she pushed him away. 'Don't touch me! Don't touch me! I am not a thief or a criminal. Sister Marie, give me your hand.'

The procession marched back along the dim corridor to the entrance where a crowd of about a hundred had gathered, mingling with the journalists hungry for news about the figures emerging from the prison in the weak light. At the exit to Saint-Lazare Mata Hari said softly to Sister Léonide, 'All these people! What a success!'[64] A gendarme led the two women to their car where Massard had pulled the window blinds down. Mata Hari sat in the back, Arboux at her side, Sister Marie and Sister Léonide on the jump seats. Massard gave the signal for the cars to start and the five vehicles – including an ambulance – rumbled away. They drove quickly through the deserted streets while the journalists followed and then rapidly passed them.

However, the press had miscalculated when they headed for Vincennes. The official cortège lost them by doubling back towards the Caponnière, the fields used for cavalry demonstrations which were contained within its walls. A few journalists managed to follow the entourage through the gates before they were closed but Bouchardon insisted the press vehicles make an about-turn. The official cars advanced slowly through the mud as the dawn began to break. The firing squad, composed of twenty-five- to thirty-year-old battle-hardened soldiers – six Zouaves in khaki with bright red fezzes, and six riflemen clad in marine blue uniforms with black berets – had already formed three lines of a square.[65] Mata Hari's car pulled up at one end. Pastor Arboux descended unsteadily from the car followed by Mata Hari who turned to take the hands of Sister Léonide and Sister Marie.

The commandant called out, 'Sabre – to hand!'

Two gendarmes appeared at Mata Hari's side. 'Come, little Sister Marie,' she said, 'take me strongly by the hand.' Sister Léonide walked next to her with Arboux just behind.

'Present – arms!' the commandant shouted. The artillery trumpets sounded the march. The soldiers fixed their bayonets to their guns while the cavalry steadied their horses behind them. The morning fog was just beginning to lift.

Mata Hari stood less than a dozen metres from the stake, a striking figure in her tricornered hat, her bright blue coat against the sea of grey mud. She looked at the soldiers, her executioners.[66] She embraced the sobbing Clunet, who gave her a lingering kiss on the mouth, while next to Bouchardon someone murmured, 'Poor Mata Hari! The Council of War didn't condemn her to this!'[67] She then calmly turned to Sister Léonide, kissed her and gave her the coat from her shoulders. 'Embrace me quickly and let me be. Stand to the right of me. I shall be looking at you. Adieu!'[68] She then touched her lips to Sister Marie's wet cheeks, shook Arboux's hand and ordered them all to move away from the firing line.

Captain Thibaud read the judgement. 'By the order of the Third Council of War the woman Zelle has been condemned to death for espionage.'

A gendarme led Mata Hari to the post and tied a cord round her waist but she stopped him when he bent to tie her wrists; she would stand before the stake rather than be tied. The blindfold, she said, was also unnecessary.

The adjutant raised his sabre and commanded, 'Take aim . . .'

Mata Hari smiled and from her open palm blew kisses to the pastor and to Clunet. She waved to the two nuns who were on their knees, deep in prayer.

'Fire!'

She fell heavily and motionless to the earth in front of the stake. Eleven bullets were fired and then a cavalry sergeant walked towards the body and delivered the *coup de grâce* – a final shot into her temple.[69]

The firing squad turned and marched past while the trumpets sounded and the soldiers passed what was now only 'a pile of petticoats'. Dr Socquet approached the body, and as he unfastened the white bodice, blood spurted from the chest in a crimson stream. 'The death has been determined by a bullet in the heart,' he said, his hands and arms now drenched in red. In a final act of discharging her duties, Sister Marie approached the body, and sobbing softly, gently twisted the wedding ring from Mata Hari's finger.

'Who claims the body?' asked Thibaud. But there was no one to take it and when Massard looked at Clunet, the elderly attorney said nothing. He had not thought to make burial arrangements. After a funeral presided over by Arboux, Mata Hari's celebrated body was sent to the University of Paris medical school for dissection.[70]

The press were quick to proclaim the execution as a coup for French justice. 'The Spy Mata Hari paid yesterday for the crimes to which she had confessed,' trumpeted the *Excelsior* in Paris, while *Le Gaulois* revealed that 'in the face of material proof' she acknowledged everything, and in London the *Daily Express* celebrated the shooting of a 'lovely spy'. A report on German reaction to the event had already emerged. On 6 October the German news agency Wolff had accused the Allies of hypocrisy in the Mata Hari case. The agency stated that:

the famous Dutch dancer has been shot in Paris following martial law under a charge of espionage. She was killed even though the judiciary process was unable to prove her culpability . . . She was killed by the same government that formerly made a martyr of Miss Cavell, the English spy, who confessed to her crime: the same government that reproached the execution of this [woman] to the German nation as an act of extraordinary barbarism.[71]

Le Gaulois suggested that while Mata Hari, 'the hired spy who yesterday paid her debt to society', would be consigned to a 'mercifully forgotten tomb', Edith Cavell, 'the noble and saintly woman', would be raised upon a pedestal. Readers were reminded that during the war female spies – 'there has never been a French woman [among them]' – had faced firing squads at Vincennes, Lyons, Marseilles,

Grenoble and Belfort. This was a true sign of women's equality, concluded the article's author, '[women] have to be equal in their work and also equal in their punishment'.[72]

The Paris journalist who predicted that Mata Hari would fade into the shadows of history had greatly underestimated the power of her story. She would become the perfect foil to Nurse Edith Cavell who was executed by the Germans in Brussels on 12 October 1915 for helping Allied prisoners to escape. But these two figures, whose lives would become imbued with mythic qualities, vividly represented the *fin de siècle*'s understanding of womanhood. Every woman had within her the elements of whore and madonna – Mata Hari and Nurse Cavell. Allied governments appealed to their female population to profess the ideals of self-sacrifice, nurturing and mothering on a heroic scale. They were urged to kill off their own Mata Hari-esque desires to reject maternal claims, to divorce brutal husbands, take to the stage or sell their bodies to maintain independent lives. But even as women were exhorted to model themselves after the martyred Nurse Cavell, the fear lingered that underneath their pristine uniforms beat a longing for the other's sexual rapaciousness.

To the men who controlled intelligence during the war, espionage and sexual perversity went hand in hand. While the Allies maintained that it was only the Germans who used the spy-courtesan, she is a powerful figure in the literature, press reports and documented history of the war. The second part of this book will explore the legacy of Mata Hari who had so perfectly married the themes of female treachery and political intrigue. The other players in the game will also emerge: Marthé Richard, the French double-agent who Captain Ladoux ordered to sleep with the enemy or face a firing squad; the mysterious Dr Schragmuller who allegedly trained Mata Hari in Brussels but who bears a striking similarity to the morphine addict and German agent, Madame Maria de Victorica, who was charged with plotting treason in the United States in 1917. Their stories and the experiences of intelligence officers themselves will reveal how the seductive *femme fatale* was created, what purpose she served and why she survived to become an enduring icon of the century.

While the body of Margaretha Zelle MacLeod was consigned to its fate on the dissecting tables of a Paris university, Mata Hari endured, performing an endless dance. Each new generation would have their own fantasy of female seduction, betrayal and revenge that they would project onto women playing her part. Films, plays, books, innumerable magazine articles and even official documents kept her alive. The firing squad at Vincennes provided the setting for her greatest debut.

CHAPTER SIX

THE AFTERMATH

Women and wine! The old, old story! Impecunious young officers drinking and gambling, lured away from their loyalty by cunning female spies and then, when they have been sucked dry, callously left to their ruin.

GUSTAV STEINHAUER, *Steinhauer: The Kaiser's Master Spy* (1930)[1]

T HE TRIAL AND DRAMATIC EXECUTION of Margaretha Zelle MacLeod, aka Mata Hari, cannot alone explain her phenomenal reputation as the century's most famous *femme fatale*. Immediately after her death, the myth-makers – the novelists, playwrights and spy masters – would breathe new life into her corpse. Her punishment was a gesture on an international scale that turned the world's glance to other equally dangerous and elusive female spies. She became a universal anti-hero who defied convention, became an outlaw and was condemned for her double crime. Audiences from Warsaw to Washington would read avidly of her exploits. But her reincarnation was controversial; she was a fractured ghost whose creators fought over her memory. Since the trial records and interrogation dossiers remained closed until the 1960s, her story was moulded to suit any purpose. Mata Hari was any woman, everywoman and no woman at all.

The remainder of this book is devoted to exploring why and how Mata Hari's story was kept alive; what she came to mean during the First World War and afterwards; who her fellow agents were and how their experiences contributed to her legend and how the forces that condemned her to death swept hundreds of other women along in their path. Cases of women shot as enemy agents in France, and those tried in England and the United States, also attest to Mata Hari's significance. Her story had irrevocably linked the international woman to espionage and prostitution. The legend of the exotic Oriental had outlived her and was embroidered to entertain and warn future generations. But without a phalanx of espionage writers, as *Le Gaulois*' columnist in October 1917 suggested, Mata Hari might have fallen into a silent tomb. Like a shadow on a blank screen, she mimed Salome, the powerful but deadly female, an enduring nightmare of female betrayal.

In the immediate aftermath of Mata Hari's demise, with more than a year until the Armistice, spy paranoia was still rampant. On 19 October 1917, four days after her execution, Captain Georges Ladoux, the head of French counterespionage, was himself arrested on charges of spying. When his agent Pierre Lenoir was taken into custody as a collaborator, Ladoux had been named as his accomplice. A morphine addict, Lenoir was originally hired as a driver by Ladoux to please Pierre's father, Alphonse – an influential millionaire advertising agent working for the finance minister and several French banks. Once Lenoir was promoted from chauffeur to spy, he negotiated with enemy agents for ten million francs to buy a controlling interest in the Paris daily, *Le Journal*, as a vehicle for anti-Allied propaganda.

While Lenoir was found guilty and executed, Ladoux was never convicted. He was dismissed from the Deuxième Bureau, released into custody and placed under house arrest to spend the remainder of the war undergoing interrogations. His case was dropped on 1 January 1919. But during the Third Tribunal heard that day, it was revealed that in 1916 a cryptogram had been sent through the mail under cover of an anonymous letter signed 'a good Frenchwoman' to Senator Charles Humbert, vice-president of the Senate Army Committee and manager of *Le Journal*. The encoded message accused Ladoux of passing information about the security of the state on to another country. Ladoux claimed he ignored the 'cryptogram', refusing to bother his superiors with it, because he thought it was a joke. Only a photograph of the original remained since he had burned it as if he was destroying incriminating evidence.

'Perhaps I burned it with other fantastic documents from anonymous sources involving politicians when I was transferred from one service to another,' Ladoux told the court.[2] But whatever his reason, it was a serious breach of conduct and contributed to the charges laid against him. However, although the former spy-chief was acquitted he was rearrested on 2 January and subjected to further interrogations until he was finally court-martialled and cleared of all charges on 8 May 1919.[3]

Once Ladoux was suspended from the Deuxième Bureau, his agents were left without instructions, funds or contacts. His most successful double-agent in Spain, Marthé Richard, only discovered what had happened when she returned to the Paris secret service headquarters in November. Ladoux had been replaced by Colonel Goubet who was furious with Richard for returning to France without permission, although she had received no instructions for several months. She found the service poorly paid, inefficiently run and dangerously riddled with paranoia. As she would later write, '[it] had so frequently adopted an exasperating suspicion towards me that I felt that it was necessary for me to protect myself.' After her confrontation with Goubet, Richard left the bureau in disgust.[4]

Ironically, the downfall of Ladoux caused no one within the French Department of Justice to question the judgement in Mata Hari's trial. Far away from the highly publicized trials in Paris the legend of the spy-courtesan that Ladoux had helped to build would still be played out in very different circumstances. There were a large number of women accused of, and even condemned for, crimes they had not committed. While hundreds of individuals were arrested during wartime spy scares in Paris, London and Rome, less than ten per cent were convicted or even charged.[5] Unlike Mata Hari, the women the Germans recruited as agents or informers received small sums for the risks they ran and found little glamour on their missions. Despite later claims to the contrary, many were motivated by money or even desperation to sell information to the enemy. But if spy-catching on the Western Front was grim, sordid and chaotic, Allied investigators kept alive its heroic legend.

D. Manning, a British intelligence officer, kept a war diary which offers a rare glimpse of the yawning gap between the romance and the reality. A fluent French and German translator, Manning had originally been turned down as an interpreter by the War Office but promised a post if he joined the bicycle corps. He was stationed at corps HQ at Moreuil in 1915 where he enrolled as a probationer on Intelligence B. His diary notes on his fellow interpreters and intelligence officers were sensitive to episodes that illustrate how deeply the myths had penetrated. He noted wryly that the lieutenant in charge 'was hot stuff, used to take his job seriously, sort of Sherlock Holmes stunt but his acquaintance with French was slight'. His friends recounted an incident involving two intelligence officers equally worthy of Conan Doyle.

> Firstly they let a valuable suspect get away to Paris and then arranged a Sherlock Holmes stunt; they would burgle her house while she was away and so obtain the incriminating papers. It was a scream, both were chockful of importance and secrecy. The stunt was pulled off in style and would probably have succeeded (visions of laurels to come) except for one little thing – they burgled the *wrong* house![6] [emphasis in original]

Manning described another fellow officer as 'a mixture of bombastic empty-headedness with cunning and intelligence'. Sergeant Young, who was covered with phoney ribbons from the Boer War, and 'a mystery medal, not to be taken seriously', told 'romantic lies that would fill a book and put Munchausen in the shade'. Intelligence officer Captain Langley embroidered his experiences in articles for *Punch* under the pseudonym 'Watch Dog'. The Americans, however, fell even harder for the 'story book' ideal of espionage. Manning commented on the 27th New York division's arrival in the spring of 1918: 'I had more spy scares to investigate while those Yanks were around than the rest of the time I was on the intelligence.'

Defining who was a traitor, however, was a complex undertaking. In French villages recently liberated from German occupation, Manning found textbook definitions were useless. 'What a state that country was in,' he wrote at Voyennes. 'There was not one *man* or *woman* you could call a true patriot. Still, it would take a very determined person to stick out old Fritz with his scientific cruelty for nearly three years.' [emphasis in original][7] He interviewed people who had been 'too friendly with Fritz', including women given special privileges by their German lovers. However, while Manning was concerned with what information had been exchanged between these couples, the French were routinely jailing any woman for betraying her country, who had given birth to a child with a German father.

Often those accused of spying were lowest on the social and economic scale with few resources to defend themselves. Belgian refugees were particularly vulnerable since they had just come from the war zone where German agents might easily have slipped into their camps, forcing or bribing them to act as informers. One Territorial Army soldier, Harold Stainton, described rumour as an 'occupational disease' which had produced a spy mania along the Belgian border. But when Stainton met a refugee along the road from Kemmel, his suspicion was immediately aroused:

We were joined by an extraordinary-looking figure. This was a young woman, blue with cold, emaciated and half-starved who said she was a refugee. She was dressed in some black garment, the general effect being what one might expect to see if one covered a skeleton in a simple black shroud. After hungrily devouring the food we were able to give her, she trudged along behind us and spun some disjointed yarn which we could not properly understand. She asked questions too, to which we had the sense to give evasive answers. Personally, I thought she was a spy – although any real evidence to that effect was lacking – and I kept my mouth shut.[8]

Despite Stainton's earlier scepticism about 'spy mania', he clung to his belief that any woman found near the battlefield must be part of a well-orchestrated campaign. This idea was reinforced in the public mind by journalists at the front relaying apocryphal tales about clever women who devised intricate methods of communicating with the enemy.

Mr Fred B. Pitney, the Paris correspondent of the *New York Tribune*, interviewed a soldier on leave from the Somme who had encountered a grandmotherly spy. An old woman had stayed behind at Bouchavesnes when the civilian population left to avoid an Allied bombardment. She washed clothes for the French soldiers, taking a keen interest whenever the troops went through the village, and often chatted with the men about where they had come from and where they were going to. 'She was a wonderful washerwoman,' said the soldier. 'It was a mania with her, having everything just right for the French soldiers who had won back her home.'

However, an investigation was instigated once the Allies realized the enemy knew every concentration of troops in the region, and that German air raids over Bouchavesnes had increased. It led to the old woman, who had been laying out her washing in coded patterns which gave away the position of French troops. Although she denied everything, the enemy's bombing accuracy ceased when she was imprisoned. She declared eventually that she was German and even though she was well paid, she had been threatened with reprisals unless she agreed to spy. She was sentenced to twelve years' hard labour.[9] This report, which provides neither specific dates nor details of how the washing-signals worked, seems rather far-fetched. However, it illustrates the extent to which the woman-spy had become a facet of lore on the Western Front.[10]

Elsewhere, French intelligence officers arrested and even executed women on equally circumstantial evidence. General Walter Kirke noted in his diary on 23 December 1914 that the French had caught a woman sending up a rocket, 'but had not shot her as she was expecting a child'. Her interrogators believed she was obeying instructions from a lover or husband since she refused, in spite of promises to save her life, to divulge anything.[11] Marguerite Schmitt was convicted of espionage charges and executed in Marseilles on 22 March 1915. A French national, aged twenty-five, she was allegedly caught sketching a gun at a military installation and found to be carrying incriminating papers when she was arrested. She was recruited in Anoux, near Briey, which was under German occupation, and assigned to obtain information about British troops in Nancy and regiments camped between Bar-le-Duc and Sainte-Menehould. Under interrogation she said a friend 'had put her into relations with the

Germans' who offered her 200 francs [£8] which she refused. Her intention was not to spy on the French, she said, and she was going to tell the Germans that she had changed her mind when she returned to Anoux. Speaking at her trial by the War Council, she said only, 'I am sorry.'[12]

During the spring of 1915, Marie Louise Welsch, known as the singer La Belle Lison in the music halls of Paris, was charged with espionage and having relations with another spy. Welsch was the former lover of a French naval officer, Lieutenant Charles Ullmo, who was found guilty in 1907 of selling naval plans to a foreign government. Ullmo asked for clemency on the grounds that he was an opium addict who 'had fallen under the power of an unscrupulous woman for whom he had squandered his fortune and ruined his life'. Welsch was blamed for the downfall that forced Ullmo to serve twenty years on Devil's Island where he became known as the Second Dreyfus.[13] In August 1915 a Mademoiselle Lallart was condemned to death, and the following January Marie Jose dei Basi, an Italian-born woman naturalized in the Argentine and Switzerland, was consigned to the firing squad in France on espionage charges. She was executed on 23 February 1916.[14]

Although capital punishment for women in France was ended in 1887, Hirschfeld notes that the execution of female spies was 'carried on with particular fanaticism'. Even when it was evident that a woman had been exploited by her lover or had no concept of her crime, the courts were rarely lenient. Madame Tichelly was executed a few months before Mata Hari on 15 March 1917, completely uncomprehending of the crime she had committed. This forty-four-year-old mother of a French soldier had worked in a munitions factory in a Paris suburb and reported details of its operation to the Germans. She then left the munitions works when she had acquired whatever information she could, and moved on to another industrial plant. Her reports escaped the censors for months because they were written on thin slips of paper and inserted between two postcards.

She was eventually caught after a censor became suspicious that she only ever wrote postcards to friends in Switzerland. Madame Tichelly had also gathered information from women with sons and husbands at the front by persuading them to show her their letters. At the trial, it was revealed that she did not understand the consequences of her actions and was stunned to learn that she would be shot although she had not killed anyone. 'It seems very likely,' writes Hirschfeld, 'that this woman was executed as a sort of theatrical gesture which the circumstances of time dictated, for, at the turn of the year between 1916 and 1917, conditions on the Western Front were especially bad for France.' Madame Tichelly was shot at Poteau on 15 March 1917 as her son lay dying in an army hospital at the front.[15]

Espionage became a convenient excuse for a neighbour or colleague to vent their prejudices, petty jealousies or misdirected patriotism. However, since women had so much less access to military information, the charges brought against them often seemed disproportionate to the crimes they might have committed. A Prussian woman in England who was naturalized when she married a British subject was caught in a dilemma. Suddenly her family at home was the enemy and she could not write to them freely about the war without arousing the suspicions of the censor. Since many intelligence officers believed women had little patriotic spirit, those with divided loyalties were thought most likely to pass on information. In Britain there were several cases of women with family in Germany who stood trial for passing information to their relatives.[16] Martha Earle, a German-born widow of a Prussian officer, was charged with conveying news in code to her sister, the Baroness van Bothmer, in Dresden. Earle wrote two or three times a week through intermediaries in Switzerland and Holland but protested that the Latin code her sister invented for their wartime correspondence was 'only for the family'. As she told her interrogators in an interview on 14 May 1918 at Holloway prison, 'I never thought my letters to my sister would be taken as a crime . . . my sister is not an enemy.' But in Britain, this was considered a violation 'of the very greatest order, a war crime'. Yet, to put it in perspective, the information these women passed to their relatives had virtually no military value and in neither case was there proof it ever went beyond the family.[17]

Did Mrs Earle's letters to her sister constitute spying? According to most definitions, probably not. Mrs Earle was never recruited into the secret service nor paid for sending information which only her sister received. However, her case reveals the contradiction inherent in prevailing theories about women's relationship to the state. While all German women were thought to be potential spies, particularly those living abroad, American, English or French women were thought to be infected with Teutonic fervour if they had a German husband. While one theory proposed that race was so closely tied to blood that loyalty to the Kaiser was inbred in anyone born in Germany, Allied women could be tainted by association. The female spy embodied such inconsistencies, which made women from neutral countries or with mixed ethnic parentage so vulnerable to suspicion.

The rhetoric of war demanded that all women visibly demonstrate their national loyalty. Those who refused to claim a single nationality and continued to move from place to place throughout the war years created awkward scenes with customs officials and local police. The *femme vivante* was likely to travel, to use different names, to lie about her circumstances to officials and to claim more than one country as home. Many courtesans had fled to capitals in neutral countries such as Spain, Sweden or Switzerland at the outbreak of war where they could continue their profession.[18] Since these countries were often considered hotbeds of espionage, stories about women who combined both trades seemed entirely believable. However, the legend of the spy-courtesan inevitably focused on the women's perceived desire for exotic stimulation.

The German spy master Gustav Steinhauer cites, as an example, the Allied spy Mary Sorrel who would have spied for anyone, 'if only for the sheer lust of excitement'.[19] A Spanish senator who knew Mata Hari claimed she became a spy to satisfy her 'lust for fresh sensations' that endless sexual adventures had dulled. Like a drug addict, Mata Hari needed ever stronger stimulants which finally only the thrill of espionage intrigues could satisfy.[20] Hirschfeld's research revealed that the best women spies were either mistresses of powerful men, *femmes galantes* or world-weary prostitutes.

However, the spy-courtesan and those international women on the upper social scale had much in common. After all, in every European country it was the daughters of the aristocracy who were expected to make the most visible public gestures in supporting the war effort. But the women whose wealth and social position had enabled them to indulge in avant-garde sexual practices without scandal in peacetime were precisely those whom the intelligence agencies feared the most. Since they were susceptible to blackmail, they might be lured into working for the enemy in exchange for certain incidents and reputations being kept quiet.

Propagandists often described how the Germans intended to disrupt the 'moral balance' in Britain and France by using these well-born women to blackmail political and military leaders. In 1916 a pamphlet by the French author Henry de Halsalle graphically described deviancy as the bedrock of German society. Berlin had replaced Paris as the 'first pleasure city in Europe' where nightclubs had become 'tombs in which our young men are buried alive'. But to reconstitute Berlin as a breeding ground of moral corruption, de Halsalle had to draw a veil of silence over the courtesans, demi-mondaines and aristocratic lesbians of Paris. German cities had far surpassed the French in decadence, he argued, and Berlin was now rife with homosexuality; it was 'the world's chief plague spot for this abject depravity of the human male and female'.[21]

The great threat to social order in Germany described by this author, however, mirrored the sexual anarchy that many believed the Allies were facing at home. Although lesbianism among Europe's best-bred daughters had been discreetly practised in pre-war Paris, it had occasionally sent shock waves through the establishment. Before the war the city's most talked-about scandal was the open relationship between the Marquise de Belbeuf – 'Missy' to her friends – and the writer Sidonie Gabrielle Colette. A constant stream of wealthy and cosmopolitan lesbians also visited Missy's home in the rue Georges-Ville. As Colette noted, they were invariably 'baronesses of the Empire, canonesses, female cousins of Tzars, natural daughters of grand dukes, refined Parisian bourgeoises, elderly horsewomen, products of the Austrian aristocracy with eye and hand of iron'.[22] It was these 'daughters of grand dukes' who were later called upon to run canteens for soldiers, staff hospitals and organize funds for medical supplies. Ida Rubenstein – Diaghilev's greatest Salome and a well-known lesbian – commissioned Leon Bakst to design a nurse's Red Cross uniform for her at the outbreak of war. She wore it while on duty at the military hospital in the Carlton Hotel in Paris that she funded and ran. The uniform was immortalized when her lover, Romaine Brooks, painted Ida against a background of 'barbed wire, mud, flames, the essence of destruction [that was] also symbolic of France's determination to survive'. By 1914 the reigning lesbians in Paris were no longer considered sinners, forced to hide an irredeemable vice, but were now regarded as useful women who could effectively marshal scarce resources and boost morale.[23]

But while the sexual practices of the French, Belgian or English aristocracy were overlooked for the sake of the war effort, anxiety about corruption was redefined as an enemy trait. Women's rejection of marriage, according to de Halsalle, was the clearest sign of degeneracy and vividly revealed in statements from the young German Fräuleins who preached a doctrine of free love. A Frau Kestner told the author, 'It is well known in Berlin that there are "secret" societies composed of strictly women only and to some of these societies belong many women whose names figure prominently in the daily press in connection with fashion functions.' There were further reports about places 'unhealthy in the extreme' that catered exclusively for women indulging in 'homosexual licentiousness'.[24] Missy's former guests who had returned home might have been well disposed to force their friends into handing over useful information, if they chose. In England rumours that aristocratic women with German relations were poisoning the war effort provoked Lloyd George in early 1917 to 'expose the odious influence of . . . the "Petticoat Scandal" hinting at treasonable correspondence with Germans in high places and implicating so-called society women'.[25] Even the royal family, who had only just changed their name to Windsor, stood accused of secretly aiding the German cause.[26]

Logically, if all Hohenzollerns, including the British royal family, were Germans, and all Germans were spies, what hope was there? Britain, many critics feared, was ruled by a family whose sympathies were divided and there-fore untrustworthy. Even worse, there was speculation that the King's sexual indiscretions might have jeopardized the nation; perhaps even he was being blackmailed by the Kaiser's agents into handing over valuable information. Since the Kaiser himself was morally corrupt, he used his subjects to further his own perverse ends – including spying. German wives, governesses or teachers living in Britain or America were therefore swept along on a powerful tide of paranoia which included a host of social evils. 'The women of Germany today,' wrote de Halsalle, 'are characterized by a degree of moral perversion and licentiousness that has never before been approached since the days when the decadence of Rome shocked the conscience of mankind.' The good old-fashioned housewife had been replaced by vamps who worshipped strange aberrations of sex which '[have] helped to rot the soul of German women'.[27] Whether at home or abroad, she was equally dangerous.

The author included comments from anthropologists who had influenced the *fin-de-siècle* discourse on prostitution, to describe the enemy's innate moral corruption. He quoted the famous Turin criminologist Cesare Lombroso who believed that female criminals were like savages, suffering from 'psychic degen-eration'. German women shared these traits, making them an entire nation of 'born prostitutes'; they lacked maternal feeling but were violent, jealous, yearning for revenge and devoted to their pimp/husbands 'as a dog [was to] a master'.[28] For their real master – the Kaiser – these women would do anything. 'Every German is a potential spy,' Georges Prade, a French detective, wrote in *The Times* in May 1916. 'The servile character of the race, its profound contempt for all self-respect makes it consider espionage as a service to the state, honourable because it is useful.'[29] Captain David Fallon, MC, noted in a New York newspaper that spying was an essential ingredient in the Prussian character.[30]

During the war writers and propagandists revived earlier myths about German efficiency in using these seductive spies. Hamil Grant published a book in 1915 that described how several thousand pretty barmaids or cashiers were recruited as agents during Bismarck's unification campaign. Women with a 'high type of morality' were rejected because all agents were ordered to 'extract information from drinking soldiers'. He claimed that more recently the Germans had limited the number of female spies to those with well-honed seductive powers.

In matters of love or revenge, where her deepest feelings are concerned, she is capable of a sustained effort calling for the application of whatever analytical powers she may possess, but seldom in other cases . . . an appeal to, say, her patriotism leaves her almost invariably cold and unenthusiastic, since love of country is a quality which depends too largely on an essentially platonic and impersonal principle to attract and hold for long her undivided interest and attention.[31]

Grant believed women hadn't the intellectual capacity to understand politics so they joined the secret service to exploit their libidinous natures. Since Grant's book appeared on Vernon Kell's recommended reading list for intelligence officers, it was probably one source of MI5's attitude towards female agents. Captain Ferdinand Tuohy contributed to the myth about German 'beauty specialists' employed in secret doings by describing their special training, 'to emulate the dark and bestial days . . . in Berlin where the highest in the land consorted and were duly blackmailed for their sins.'[32] The courtesan and the foreign female spy were interchangeable, each using her statelessness to search for male patrons.

Before the publication of Grant's book, the courtesan-spy and her pimp-accomplice made their debut in Edwardian adventure stories which were thought to be based on real cases. They had proved so popular that 'Candida', writing in the London *Graphic* in 1914, could confidently claim these romantic villains were completely familiar to the 'average person'. 'He had read all about them, and has seen him repeatedly on the stage . . . it is the duty of the drama to teach us real life.' The spy's female accomplice was 'the more extravagantly humorous type', with a foreign accent, 'daring Parisian' wardrobe and evil intentions. She was always unmasked, 'to the huge approval of the gallery', who saw through her from the start.[33] While adults delighted in the stage antics of 'bogus architects and contractors and sham waiters of German origin', children followed the adventures of characters like Pontifex Shrewd in the boy's comic, *Lot-O'-Fun*. Captain Shrewd, Chief of the Southern Command's Secret Service, and his Chinese sidekick exposed nefarious Hun schemes to entrap innocent young British officers.[34]

In 'Mystia the Witch', Lieutenant Harland who is about to enlist with a 'Blankshire Regiment' disappears and the War Office sends Shrewd to investigate. He soon discovers that the young officer has fallen for music-hall artist Miss Daisy Delant, who flaunted 'a wealth of jet black hair, and large commanding eyes'. Also known as 'Mystia the Witch', she specializes in hypnotizing her audience and has soon mesmerized the unsuspecting Harland into handing over valuable military code-books. Pontifex tracks Miss Daisy to a large country house where she sets a tiger and a brown bear – part of her stage act – upon him. But Weng Fo quickly subdues the animals with a valerian-soaked sponge while Shrewd apprehends Daisy just as she bites into a poison capsule and cries out before her death, 'For the Kaiser.'[35]

Such wartime adventure stories, while blatantly reminding boys that 'England wants every one of her sons who can go', drew upon well-established myths. German women were often portrayed as so feverishly patriotic that they happily laid down their lives for the Kaiser. Like the French dancer Marie Madeline who was a Munich hit in 1908, these seductive spies were thought to employ hypnosis and other psychological tricks to ensnare British men. The stories also reinforced the notion that female music-hall performers, who were often foreigners, were involved in sinister activities. Whether it was prostitution, the white slave trade, drug dealing or espionage, the enticing entertainer promised illicit thrills. For middle-class male readers, these espionage stories offered striking parallels with Edwardian pornography in its depiction of a mirror world that played out a magical form of wish-fulfilment 'through a series of bizarre images and irrational acts'.[36] Like Pontifex Shrewd's visit to Daisy's home, in these stories time is suspended, fantastic events occur – wild animals leap from closets – and evil wears a sexually enticing face.

Many intelligence officers in England and France were also seduced by the spy romance. In Britain, Erskine Childers' novel about a German invasion of England, *The Riddle of the Sands*, provoked Lord Selborne to demand a detailed report on its feasibility. Winston Churchill later credited it with prompting the government to establish naval bases in Orkney, the Firth of Forth and Invergordon.[37] Novelist William Le Quex, author of *The Invasion of 1910* which appeared in twenty-seven languages and sold more than a million copies, played a crucial role in forming Britain's civilian intelligence agency. Colonel James Edmonds, then director of military operations on secret service, hired the amateur spy hunter, Le Quex, to form the Voluntary Secret Service department. Edmonds' arguments, which Le Quex supplied, convinced the government to direct the committee of Imperial Defence on 20 April 1909 to establish a counterespionage bureau, MO5.[38] In several cases, former spy-chiefs turned novelist to give their readers access to the 'professional secrecy [that] binds all those who have participated in the secret drama'. Georges Ladoux, who turned to writing fiction after the war, confessed that even his 1932 biography of Marthé Richard was profoundly influenced by writers such as Fenimore Cooper, Mayne Reid, Conan Doyle and Maurice Leblanc.[39]

The Germans also acknowledged the British love of espionage stories. Former agent Felix Gross claimed the Germans were able to expose an English agent disguised as Erik Erikson, a Swedish timber merchant, because of his library. 'Erikson' was so convincing that he had acquired an authentic Swedish passport and travelled into Germany during the war. But his cover was blown after a German agent disguised as a telephone repair man entered his house in Stockholm and found shelves full of novels by Emerson, Carlyle and Phillips Oppenheim.[40]

The spy romance influenced both Allied and Axis intelligence officers. Gustav Steinhauer, the former private detective responsible for pre-war espionage in Britain, once met William Le Quex whom he described as having 'more than a nodding acquaintance with most of the spies in Europe'. Just as Steinhauer paid tribute to Le Quex, his 1930 memoirs tellingly juxtaposed the fantasy of his espionage work with the reality of domestic life. Hot on the trail of Allied spy Baroness Lilika d'Audreve Sevillja, aka the Baroness in Green, he disguised himself as Baron Jan van Leuwarden, to woo this dangerous vixen.[41] They met at a luxurious Berlin hotel in 1917 where Steinhauer was a nobleman by day and suburban father by night; he addressed the Baroness directly in a chapter that described their affair:

> You thought that your Baron was in love with you – and so he was, but
> he also had to remember that in reality he was nobody more than Kriminal
> Kommissar Steinhauer who lived in three modest apartments just outside
> Berlin with his wife and three strong boys. He was really playing Cinderella,
> was Baron Jan van Leuwarden. When the revels were over, he had to leave
> his fairy princess (that was you) and make his way home, where he could
> look at his sleeping children, bring the coals up from the cellar, and when
> that had been done, tumble into his modest bed.[42]

Espionage allowed Steinhauer to experience what was otherwise beyond his social and financial means. The beautiful Baroness offered Steinhauer all the demi-monde's excitement so that a lowly naval intelligence officer briefly savoured the decadent pleasures of the rich, while fulfilling his duty to the Fatherland. But while Steinhauer acknowledged that he was only playing a part, the Baroness was portrayed as the real thing. There is never any suggestion that the female spy might also have a husband or children waiting for her somewhere or that she might be performing as well. These stories had an enormous appeal to their middle-class male readers who themselves dreamed of a Cinderella-like escape from children, coal bins and modest beds.

Former spy masters-turned-authors often described the world of espionage as an élite male cadre that occupied the equivalent of an exclusive club. To Ladoux 'the secret war' was a 'gigantic poker game, the stake for which is the very existence of nations' where the victors 'need not even put down their cards, that is, sacrifice the flower of their race'.[43] Rupert Grayson, in a foreword to German agent H.R. Berndorff's book, also evokes the atmosphere of the gentlemen's club to describe two former enemy agents meeting after the war. 'It is a dangerous game, kicking down screens or tearing aside curtains . . . or is it just whispers, suspicion, masked to the teeth yet pregnant with suspicion? Which will it be?'[44] In these books, when the opponents finally reveal their identity, they greet each other with mutual respect, even admiration for their intricate deceptions. The espionage writers spoke to a male audience; their female characters may have occupied a crucial role in the plot, but they never penetrated the men's cosy world of mutual understanding.

But if female agents existed on the periphery, espionage writers claimed that any woman who held a job or occupied a public position might be a spy. Winifred Ludecke argued that actresses were especially adept at spying since agents were most often 'adventuresses or ladies of the demi-monde, actresses, dancers, artists from the music halls, and cabarets'. But 'aristocrats, school teachers, seamstresses and laundry maids' were also employed with varying degrees of success during the war.[45] Former British agent Captain Ferdinand Tuohy concurred with Ludecke in his memoirs which boasted of 'facts which transcend fiction'. 'Quick-brained actresses artlessly made their soldier adorers chatter on while brainless princesses, minutely schooled by rusé statesmen, asked questions – "you interest me so" – of officers and other commoners only too honoured, after the manner of the age, to distract a royal highness.'[46] Tuohy's career as war correspondent and intelligence officer lent credibility to his rather fantastic observations. His 1920 history of espionage was credited with offering rare insight into British intelligence. After its publication, the Army Council announced that it 'look[ed] with disfavour on any premature publication of the facts relating to the work of intelligence', which would have deterred a less stalwart writer.[47] However, a decade later Steinhauer flatly denied Tuohy's claims that the Germans had an 'army of highly paid spies in your country when the war came'.[48]

The spy paranoia which had flourished in France and Britain was exported to America and influenced newspaper reports before its entry into the war on 6 April 1917. Sensational accounts of enemy agents fell on fertile ground among those politicians and newspaper editors determined to break what they perceived as American isolationism. They were aided by Admiral Sir Reginald 'Blinker' Hall who regularly sent Captain Guy Gaunt, the British naval attaché in Washington, DC, messages that had been intercepted between the United States and Germany. Early in 1916 Gaunt began to forward names of those officials, individuals and their friends whom the Germans considered important, to John R. Rathom, editor of the Providence, Rhode Island, *Journal*. Since *The New York Times* had publishing rights to Rathom's spy scoops, the Germans soon became the focus of much unwanted attention. American Secretary of State Robert Lansing recalled that these stories fostered a mania for hunting German spies comparable to the seventeenth-century witch hunts. According to Lansing, 'certainly nine out of ten, and probably ninety-nine out of a hundred of these suspects were guiltless of any wrongful act or intention.'[49] Among the victims were several wealthy but 'dissolute' women.

In early 1918 the spy-hunters had captured what the *San Francisco Sunday Chronicle* headlined 'one of the Kaiser's "Vampire" Spies'. The American-born Baroness Iona 'Nonie' von Zollner, the wife of a Bavarian officer, was charged with violating the espionage act. Even worse, she had seduced an officer who was exactly half her age. The case exposed 'a sensational love affair between the forty-four-year-old beauty and a young United States army lieutenant of twenty-two, in the course of which suspicious codes, and dangerous wartime secrets were involved'.[50] Baroness 'Nonie', whose father was the New York millionaire William Pickhardt, stood accused of using her beauty to exploit her contacts with high society for the German cause. Although she was suing the Baron von Zollner for divorce and her son was enrolled at the US Naval Academy in Annapolis, it was believed she was sending her husband secret coded messages through a Dutch intermediary.

The packed courtroom, filled with women defiantly clicking their knitting needles as they stitched socks for the troops, heard how 'Nonie' and a young officer had been caught at Chatanooga's Patten Hotel. 'The house detectives . . . found the baroness lying disrobed on her bed, and underneath the bed, in a nude state, his clothing in his hands, was Lieutenant Spaulding.'[51] On the morning the trial opened, Spaulding broke free of his jailers to embrace Nonie and 'cried aloud to the world his love for the woman, twice his age'. Like Mata Hari, the Baroness admitted to having enjoyed the opportunity for being 'intimately acquainted with high military officers' and bedding a younger man. With relish, the court, filled with Mesdames Defarges, watched as the reputation of an extremely privileged woman, whose beauty was comparable to that of 'the Duchess of Gainsborough', was ruined. Petty jealousies often formed the basis of such accusations which, combined with a righteous indignation about a woman's sexual conduct, formed a potent conduit for releasing social tension. The spy-courtesan's trial masqueraded as a new form of patriotism. Now the Americans were having their war for purity.

On 19 March 1918 another nest of aristocratic lady conspirators hit the headlines.[52] 'Two women in luxury' were seized from their expensive hotel suites at the Biltmore and Waldorf in Manhattan, along with their aristocratic lovers. The French Count Robert de Clairmont was arrested with Madame Elizabeth Charlotte Nix, described as 'tall, stately, even haughty, she plainly is of the aristocratic junker class of Berlin'.[53] Their accomplice, Madame Despina Davidovitch Storch, who would later be immortalized as 'Turkish Delight' in spy literature, was taken in on suspicion of committing activities in the interest of an enemy country.[54] An amateur detective, Mr Van der Poel, had befriended Madame Storch several months before and his private investigation led to her arrest. He had become suspicious about her spending habits, in particular how she afforded the five-hundred-dollars-a-month Waldorf suite without any visible income. He was equally curious about what she kept in a safety deposit box at the bank.

Madame Storch, who was arrested with her lover the Count de Beville, was a glamorous attraction for the press – a variation on Mata Hari's theme of exotic other. Born in Constantinople, to a German mother and Bulgarian father, she was described as aged twenty-three, with an olive complexion, jet black eyes and 'the mass of heavy black hair from the Orient'. Moreover, she reminded the reporters of silent screen star Theda Bara; 'it was easy to see how men would fall under the influence of that smile and those brilliant black eyes.' The Hollywood-like atmosphere heightened when Madame Storch fainted upon hearing she might be deported to France. The faithful Count rushed to her side, administering reassuring pats to her back. That day the Theda Bara lookalike and Elizabeth Nix were transferred to Ellis Island.

Ten days later Madame Storch was dead and Clairmont was said to be dying in his Manhattan apartment.[55] Although it was rumoured that Storch had committed suicide by swallowing poison, immigration inspector Bryon H. Uhl announced she had simply caught pneumonia. The press also speculated that she had deliberately stymied her interrogators, knowing that she faced execution in France.[56] Moreover, the Justice Department had identified Madame Storch as the leader of an extensive spy network.

The script for Despina Davidovitch Storch is remarkably similar to that of Mata Hari; both were believed to have trained as spies before the war in the art of exploiting their sexuality and social connections to gather vital military information. Despite Mata Hari's invented Orientalism, there were comparisons with Despina's dark-eyed beauty and notorious reputation. Just as Paris gossip claimed many important men breathed a sigh of relief at Mata Hari's execution, Manhattan greeted the news of Madame Storch's death with equanimity. According to Justice Department officials, 'the woman's career here brought to light an astonishing list of Americans of wealth, standing and political influence, who had evidently allowed themselves to be used as instruments by Madame Storch.'[57] Meanwhile, the US Congress was set to pass legislation placing women enemy aliens on equal footing with men, to allow for a round-up of the Kaiser's agents throughout the country.[58]

Tragically, if Madame Storch had not succumbed to pneumonia, her case would probably have been dismissed. Her alleged 'accomplice', Elizabeth Nix, wrote to the US Attorney General Gregory from the military hospital on Ellis Island, declaring their innocence. There was no spy ring. Nix swore – 'you have my word of honour and I want to be shot if anything I tell you is not true' – that she first met Madame Storch when they were taken to Ellis Island. Madame Nix faced Mata Hari's dilemma: her prosecutors refused to believe she had nothing to confess.[59] The catastrophe had already claimed Madame Storch; her safety deposit box contained only a few love letters from the Portuguese ambassador in London, not military codes. They were all victims of malicious gossip, said Nix. 'The whole case is a make-up [sic] but who has done it? Some enemies, jealous women or so?'

The Justice Department file on Nix reveals that the state's espionage investigation depended on gossip and amateur spy-catchers. Witt K. Cochrane, head of a large Chicago advertising agency, wrote to the Attorney General on behalf of Mrs Carl Hartman, whose American husband was an aviation officer in France. A month after the arrests of Nix, Storch, Beville and de Clairmont, Mrs Hartman offered further evidence of their crimes. As a well-known New York hostess for several years, she had met 'a vast number of German and Austrian "noblemen", their consorts and mistresses and wives'. Mrs Hartman claimed to have investigated those acquaintances she now accused of working for Germany.

Even Elizabeth Nix's teenage son Herbert was implicated in the spy ring. According to Cochrane, 'the boy ... is thoroughly supplied with money by Seligman, the banker, of whom she tells a story that is strikingly immoral and degenerate.' Mrs Hartman also recalled meeting Mrs Nix and Herbert at the Ritz-Carlton hotel where the boy was 'quite outspoken in his loyalty to Germany'. Count von Bernstorff, the German ambassador to Washington who was expelled from the United States, was great friends with Mrs Nix, and often lent her money. After Bernstorff's departure, Seligman supported the family financially and according to Mrs Hartman, 'use[d] young Nix in some degenerate way'. Cochrane concluded that all this information 'might prove valuable ... particularly in this shifty crowd of foreigners [who] are a highly immoral and dissipated lot'. Long-haired musicians, intellectuals, doctors with mistresses, gamblers and phoney aristocrats all fell under Mrs Hartman's piercing gaze.[60]

The charges of immorality and degeneracy formed a pernicious theme during the spy scares in America. But the double standards which informed codes of sexual practice during peacetime were elevated into a moral crusade during the war. Young Lieutenant Spaulding fell victim to Baroness Nonie, Madame Storch was an adulteress, and Elizabeth Nix stood accused of allowing her son to prostitute himself to an elderly banker. Teutonic deviance had brought forth women's most evil desires and used them to terrifying effect. Every New York hostess knew this and was encouraged, as Mrs Hartman was by Cochrane, 'to keep right on gathering information and report ... as rapidly as possible if anything occurs worthy of note'. Though Cochrane could vouch for none of Hartman's accusations, he believed 'it may be wild stuff, but it can't all be wild'.

As was the case with Mata Hari, simple explanations were regarded as clever cover-ups. The reality, however, was that Madame Nix's funds were not a payment for espionage work but a loan she received from the German embassy. Marooned in America at the outbreak of war, with her accounts frozen, she was loaned $2,500 repayable to the Foreign Office in Berlin. A telegram from Washington, DC, to Berlin that Admiral Hall's London office intercepted on 7 January 1915 confirms this. 'Frau Ellis Nix, whose father lives at 5 Klausgrothstrasse, Wilmersdorf, Berlin, is stranded here with children on account of the war and has been up to now supported by me [Bernstorff]. Please get father to pay into Foreign Office a considerable sum, say about 10,000 marks. [$1,600 US].'[61] Although the message confirmed Madame Nix's statements, she and both her children were interned at Ellis Island for several months. By September 1918 John Lord O'Brian, the Attorney General's special assistant, would still describe Nix as 'a notoriously immoral person who in peace times would be promptly deported'.[62] However, in peacetime a woman's sexual conduct was rarely regarded as a threat to national security.

The hunt was on and there were daily reports of pro-Germans being tarred and feathered, pushed into canals or forced to kiss the American flag. Government investigators appeared to be uncovering nests of spies and on 27 April 1918 triumphed in the arrest of 'the most daring and dangerous spy in American history' at a Long Island hotel.[63]

Madame Marie de Victorica, née von Kretschman, aka Marie de Vussière, admitted that she had travelled to New York from Berlin in 1917 as a propagandist for the Germans. But she never stood trial. Instead, she turned state's witness against the Irish-American leader, Jeremiah O'Leary, whom the German military attaché had hired for sabotage operations on Sir Roger Casement's advice.[64] Victorica arrived in Manhattan where she contacted her partner, Hermann Wessels, a German naval officer who had also been sent by the Imperial Ministry of Defence (Reichswehrministerium) to organize the destruction of naval shipyards. They were employed to 'operate against England with the help of the Irish living in America, that is, to win over Irishmen in the United States who were supposed to perform acts of sabotage in England or in the English fleet.'[65] However, Victorica admitted that their network met without any success whatsoever.[66]

By this time, the spy-courtesan had so determined the coverage of espionage trials that every report strained to conform to Mata Hari standards. In reality, Victorica was overweight, middle-aged and hardly fitted the *femme fatale* model, but she was extremely intelligent, articulate and had extensive political connections within the German imperial government. However, espionage writers would immortalize her as 'the beautiful blonde woman of Antwerp' and MI5 had sent the American secret service a cable describing her in these terms. Moreover, during the 1919 trial of another saboteur, Willard Robinson, Victorica admitted to being a morphine addict for more than twenty years. (She had probably developed her drug dependency during an illness which required her to undergo seven operations and spend four years convalescing in various resorts.) Yet through all this, 'she retained something of the attractiveness of feature and complexion that must have made her conspicuous for beauty in earlier years.'[67] Since there was no suggestion that Victorica was a coquette for the secret service, news reports focused on her treacherous talents.

'The young woman prisoner is one of the most talented young women in the service of the Kaiser,' claimed the *New York Times*. 'She lives up to her reputation as an unusually clever woman.' Victorica, the daughter of a Prussian general, held degrees from the Universities of Heidelberg, Zurich and Berlin where she studied political economy. She had the highest contacts within the imperial government, professed an extensive knowledge of European politics and spoke several languages.[68] A German informant testified from Atlanta penitentiary that she was a trusted government agent who had special orders to direct Sinn Fein activities for Germany in America by helping fund Irish newspapers.[69]

In the iconography of female agents, Victorica was extremely unusual. She was, as she wrote to a friend, 'a very fierce patriot', who counted among her colleagues Matthias Erzberger, the German parliamentary secretary from 1918, the author Count Ernst zu Reventlow, Maximilian Hardern, editor of *Die Zukunft*, and Wilhelm Solf, chief of the Berlin colonial office.[70] She considered herself neither a spy nor a sabotage agent but a 'German propagandist caught and gotten stranded by the war'. According to Victorica's account, her American investigators considered her a patriot and 'even complimented [me] for being plucky and standing up for my country!' For the benefit of the district attorney, she began an autobiography in 1919 and during her sentence entertained herself by writing political essays 'that will be quite valuable as historic material later on for me'. She also kept an eye out for suitable material for her other passion – the movies. In Germany, she had written and produced a few silent films.

However, Victorica was aware that, since she couldn't be categorized as a spy-courtesan, she had become an enigma. As she wrote to a friend, identified only as 'Mitzi':

> A real hell of a time I had with the newspapers here by becoming their victim in their quest for sensations, they called me the personal messenger of the Kaiser, the most dangerous German spy, and the 'mysterious woman in black', you will laugh when I show you some of the clippings I collected. American notoriety is hell for any decent person, and to be a witness in Court in a sensational case is worse than being a defendant oneself.[71]

The press coverage varied and, according to Victorica, 'while one part . . . represented me as a government-sleuth, another part described me as an awfully dangerous and powerful messenger of – the Emperor!'[72] Victorica was portrayed as an intellectual who ruthlessly controlled hundreds of agents and punished any failure with death. She became the antithesis of the courtesan, a beautiful but frigid woman who hated men. In several spy stories, she appears as a sexual sadist or a lesbian, signalling ever further degrees of moral corruption. Conveniently for the espionage writers, Victorica died of pneumonia in 1920 before she could reveal the full details of her espionage career.

At first there was speculation that since Victorica and Madame Davidovitch Storch had succumbed to the same illness, they must have been killed by a 'scientific murderer of the Imperial German Government'.[73] According to one report of Victorica's testimony in April 1918, she knew Madame Storch and Madame Nix who was 'an intimate friend of the Kaiser'.[74] With Victorica's death went the last chance to resolve the mystery surrounding her propaganda operations in the United States during the war. However, Herbert Yardley, who was the leading expert of America's cryptographic bureau, known as the Black Chamber, supplied the missing details in a book published in 1931. Yardley claimed to have decoded the intercepted messages from German agents which led to Victorica's arrest. According to Yardley, she was the genius who organized the importation of explosives into America stuffed into religious altar figures which relied on a network of Catholic priests to convey instructions. 'That this was feminine and not masculine subtlety I have not the faintest doubt,' he wrote. 'It is too much to believe that Madame Victorica's masculine master was so clever.'[75] Yardley imagined himself locked in battle with a beautiful but brutal woman.

Finally, she gave in to her interrogators. '[A] pitiable, broken creature, her beauty and charm gone, she died . . . Though a pathetic figure in death, may she remain immortal in the annals of espionage.'[76] Yardley's description of her demise contrasts sharply with the confident tone of the letters she wrote from Ellis Island in 1919. Although her case fell apart because of the Armistice and the slow pace of the American legal system in dealing with espionage cases, Yardley's book graphically illustrated a defeated woman whose drug dependency stemmed from the constant stress of intelligence gathering. Instead, Victorica often commented in her letters from prison on the kindness of Justice Department officials, who had carefully arranged for the continuation of her 'medical treatment'.[77]

Neither did Victorica's experience conform to the usual spy story which pitted the vamp against the lone male sleuth. Mrs Jentzer, a Justice Department detective, had met Victorica casually at Manhattan's Waldorf Hotel where they discussed the merits of secret inks over tea. The undercover government agent was 'a nice little woman whom I consider as one of my best friends in this country', Victorica wrote to Mitzi. 'She is a very interesting self-made woman, the only female member of the Secret Service. She was the one to trail and finally arrest me, but I bear her no grudge for this.'[78] All of Victorica's testimony suggests that Herbert Yardley's involvement in the case was probably limited to his cryptography work.

Following adverse reaction from government officials in America and Britain after the publication of Yardley's book, he wrote a novel based on his experiences, entitled *The Blonde Countess*. Through fiction, he was able to flesh out his espionage fantasies and build Madame de Victorica into a cold-blooded Mata Hari. The plot revolves around the search for the enemy spy, J37, who is 'a woman more to be feared than half a dozen military attachés'.[79] The story shifts back into familiar territory with Nathaniel Greenleaf, chief of the Black Chamber, heading an investigation which eventually leads to his former lover, the Countess Thorlund. They are locked in an intellectual but deadly struggle and when Nathaniel finally confronts the Countess, he realizes how deeply she hates him. Yet he still prefers this witch-like figure to any other woman; the fascination is 'two parts fear and detestation' while her power is an 'evil spell'.[80]

Yardley's fictional account transformed Victorica into a creature which the espionage writer needed to tell his story. Her intellectual and political interests were trimmed away, her physique was refashioned and her sexuality placed uppermost in the plot. Other post-war novels written by former spies conformed to the same mythology: attractive female agents were used to extract information from men through pillow talk, and stood accused of a double set of crimes. The tension which existed between the need to maintain the status of the good woman and devoted wife with the desire for a heartless mistress was played out in endless variations within this genre. Whether it was Baroness Nonie, Madame Nix, Marie de Victorica or Mata Hari, these carefully constructed vamps enacted an eternal drama.

Early on in the war, the Allies had seized upon the Germans' execution of the English nurse Edith Cavell and condemned it as barbaric. Couched in the rhetoric of sanctifying womanhood, press reports about the execution made convenient copy for army recruits in Britain and, later, in America. However, the anger which Cavell's death provoked posed an awkward question about the French penchant for shooting women spies, sometimes on thin evidence. One woman's death was another's martyrdom. As the next chapter explores, Mata Hari and Edith Cavell became the war's most potent female icons in the long-drawn-out propaganda campaign waged on the home front.

CHAPTER SEVEN

A BATTLE FOR HEARTS, MINDS AND RECRUITS

No incident of the war has filled the mind of the public with greater horror and detestation than the execution of this heroic woman, Edith Cavell.

THE LORD MAYOR OF LONDON (1917)[1]

A beautiful young woman, the Dutch dancer, Mata Hari condemned purely on suspicion of espionage, has fallen under the muzzles of French rifles. This cruelty is made even worse by the sentimental tirades, furious condemnations and humanitarian protests that France made when the English spy, Miss Cavell . . . was subjected to the rigour of a trial.

ABC DOMINGO, *newspaper, Madrid* (1917)[2]

WITHIN THE CONTEXT OF THE WAR the two greatest figures in the history of espionage that powerfully represent the dichotomy between good and evil women are Mata Hari and Edith Cavell. More clearly than any other cases, they raise the propaganda value of the female spy whose crimes allude to other battles between the sexes. The idealized, self-sacrificing mother which Cavell symbolizes is, in reality, difficult for any woman to sustain. But when women – whether suffragettes or Red Cross nurses – demanded more autonomy and a voice in public life, they faced accusations of being unsexed. Mata Hari and Edith Cavell were polar opposites that, in the public discourse, worked in tandem; the spy-courtesan and the power-hungry nurse became two archetypes of female independence. Whether revered or reviled, neither woman was 'natural' but had rejected home and family to pursue her ambitions.

After Mata Hari's death, comparisons with the English nurse Edith Cavell, executed by the Germans in 1915, were inevitable. A Dutch newspaper received complaints from readers who felt the unsentimental reports of Mata Hari's death compared unfavourably with the indignation expressed about Cavell.[3] The German government was quick to exploit the hypocrisy of the Allies who denounced Cavell's execution as an abomination because a woman's life was sacred, yet applauded Mata Hari's death at Vincennes. In neutral Spain, the pro-German press praised the Dutch dancer, while pro-Allied newspapers resurrected Cavell's memory to criticize the Kaiser. *El Parlamentario* portrayed Mata Hari as Judas, selling 'the soldiers for 30 pieces of silver',[4] while *La Tribuna* accused the 'successors of Jeanne d'Arc' of having shot several German women for pleasure since 1914.[5] The newspapers sympathetic to the Germans – known as the *germanofilos* – the *Protesta*, the *Dia*, the *Correo Español*, all lamented the brutal killing of a 'beautiful dancer'.[6]

But if the women were painted as sinner and saint respectively, their tragic deaths were used for the same ends. The Germans shot Cavell at 2 a.m. on the morning of 12 October 1915, without considering an appeal for clemency. In Britain, government and press reports provoked a huge outcry against the execution; monuments were built, films produced, plays written and Cavell's portrait hung in schoolrooms throughout the country. The French government minted a souvenir Cavell medal that depicted the execution scene against the background of a mutilated church and a burning village. By November 1915 the Morality players had produced a film entitled *The Killing of Nurse Cavell* and by the following spring a Spanish exporter was sending 'Cavell oranges' to England, wrapped in tissue with etchings of her final hour.[7] Her popularity lasted throughout the war. By 1918 Sir Hall Caine's 'patriotic picture play' was still touring the country and John Tussaud reported that 'Nurse Cavell' remained the most popular wartime figure in his waxworks museum.[8]

While the Allies had Cavell oranges and medals, the Germans seized upon Mata Hari for their own propaganda purposes. They produced a glamorous portrait on a postcard with the inscription, 'A Victim of War-Madness, MATA HARI, the beautiful Dutch dancer who was shot guiltless in France, October 15, 1917'. According to Mr Frankenhuis, a Dutch collector of war curiosities, 'the propaganda object is to counteract the sentiment caused by the shooting of Miss Cavell; the Germans thus aim to prove that for every crime committed by them, a corresponding one has been committed by the Entente.' The Germans also manufactured 'a small change purse one side of which is a photograph of Miss Cavell and on the other side, a photograph of Mata Hari'.[9] Every German housewife was to be reminded of British hypocrisy whenever she reached for a few pfennigs.

Louise Thuliez, a Lille teacher who was involved with Cavell's Belgian escape network and whose death sentence was commuted to hard labour for life in 1915, described the German propaganda in Brussels:

> In trying to defend themselves the Germans have pushed their insolence so far as to compare Edith Cavell to Mata Hari. Edith Cavell had worked for her country, consecrating to this noble task all her career of faith and sacrifice. Mata Hari, thinking only of her own personal charms, had sold herself to the highest bidder. While Edith Cavell, at the bedside of the wounded men she was tending, wept over the sufferings of her fellow-countrymen, Mata Hari in the luxury of palaces betrayed indiscriminately all who approached her. Which of these two women deserves to be called a 'spy'?[10]

German reports about Mata Hari were intended to embarrass the Allies over their double standards rather than provide sufficient evidence to clear her name. Even critical newspaper readers like Thuliez took Allied press reports about the Mata Hari case at face value. The image of the decadent, erotic spy tugged at a deep moral chord, throwing Cavell's selflessness into sharp relief. In the propaganda battle, the British would prove more adept, as MI5's first head Sir Vernon Kell once described it, 'at keeping the public sweet'.[11]

In Holland, however, awkward questions were raised about the outrage over the Cavell affair. General Snyder wrote to the British minister in The Hague to ask about parallels between Cavell's death and the French execution of Félice Pfast, whom the French Third Council of War found guilty on 10 July 1915 and executed a month later. Pfast was a Frenchwoman, aged twenty-five, from Metz, near the German border, who was granted permission to visit her mother in Belgium where she met a German official. She was recruited to gather information in Paris and she reported her results on her next visit to Belgium three weeks later. The official was pleased with her success and paid her 5,000 francs for another mission before she was caught in Marseilles. The British minister replied to General Snyder that 'as Miss Cavell's offence was merely that of aiding Allied subjects to escape from Belgium', it bore no relation to the Pfast case.[12] However, George Barton, whose world history of military spies was published in Britain and the US in 1917, confirms that Pfast's execution was widely compared with that of Edith Cavell.[13]

If both Cavell and Mata Hari had lost their lives to 'war-madness', the British claimed the high moral ground in their treatment of female spies. Sir John Simon, the government's chief prosecutor, rejected claims that Cavell's sentence was similar to the punishment of women spies in Britain. In 1915 Simon stated that even in cases where espionage had been clearly proved, no woman had ever been sentenced to death for this crime.[14] However, an English court condemned a Swedish secretary, Eva de Bournonville, to hang in January 1916, only three months after Cavell's death. She was only reprieved after the government realized how valuable her execution would be to the Germans in the propaganda battle.[15]

Justice Archibald Bodkin influenced this decision by writing to the Director of Public Prosecutions on 16 November 1915 suggesting that de Bournonville should not be hanged. Bodkin attempted to put the case in perspective:

> The case so far as 'information' is concerned is not very serious. She might perhaps have happened upon something 'good' but has not done so. What possible reason therefore is there for having three judges, presided over by . . . a jury; the scandal about Count Reventlow [the Danish Minister in London who supplied her with letters of recommendation] made quasi-public property – merely because she is a woman alien and not a man? *Since Miss Cavell's death, things are different* – let us show the Germans *our* courts martial do not shoot women because the Germans do. But do see the Attorney General and get the very sentimental direction that all women are to be tried civilly unreserved.[16]

Although the presiding judge at the Central Criminal Court originally dismissed Bodkin's advice, his letter reflects the impact that Cavell's case had on the treatment of women spies in Britain. It was now injudicious to execute women, especially those who had gathered relatively unimportant information. In fact, during her interrogation, de Bournonville had divulged a valuable 'accommodation address' which had served German intelligence well and the address of a Belgian officer who was actually a POW in Germany.[17]

However, although de Bournonville's sentence was reduced to penal servitude for life, rumours continued that the British had a different set of rules about the preservation of female life in the war zone. After the House of Commons learned that 'a woman spy' had been convicted, a Labour MP suggested an investigation to determine whether prosecutions under the Defence of the Realm Act were being 'too severe and arbitrarily applied'.[18] It was also believed that since no

English court would condemn a woman to death, Sir Basil Thomson had sent Mata Hari back to the French authorities, who would.[19] The British government never executed a woman during the war, but its judges had certainly tried to; whether a convicted female agent lived or died was a matter of politics, not humanity.

Although British newspapers were convinced their nation was chivalrous enough to pardon women spies, the lack of comment on Mata Hari's case contrasted sharply with the poignant detail in reports about Edith Cavell. Both women died in equally grim circumstances. Cavell, who ran a nursing school in Brussels, had helped many Allied prisoners to escape over the Belgian border into Holland. On 5 August 1915 she was arrested, taken to the city's Saint-Gilles prison and placed in solitary confinement where visitors were refused. A German military tribunal at the Salle des Députés on 8 October found her guilty of helping prisoners to escape and sentenced her to death along with four others.

At about 8 p.m. on 11 October, Hugh Gibson, secretary of the American legation in Brussels, received word that Cavell would be shot before dawn. Gibson and the Spanish minister, the Marquis de Villalobar, pleaded with the Germans to stay the execution. The American, whose legation represented British interests, 'emphasize[d] the horror of executing a woman, no matter what her offence'. But Baron von der Lancken was adamant that 'even the Emperor himself could not intervene'.[20] Eventually von der Lancken was persuaded to wake up General von Sauberzweig, the military governor of Brussels, and argue their case. However, the general brushed aside von der Lancken's objections and ignored all pleas for clemency.[21] Even Baron von Bissing, Belgium's governor general and the man whom Mata Hari had planned to seduce, refused to answer the American's final appeal for Cavell's life.

She was taken from Saint-Gilles prison just after midnight, driven to the Tir National outside Brussels and shot at 2 a.m. on 12 October.[22] Dr Benn, the German government's chief medical officer in Brussels who witnessed the execution, commented: 'She went to death with a poise and a bearing which is impossible to forget. She had, however, acted as a man towards the Germans and deserved to be punished as a man.'[23]

The Belgian government under German influence regarded Cavell's execution as a warning that women enjoyed no special protection. 'The sentence was executed in order to give a lesson to all women who, sheltering behind the privileges due to their sex, take part in work that is punishable by death,' La Belgique reported in October 1915. 'If we were obliged to recognize such privileges, we should open the door, purely and simply, to the machinations of women who are often far more cunning, far more adroit in these matters, than the most accomplished masculine spy.'[24] Like the French, the Germans believed women were inherently far more deceptive and, therefore, dangerous. But Baron von der Lancken would describe the incident as 'a grave political blunder which rendered inestimable service to English atrocity propaganda'.[25]

Edith Cavell might have been 'punished like a man' but throughout the Allied nations she was hailed as the new madonna. Press reports often evoked maternal images that placed Cavell in a panoply of female saints who supported and nurtured male endeavours. Sadi Kirschen, one of the Belgian defence lawyers at her trial, said she was 'like a mother' to the soldiers whom she nursed 'with

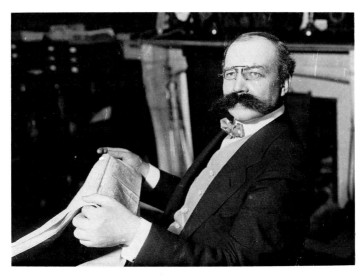

PLATE 9 *Mata Hari's lover, General Messimy, the French Minister of War.*
(COLLECTION ROGER-VIOLLET, PARIS)

PLATE 10 *Georges Ladoux, 'the fat little man' who was head of French
counter-espionage during the war and responsible for Mata Hari's demise*
(COLLECTION ROGER-VIOLLET, PARIS)

PLATE 11 *Mata Hari's prison photograph taken on the day of her arrest in 1917. (ULLSTEIN BILDERDIENST, BERLIN)*

PLATE 12 *Captain Pierre Bouchardon, Mata Hari's interrogator (left), with prosecutor Lieutenant André Mornet (right) during the 1917 trial.*
(COLLECTION ROGER-VIOLLET, PARIS)

PLATE 13 *Marthé Richard, the aviator and French double-agent who protested Mata Hari's innocence after the war.* (BRITISH LIBRARY, LONDON)

PLATE 14 *The last photograph of Mata Hari, taken at St Lazare prison, 1917.* (COLLECTION ROGER-VIOLLET, PARIS)

PLATE 15 *A re-enactment of Mata Hari's execution in 1917, probably from the 1922 French silent film about her life.* (COLLECTION ROGER-VIOLLET, PARIS)

PLATE 16 *Sister Marie-Perpétue, one of the two nuns who accompanied Mata Hari to her execution from St Lazare prison.*
(COLLECTION ROGER-VIOLLET, PARIS)

MURDERED

OCTOBER 12TH, 1915

By THE Huns

MISS EDITH CAVELL

ENLIST IN THE 99th

AND HELP STOP SUCH ATROCITIES

8 PUBLISHED BY THE ESSEX COUNTY RECRUITING COMMITTEE

PLATE 17 Recruitment poster using the martyred Edith Cavell as a rallying point, 1915. (IMPERIAL WAR MUSEUM, LONDON)

PLATES 18 & 19 These British posters, which were widely circulated during the Second World War, illustrate that the female spy was still linked with myths about the danger of 'pillow talk' which Mata Hari's case had spawned. (IMPERIAL WAR MUSEUM, LONDON)

PLATE 20 *Mata Hari's story has been recreated in several films, including this 1964 production starring Jeanne Moreau. She commented to Marguerite Duras, 'The greatest moments of her life unfolded like a series of illusions and deceptions.'*

a fanatical devotion'.[26] A nurse who had once worked with Cavell in London described her as a 'heroine of the Joan of Arc type'.[27] In the *Daily Express* she was a 'Florence Nightingale', who 'loved humanity and was also fond of dogs', and in the *Morning Post* her compassion had a 'womanly quality'.[28] The reports were unanimous in condemning her death as 'the bloodiest act of the whole war', which no civilized nation could condone.[29]

As Cavell was turned into a martyr for the Allied cause, all the complicating elements of her story were stripped away. Her knowing involvement in the escape network was ignored and commentators explained away her belief that 'patriotism is not enough' as evidence of her strong religious conviction. In its simplified version, Cavell's death became a rallying point for British propagandists. The Germans had stooped to shooting the revered angels of the hospital ward and must be stopped. 'Is it possible there is one young man in England today who will sit still under this monstrous wrong?' the Bishop of London asked his congregation on 21 October. 'God's curse is on the nation that tramples underfoot and defies the laws of chivalry which once relieved the horrors of war.'[30] At a London rally the following week, *Daily Mirror* journalists handed out photographs of Miss Cavell and 'the response was a large number of recruits who joined in order to avenge the brave martyr'.[31] Meanwhile the *Daily Mirror* and the *Daily Telegraph* ran competing fund-raising appeals to build a Cavell memorial, while boosting their circulation.

Cavell was chosen as the perfect vessel for conveying the message about the need for women's heroic self-sacrifice. As a childless, virginal mother-figure, it was often claimed that she represented all the Huns' anonymous female victims. The Belgians associated Miss Cavell with 'the many Belgian women who have already fallen martyrs to German barbarism and from whose innocent blood will arise new heroism for the defence of civilization'.[32] In Rome Signor Altobelli told the Italian Chamber of Deputies that she represented his country's suffering women.

> The thousands of children in their mothers' arms who have been butchered or mutilated, the thousands of young women who have been violated in the presence of fathers or brothers, bound hand and foot . . . were mostly anonymous, but in Miss Edith Cavell, we have a concrete figure.[33]

When the French unveiled a memorial to Cavell a year later, they praised 'a heroine who not only shed lustre on the women of her race but upon all women'.[34] Such accolades denied the reality of Cavell's experience, reducing her to the perfectly passive female, whose death was the ultimate self-sacrifice. This imagery upheld the reigning divide between the sexes reinforcing the equation of women's purity and innocence with male virility.

Edith Cavell was unfairly tried and convicted but she was not a victim of circumstance. However, as the woman who died for 'the right of womanhood to help men in distress and danger', her execution provoked a backlash against this fusion of feminine devotion with masculine, patriotic action. Despite the tributes, many people began to question her martyrdom. An English physician, P. Macleod Yearsley, spoke with several suffragettes who argued that Cavell 'knew what she was risking and what penalty she would incur and therefore fully deserved her fate'. Yearsley's friend, RAMC Dobbs, who was stationed on the Western Front, thought that she did 'her best for her own side' but the death sentence was justified. As Dobbs told Yearsley in 1919:

> The Germans . . . repeatedly warned her that she must not act as a spy but could do all she wished to help the wounded and distressed . . . The real crux in Nurse Cavell's case was that she persisted in acts which, done in an enemy's country, were simply spying and she would have been arrested by any belligerent. The outstanding point was that *we* do not shoot women. There is no denying her acts were patriotic and that she died a patriot's death; but her imprisonment would have perfectly well met the case. [emphasis in original][35]

An article by Robert Ach on 30 January 1919 agreed that Cavell's crime deserved capital punishment since neither the Allies nor their enemies could accept 'the privilege of sex'. 'It is time that we recognized this,' he wrote, 'and admitted that Miss Cavell heroically ventured her life and died for her country but that she was no more and no less "murdered" than thousands of men who fell in honourable fight on the field of battle.'[36] Ach ignores the outstanding differences between a soldier and a nurse like Cavell, who worked in a private hospital. Despite her contact with British intelligence, she was a civilian who had never been officially recruited or trained for the 'honourable fight'. Former espionage officer Captain Ferdinand Tuohy agreed with Ach that 'It was a woman who gave away most of the French espionage system in Belgium in 1915 . . . It would be idle now to trace the cause of this collapse other than to where it belongs – the trial of Miss Cavell.'[37] These comments expose a deep contradiction: Cavell was expected to play the quintessential feminine role of nurturer while accepting punishment as if she were a soldier.

Whether Cavell was a spy also remains a moot point. Captain Sigismund Payne Best, an officer in the British Intelligence Corps in Belgium, was the GHQ contact for the agents Alexandre Franck and Joseph Baeckelmans, who worked with Cavell. These men were caught, condemned to death in Brussels on 18 September 1915, and executed five days later. Best recalled how the Belgian spy network was dismantled following their arrest:

> Unfortunately [Franck and Baeckelmans] had got in touch with Miss Cavell and had helped her in connection with escaped prisoners and the evacuation of British people. It was at that time when Miss Cavell was being arrested and these two men were caught by the Germans and executed. Well this put me against the whole idea of helping prisoners to escape. Nurse Cavell was in a way responsible for the breakdown of the Belgian Intelligence Service in 1915.

After this incident, Best instructed his soldiers to turn over escaped prisoners to the Germans and later in life wrote with bitterness that, '[Edith Cavell] was in truth a damned nuisance + caused us many a headache + it wd have been better for everyone if she had stuck to nursing.'[sic][38] Best hinted that women had no place in the male business of espionage, and that Cavell was a disruptive and even dangerous influence.

British intelligence must therefore share at least partial responsibility for Cavell's capture, but Best's antipathy towards her reflects an ambiguity towards nurses that often surfaced during the war. Imbued with the most sacred maternal qualities, nurses and their organizations were often distrusted by military men who feared they perverted the masculine mission of war. This 'petticoat soldiering' could only encourage women to ignore male authority, creating anarchy and chaos. An article in the *Leipziger Neuste Nachrichten* about Cavell's case suggests that men on both sides during the war shared this suspicion. The British were criticized for funding Cavell's operations that 'encouraged her to conduct her unholy mission behind the shield of her womanhood, and with that mask which in England is most beloved of criminals – the Red Cross'.[39] General Walter Kirke, who organized British intelligence on the Western Front, worried that nursing might provide a cover for enemy activities. 'Now the whole country full of secretive females with fancy Red Cross outfits, subject to no form of control,' he fumed in his diary on 10 December 1914. 'Many undesirables must be included amongst their activities and it is an obvious means of access for hostile agents.'[40]

During the war, however, nurses were accused of more than hampering military operations. Even before 1914 sexologists had determined that, especially for upper-class women, nursing activities were intimately connected with sexual pleasure. These 'spinsters or virgins, half or totally withered' often entered the profession 'to observe closely the intimate details of the male organism'. Frédéric Masson, a French academic, produced a pamphlet in 1915 that claimed certain women were aroused by ailing men, giving rise to a 'cult of the wounded'.

Once in a position of authority, these sadists abused their power, tyrannizing the sick men in their care. After 1918 German sexologist Dr Magnus Hirschfeld heard from dozens of French and German soldiers who described being humiliated by these prurient women. One recruit thought a nurse deliberately embarrassed a group of naked men waiting for their medical by giggling and smirking as she walked past. A German prisoner-of-war remembered two French nurses insisting he kept the lavatory door open so they could watch him urinate and another claimed nurses often took more than a clinical interest in his genitals when he used the bedpan. These comments often reflected the division between the working-class enlisted soldiers and middle- or upper-class nurses. The men described the discomfort and resentment they felt at being attended by women who they thought used their social status as a means of control. But the nurses were also a convenient target for the resentment men felt towards the injuries they had suffered; the women were literally and metaphorically perceived to be profiting from men's misery.

Rumours persisted throughout the war that nurses were sex-mad or even disguised prostitutes who exploited the chaotic atmosphere of the front line to ply their trade. A popular song in Hungary hinted at the 'more than doubtful reputation of the nurses' and in German cities prostitutes bought nurses' uniforms on the black market in order to enter military barracks. The war nurse – the only woman a soldier might meet on active service – was an emotionally loaded female figure, as Hirschfeld argued:

> Protagonists of the theory that in women all the expressions of life are far
> more deeply rooted and anchored in sexuality than men may find in such
> cases support for their position ... In general the impression created was
> that the nurse had to be either an angel or a whore. That the evil reputation
> proved itself in general to be stronger than the idealizing tendency is partly
> due to the physicians who in general had a very derogatory opinion concerning
> female help.[41]

The patronizing attitude of doctors and officers, however, reflected attitudes in
society as a whole.[42] The war had challenged the belief that daughters of the
bourgeoisie must be confined within the 'sanctity of the fireside'. Once these
respectable ladies had entered the public sphere, it was feared, they would
unleash sexual urges that fathers and husbands had carefully controlled. A
suspicion remained that nursing – the most prestigious women's service in the
Allied countries – was full of females whose Janus face hid her true instincts. Her
other dark, libidinous side wore the smile of the spy-courtesan; Edith Cavell and
Mata Hari, madonna and whore, inhabited the same female body.

Several intelligence officers claimed to have uncovered cases of field nurses
working as enemy agents that lent credibility to this theory. Captain Ferdinand
Tuohy, the British intelligence officer on the Western Front, recalled how a
vivacious young Polish woman had disguised herself as a Red Cross nurse
to extract information from unsuspecting Russians. For two years during the
war she resided at the Hotel Bristol in Warsaw, which was a reputed espionage
centre. The charming nurse was popular with the guests, particularly the Russian
officers, 'just in from the line and hypnotized by the prospect of a love affair'.
Listening with rapt attention the nurse coaxed the exact details of his military
position from an admirer, so she would always know where he was. Above her
bed hung a map of the front where each officer marked his company's position
with a small flag. Eventually, one of her lovers became suspicious of her interest
in military tactics and informed the Polish authorities.[43] She was arrested and
revealed to be a German spy.

In other accounts, the nurse appears as a patriotic Frenchwoman who has
been manipulated into working for the enemy. The aristocratic Mademoiselle
Solange joined a nursing corps at the outbreak of war and was sent to the
Argonne where she was praised for her dedicated service. However, several
fellow nurses began to wonder why she kept such a large map of the Western
Front in the bedroom of the cottage where she was billeted. They also noticed
that after long conversations with the soldier-patients about their battle experiences, the flags on her map were shifted accordingly. In another version of the
story, Solange had several officer-lovers who took turns in her bed; it was their
regiments which she carefully moved about her map. She was a prolific correspondent and frequently asked patients or hospital orderlies en route to the
interior to post letters for her. An Allied agent traced the leak of vital military
information to the Argonne, so that even the dedicated Solange's letters were
opened. A note to her 'foreign' dentist in Paris was tested for secret ink, and
was found to contain incriminating evidence.

Solange was arrested but refused to answer any questions and complained
of violent headaches. 'One day she broke down and confessed between violent

sobs that she loved France . . . but a mysterious, invisible power forced her to betray her country.' She admitted that, through hypnosis and drugs, her dentist had compelled her to gather information for the Germans. She was conscious of her actions, but powerless to stop herself. The French military authorities were lenient and she was eventually released into the custody of her family who hushed up the affair.[44] However, Dr Hirschfeld claimed that Solange poisoned herself with veronal before the Third Council could try her.[45]

Although there is no documentary evidence to prove the Solange case, there was a popular notion during the war that spies employed such nefarious psychological methods to extract information from their prey. Leval, the legal adviser who witnessed Cavell's trial, told a London audience on 13 October 1917 that the Germans had gathered evidence against her from a somnambulist nurse who talked in her sleep. 'They mesmerized her and from her gained knowledge they would not otherwise have possessed.'[46] The allusions to woman's inherently treacherous nature are borne out in these accounts; even the selfless nurse has an evil side which an unscrupulous master could effortlessly exploit.

The Mademoiselle Solange story may have originated from an actual incident that took place during the war. One possible source was recorded in General Walter Kirke's diary. He received a report in April 1916 about Madame Ewing, a Frenchwoman who worked as a double-agent for the British. She was living in Holland when she was approached by the Germans and given instructions to infiltrate a French hospital near Calais as a nurse. Her secret service contact told her they didn't require any information about the Belgian army but requested news of the French and British forces. She was given invisible ink and told to leave the hospital after two months to avoid any suspicion.[47] Espionage writers would later add details to the story, turning Madame Ewing into either a manipulated nurse or a manipulative spy-courtesan.

Another source may have been the case of Rose Ducimetière. She was raised in a Paris orphanage and as a teenager became involved with Walter X, a Swiss German waiter who worked in a brasserie. Walter soon introduced her to prostitution, acting as her pimp while she worked the Boulevard Sebastopol. She picked up information from her soldier-customers and passed it back to Walter. She also wrote so dutifully to soldiers at the front that the Swiss Military Review eventually sent her to nurse at the Italian front. While this 'beautiful young nurse' was there, she often questioned her patients about their military experiences. On her return to Paris in October 1916, she entered the Val-de-Grâce hospital and was arrested at the bedside of a seriously wounded man. Since she was only nineteen years old, she was saved from the firing squad and her sentence was reduced to penal servitude for life on 24 April 1917.[48]

There were, however, widely reported cases in the British and American press of volunteer nurses accused of espionage. Caroline Bartlett née Gott, an American opera singer, fell into the category of 'international women' that the French believed were so dangerous during the war. The highest paid soloist in the US, Bartlett was in London at the outbreak of war and immediately cancelled her proposed European tour to raise funds and supplies for military hospitals. She adopted the name Sister Beatrice to work anonymously and designed her own purple and white uniform. Despite her humble disguise, she still used her international contacts to solicit donations from friends including Mrs J. Couts

Michie who offered a house for convalescing soldiers. Sister Beatrice originally intended it for Canadian regiments, and planned to name it in honour of Major General Sir Sam Hughes. However, when she realized the Australians were 'in special need' the residence went to them instead.

In 1915 she accompanied Dr Hayden Guest to the Belgian and French war zones to organize the distribution of hospital supplies. But after a dispute with the French authorities, she discovered that rumours that she was an agent for Germany were hindering the shipping and collecting of medical supplies. When she returned home to Boston in December that year, she was refused travel permission in Canada for a fund-raising venture because she was suspected of being a spy. Ironically, the minister of the Canadian Militia responsible for banning her was Sir Sam Hughes who had been denied the honour of having a convalescent home named after him.[49] She told the *Montreal Gazette* that she suspected French officials' gossip about her was obstructing her work in Canada.

What the war had created was a paranoia that any woman could be suspected of espionage. Whether they were foreign women who married abroad, society ladies, volunteer nurses, washerwomen or prostitutes, their loyalty could not be taken for granted. Demonstrations of national loyalty were required for men who faced pressure to enlist in Allied forces, while women were expected to play a myriad of supporting roles. As espionage cases from Britain, France and the United States have revealed, however, women who fell short of patriotic expectations stood accused of a double crime. Any suggestion that they had abandoned the passive sexual role was tantamount to a betrayal not only of their family or husband but of the state as well. Espionage and sexual anxiety, whether covert or deeply buried, appear as an endlessly repeated theme in spy literature. The mythomania that surrounded Mata Hari crystallized these fears, preserving the complex struggles about gender, identity and race which were the undercurrents of the war.

Mata Hari's execution alone had not turned the world's attention to the issue of women spies. Nefarious female schemers had always existed in fiction but were now given flesh and found to have penetrated the most cultured circles in Europe. But this female spy *par excellence* survived so long after her death because her story had struck a universal chord. Like the rumours of her escape that circulated in the Paris cafés, the condemned woman had outwitted her opponents. The anti-hero lived on. It was believed that Mata Hari, the abandoned wife, had finally found her prince who had whisked her off to a castle in Austria or Spain or America. The struggling dancer had discovered her best audience yet and eventually her memory would inspire respect, and even the admiration that had so long eluded her. As Dr Hirschfeld once wrote of her:

> Mata Hari, who was a great artist in the realm of love but only a dilettante as a spy, was shot because, in the fall of 1917, there was need for an international gesture on a large scale . . . Her fate directed the glance of the world to other female spies.[50]

As the final chapter will reveal, the artist of love would assume many guises after her death, but the realization that she was used to express deeply felt emotions was never doubted.

CHAPTER EIGHT

THE LEGACY

Mata Hari, now that romance has been busy dressing her sordid figure in frills of fancy, has become prettily effective to the imagination ... On the whole, I am heartily sorry for spies; they have a rotten time and a nasty end, unless they are exceptionally lucky.

HERBERT T. FITCH (1933)[1]

Olga Pulloffski, the beautiful spy –
The Firing Squad tenderly kissed her,
Then the Captain said 'Fire' and the smoke cleared away
And they all hollered, 'Hooray we've missed her!'
She is too young and fair to die,
Olga Pulloffski, the beautiful spy!!

R.P. WESTON AND BERT LEE (1935)[2]

AFTER THE EXECUTION, the curious drifted to the Nouveau Cimetière at Vincennes, where the notorious traitoress was believed to be buried. They found nothing but a shallow, empty grave. Had Mata Hari escaped the firing squad on horseback with a lover who had ridden through the Vincennes wood to spirit her away? The cemetery's curator himself thought she was buried ignominiously in a mass grave with forty other spies where even a modest cross was forbidden such sinners.[3] The fate of Mata Hari's corpse would not be publicly known until 1921 when Emile Massard published his eye-witness account. In the bleak winter of 1917, as the war dragged on, rumour and speculation flourished.

Whatever her crimes and however her prosecutors justified her execution, there remained a powerful desire to rehabilitate the courtesan-spy. The gossip that a wealthy Spanish playboy, Pierre Mortissac, had arranged for Mata Hari's escape, fulfilled this longing. As Mario Duplessis told *El Mundo*, Mortissac had enacted a scene from Sardou's play, *La Tosca*. Duplessis claimed that before Mata Hari left for Vincennes she handed Maître Clunet a letter from Mortissac who firmly believed in her innocence.[4] He had bribed the Zouaves to fire blanks and he made his dramatic entrance from the wood as she dropped to the ground. Like a fairy-tale couple, they were believed to have settled happily somewhere in an ancient castle. The story explained her bravado before the executioners because she had faith that Pierre would prevent her untimely death.[5] Since Mortissac was only twenty-one, he might have been the young officer mentioned during Mata Hari's trial which several newspapers wove into a tale of triumphant love.

There was, however, a much more tragic version of this story. Like the lover in *Tosca* who cannot be spared, Pierre Mortissac had failed to rescue the woman he worshipped. In despair, he joined an order of Trappist monks at Miraflores in northern Spain and retreated from the world. A miniature portrait of Mata Hari hung in a locket round his neck as a constant reminder of his failure and why he prayed for salvation. If she had achieved nothing else in her life, at least she was responsible for turning a dandy, an Apollo and the man the lesbian Princess de Polignac said she would most like to be, into a saint.[6] Since the war had claimed so many young lovers, the story of a redeeming death had an enormous appeal; even if Mata Hari died without cleansing her own sins, she had elevated one man from the demi-monde to a higher spiritual plane.

However, when reports about Mortissac's conversion appeared in Barcelona's *Correspondencia Allemana*, they seemed suspiciously familiar to the writer Camille Pitollet. She noticed that among the published stories, several bore a strong resemblance to an episode in Maurice Barrès' *Greco, or the Secret of Toledo* and Théophile Gauthier's description of Miraflores in his 1843 *Voyage to Spain*. As Pitollet commented, there was much mileage for journalists in reviving Mata Hari and she quoted the author Rachilde, ' . . . *il sera des enfants à la Reine*' [there will be children to the Queen]. She concluded that 'the true story of [Mata Hari's] treachery, the real reasons for her condemnation and the plot of her last lover Mortissac to save her from execution, make up a trilogy which will probably never be written.'[7] Pitollet acknowledged that myths, if they satisfy a collective desire, endure, no matter how carefully contrary evidence is presented.[8]

The tale of the long-lamenting Pierre Mortissac was a case in point. It survived into the 1930s when several French and English newspapers reported Mortissac's death during the Spanish Civil War after his monastery near Pentaflor [sic] was allegedly stormed by General Franco's troops. The monks had refused to open the gates when Franco requisitioned the monastery as a defence against the Republicans. Eventually, the prior persuaded all but one man to leave. This courageous monk held back Franco's troops with a machine gun from the Republicans, shooting sixty soldiers before he was caught and executed. The monk turned rebel was, of course, Mortissac who had finally died a hero.[9]

Just as the story of Mata Hari's faithful lover was adapted to illustrate a particular event, the icon of the dancer served conflicting purposes. To the Allies, she would remain a romantic villain, while the Germans continued their rehabilitation campaign as a reproach to the French for their double standards over Edith Cavell. A month after Mata Hari's death, several German newspapers disturbed Franco-Dutch relations by claiming she was a former lady-in-waiting to Queen Wilhelmina. Jonkheer Loudon, the Dutch Foreign Minister, considered these false reports so damaging that he personally sent a telegram to the Paris ambassador ordering 'the refutation of this absurd rumour'. To staunch its tide, he suggested the ambassador 'try everything possible, in case the French press also spreads this rumour, to have the newspapers point out that this person ... . had nothing to do with the Queen's court'. If necessary, he was instructed to appeal directly to the French government to deny the story.[10]

Suspicion clung to Mata Hari's case long after the war. Had she been justly tried or was her execution a diversion to protect the important men who had been her lovers? Although she had been discreet during her trial in

Paris, until her execution the possibility remained that she might divulge their names to save herself. 'She went to her death with her lips unsealed,' claimed the *News of the World* in 1924. 'Many people in Paris breathed freer when the news of her execution was made public.'[11] Raoul Deboissigne, a former 'Special agent of the French Scotland Yard', argued that she was protecting a German secret service agent, Count von Speck, to whom she was a mere puppet.[12] But the theatrical producer, Albert de Courville, countered that a French lover, who was an agent for the Deuxième Bureau, had betrayed Mata Hari. 'Yet she trusted him implicitly and would have given him anything.'[13] There were even conflicting reports about the details of her execution: Pierre Bouchardon claimed three bullets pierced her chest and Paul Allard believed only a single shot reached her heart. The truth was less poetic. Georges Godot, who was one of Mata Hari's executioners, saw a body riddled with wounds.[14] Since the French government refused to allow the public to examine the evidence, however, the rumours continued.

In the meantime, association with Mata Hari was so dangerous that the mythical Pierre Mortissac's rescue acted to assuage French guilt about the condemnation of their former star. The romantic tradition worked in tandem with the spy paranoia that continued after her execution. Once the van der Veen sisters, who owned the house Mata Hari had rented at 16 Nieuwe Uitleg street in The Hague, finally established that no living relative claimed the right to its possession, her belongings were sold at auction in January 1918. Although Baron van der Capellen's photograph featured prominently among the sale items, he stayed away.[15]

It was common for former friends to deny all knowledge of Mata Hari. The courtesan Liane de Pougy assured her milliner in April 1920 that, although she had a picture of Mata Hari taken before the war, they had never been friends. 'Mata Hari, so beautiful in her body and so ugly in her soul, who simply for love of lucre betrayed the France which welcomed her so kindly – this photo reveals her slyness.'[16] De Pougy's denial encapsulated the desire to believe in Mata Hari's guilt which, in hindsight, was used to explain her weakness of character or artistic failures. Even Maître Clunet, in an interview with a French diplomat in 1919, would state equivocally that: 'Mata Hari wasn't innocent, but she wasn't guilty enough to deserve to die.'[17]

The American Natalie Barney was shocked when her attempt to dispel rumours surrounding Mata Hari's death met with uncharacteristic disapproval from her French friends. Barney wanted to prove that she had not faced the firing squad naked beneath a sable coat. Barney eventually found and interviewed the Zouave officer in charge of the firing squad. His description of Mata Hari's plain suit, and the way she had stood so still it made him tremble, were passed on to Janet Flanner for her *New Yorker* column. This, Barney hoped, would ensure that everyone would know the truth 'about a friend she regarded as just as much a victim of the circumstances of war as the battlefields' slaughtered millions'.[18]

Mata Hari's name even had the power to embarrass and discredit public figures. During her 1917 trial General Somprou's decision not to disclose General Messimy's name as the politician who had written her love letters caused reverberations for years. The prosecution produced letters sent from a cabinet minister with the initials M-----y, which could have applied either to Messimy or to Léon Malvy, the interior minister. Léon Daudet and Malvy's other political opponents publicly accused him of being Mata Hari's mysterious lover. When Georges Clemenceau came to power in November 1917, he denied the accusation against Malvy but, nonetheless, exiled him from France for five years. It was a magnificent display of hypocrisy since Clemenceau himself was once the lover of another celebrated courtesan with an interest in espionage, Léonide Leblanc, while Malvy had never known Mata Hari.[19]

In 1926 Malvy returned to Paris from his sojourn in Spain and persuaded Messimy to admit his part in the affair. The journalist Madame Séverine joined the campaign insisting that, for the sake of history and posterity, Messimy put the record straight. Malvy was re-elected to the assembly and resumed his post as interior minister. But when the opposition raised a question in the assembly about Mata Hari, Malvy fainted and shortly afterwards resigned because of poor health.[20] Messimy then denied he had ever slept with this beautiful woman, which he now regretted, but thought Mata Hari should be taken as a warning to youthful politicians to beware the advances of *les mangeuses d'hommes*.[21]

Emile Massard joined the fray when his history of wartime intelligence, *Les Espionnes à Paris*, was published in France in late 1922. Among Mata Hari's other prestigious conquests, he claimed she had seduced the former Dutch prime minister, van der Linden, into allowing German agents in Holland to organize a vast espionage network aimed against France. Massard cited General Boucabeille, the former French military attaché at The Hague who had investigated Mata Hari's case, as the source for this major breach of Dutch neutrality. In reality, there was no evidence that Mata Hari ever met van der Linden, nor that she had any influence on the Dutch government's attitude towards German spies in their country. Boucabeille rejected these explosive accusations which had provoked rapid correspondence between Paris and The Hague.

On 2 February 1923, E. de Peretti de la Rocca, who headed the Quai d'Orsay's political department, wrote to Jonkheer Loudon, passing on Boucabeille's formal denial of Massard's allegations. The general judged that:

> all the assertions made by Massard on the relations of Mata Hari with a French Minister of War, the Duke of Brunswick, the ... Dutch [Prime] Minister, Monsieur van der Linden, on the role attributed to him, to the Prince Consort, [and] to the Queen Wilhelmina, rest on the charge of their author.[22]

Boucabeille concluded that while the claims were completely false, Massard's most erroneous charge was that the Dutch had plotted with the German secret service against France. This further implied that Mata Hari's intimacy with van der Linden had prompted the Dutch government to ignore her crimes against France in their plea to stay her execution. 'It must be said that Queen Wilhelmina forgot the affair of the Prince Consort, refusing to associate it with this proceeding,' wrote Massard.[23] By this time, Mata Hari had been so convincingly portrayed as an enemy agent to the French that even a humanitarian attempt to spare her life was equated with German complicity.

Meanwhile, Monsieur Fournier of the Deuxième Bureau assured the Dutch military attaché in Paris that the French government, while condemning Commandant Massard's accusations, was powerless to censor him. Massard, who was a publicist before being mobilized as a reserve officer during the war, had been struck off the army list in April 1919. Therefore he had not been required to submit his book to the Minister of War before publication.[24] General Boucabeille, however, offered to formally deny Massard's accusations in a press statement. When the legate in Paris, Ridder van Stuers, suggested this to Loudon, he replied that 'these smears are so preposterous to Dutch ears that I don't think it necessary to press the offered brand iron'.[25]

Ironically, while the French government officially distanced itself from Massard's claims, it staunchly refused to provide even Mata Hari's family with information about her trial and execution. The French Foreign Minister wrote to the Dutch legation on 14 January 1918 stating that under no circumstances would documents concerning her case be released.[26] Pastor Arboux confirmed that Mata Hari had left no will and the final letter to her daughter had been lost, which made her estate extremely difficult to settle. Non, Mata Hari's daughter by Rudolph MacLeod, had read in the Dutch press that her mother had written her a final letter which she longed to see. 'Accordingly,' MacLeod wrote to the Dutch legation on 10 April 1919, 'we've given up all hope of ever hearing from [Mata Hari].' MacLeod was also furious at the French government's indifferent attitude towards Mata Hari's only surviving child and bitter about the disposal of her assets.

'[Non] would have been the only inheritor of her mother's property if everything the woman left behind hadn't disappeared thanks to the French Republic,' he fumed. 'They have shared out the loot between themselves beautifully.'[27] Monsieur Henry Lecouturier, the Third Tribunal's judicial administrator, confirmed that all of Mata Hari's possessions collected from Saint-Lazare prison and the Palace Hotel were sold at auction on 30 January 1918 for 14,251 francs, 65 centimes. However, the money went 'to pay the French government which had privileged rights to it, to defray the cost of the trial'.[28] Since even this considerable sum had not exhausted Mata Hari's debts, Lecouturier advised the Dutch legate to suggest that Rudolph MacLeod, on Non's behalf, make no claim on Mata Hari's estate.[29]

The French Minister of Foreign Affairs seemed equally uncooperative in answering MacLeod's other queries. Mata Hari's former husband was anxious to have a copy of her death certificate because Non, who had finished her teacher's training course and was leaving for the Dutch East Indies, needed this document in case she wished to marry. He learned that a death certificate had been forwarded to Mrs Zelle MacLeod's brothers on 18 January 1918 and he would have to apply separately for a copy.[30] Non, now aged twenty-one, looked startlingly like her mother and would have cut a striking figure among the Dutch colonists with her jet-black hair and her height; like Mata Hari she was almost six feet tall. But a few days before Non's ship set sail, she died suddenly of a cerebral haemorrhage on 10 August 1919 and was buried at the Worth-Rheden cemetery near Arnhem. By this time, MacLeod had divorced his second wife and married Non's former nanny, Grietje Meijer, aged twenty-five, who gave birth to a daughter, also named Non, on 20 March 1921.[31] But since these events went largely unreported, journalists would later invent stories about Mata Hari's daughter either rising to her mother's defence or following her profession. The truth, as was invariably the case with Mata Hari, was much more poignant.

While the French government's guarded files remained closed, the assumption of her irrefutable guilt prevailed. Emile Massard's portrait of the spy-courtesan, *Les Espionnes à Paris*, which was serialized in 1921, was juxtaposed with an anonymous attack on Charles-Henry Hirsch's play, *La Danseuse Rouge* (The Red Dancer). Hirsch was accused of creating a sympathetic portrait of Mata Hari, played by Cora Laparcerie at the Théâtre de la Renaissance. (Ironically, Laparcerie had performed alongside Mata Hari at this venue in 1913.) Hirsch was lambasted for glorifying a spy-courtesan and transforming her into a martyr to usurp Miss Cavell's rightful position. Even though the war was over, one could still be charged with defeatism. When the curtain fell on the second act, 'the audience, agony in their very entrails, was ready to consider how the brutish French officers . . . sent to death an otherwise admirable creature.'[32] To question Mata Hari's execution was still a heresy against the Republic.

La Liberté asked if one should use the 'propaganda of theatre' for the 'rehabilitation' of a spy? Even worse, Hirsch was accused of profiting from the story of a woman who had sent thousands of Frenchmen to their deaths. The serialization of Massard's book, which concentrated on Mata Hari's trial and execution, was intended to counter the false sympathy that *La Danseuse Rouge* had aroused. But according to Hirsch the play, which was adapted from his 1917 novel *La Chèvre aux pieds d'or* (The goat with the golden feet), was never intended to restore Mata Hari's reputation. Although his heroine recounted her pitiful life before the judges, Hirsch emphasized the proof of her guilt and supported capital punishment. In any case, he argued, his works were fiction only loosely based on fact.[33] He was so concerned about public sensibilities that before the play opened he sought the blessing of Monsieur Binet-Valmer, president of the Officers and Veterans League, whose suggestions were duly incorporated into the original text.

But the following week Binet-Valmer stated in *La Liberté* that Hirsch's play was too provocative; the nation needed order and stability.[34] To settle the dispute, Binet-Valmer deputized several members of his organization to attend a performance of *La Danseuse Rouge*. Unexpectedly the veterans 'had not been offended by each moment' and endorsed Hirsch. *La Liberté* then backtracked, declaring the playwright 'a writer of great talent' who had sensitively portrayed the spy as an unrepentant assassin.[35] Despite this volte-face, elsewhere Hirsch's play was still regarded as subversive for its humane portrait of Mata Hari. When Marshal Ferdinand Foch was scheduled to appear in Nancy for a patriotic celebration in June 1922, the town's mayor banned a scheduled performance of *La Danseuse Rouge*, fearing that it might provoke riots from outraged war veterans.[36]

Mata Hari had become a potent metaphor for the war's death and destruction; her execution had operated to bind the nation's wounds. The myth that she had seduced dozens of powerful men – from officers to high-ranking politicians – went unchallenged. Criticism of her execution was deemed unpatriotic or even pro-German. But if the justice of Mata Hari's case was taken for granted, there remained a parallel desire to resurrect her as a grand courtesan from a glamorous golden age. *La Liberté* scorned Cora Laparcerie's portrait of a young *femme galante* who had risen through the social ranks to exploit her connections as a spy. The writer suggested with sarcasm that 'a prostitute is always an innocent victim of society, isn't she, and if, by chance, she becomes a spy, we haven't enough tears to shed.'[37] Mata Hari, the 'nude of art', whose erotic Oriental dances had thrilled Parisians of *la belle époque*, was much safer territory for the romance writers.

Vicente Blasco Ibanez, a South American novelist, published an extraordinary novel in 1920 based on the idea of Mata Hari as a sexual hedonist. Although *Mare Nostrum* was clearly fiction, Ibanez had researched the case and even received Madame Clunet's description of the circumstances surrounding the execution. It was said to be so realistic that it was banned in France, 'for reasons that will be explained one day'.[38] Ibanez perfectly articulated the ambiguous emotions that the spy-courtesan fantasy aroused. Mata Hari as Freya Talberg is a magnificently alluring lover whose intense sexual passion signifies her danger. The antithesis of a wife, she rejects the feminine ideals of self-sacrifice and domesticity. Her home is a hotel room where she envelops herself in beautiful clothes, heady perfumes and expensive jewels. Since she has no maternal instinct, she has divorced sex from procreation, has no family ties and never plans the future. The state means nothing to her, she is loyal only to her desires. Most compelling of all, she has the illusion of power, withholding her affection and forcing her lover into a humiliating, female position. Like Salome she has stolen a masculine trophy by reversing roles.

Ibanez's hero is a happily married Spanish sea captain, Ulysses Ferragut, whose ship is held up in Italy at the outbreak of war. On a day trip to Pompeii he meets two women, a 'dainty ash blonde' named Freya and an older Russian Pole, Dr Fedelmann. The ladies invite the captain to tea the following day where he instantly falls in love with Freya's 'passionate eyes and little tricks of malicious coquetry'. Although Ulysses has a devoted wife and young son at home in Barcelona, he begins a torrid love affair with this mysterious woman.

Ibanez vividly portrays Ulysses as a man in the grip of a destructive erotic force. Freya/Mata Hari is literally the *mangeuse d'hommes* who bleeds men of their money and their morals. She compares herself to a spider drawing its prey irresistibly into a web. 'How I would fasten my mouth against their hearts! And I would suck them – I would suck them until there wasn't a drop of blood left, tossing away their empty carcasses!'[39] Ulysses is attracted and repelled when she wraps herself tightly around him, kissing him with 'deadly and caressing lips'. But when he attempts to reassert his 'masculine authority' by raping Freya, she skilfully executes a Japanese 'fencing trick' to throw him off.[40]

Freya is the archetypical *femme fatale* of romantic literature whom her lover 'adores but detests'. Her menacing influence, like an infectious disease, cannot be contained and spills over to poison Ulysses' beloved family. She persuades him to carry petrol aboard his ship to German submarines off the Spanish coast. On his return to Barcelona, Ulysses learns that the German submarines he fuelled have torpedoed the ship on which his son was sailing. Death is the price for his torrid passion with Freya. Even Dona Cinta, his 'sweet obedient little wife', is transformed into an angry and unforgiving woman when she learns about his affair.[41] He resolves to avenge his son's death by seeking out Freya, who is held responsible for all his misery, and punishing her.

Ulysses eventually confronts Freya in a Barcelona hotel. He hits her 'without pity, concentrating all his soul in his fist' until she lies supine before him, inviting him to appease his anger. Since her conscience has begun to trouble her, she pours out her story. Her wealthy Italian father lost the family fortune when she was a girl but despite their poverty they lived in grand hotels where Freya learned to 'adore wealth as the most powerful divinity on earth'. As a young woman, she became accustomed to luxury but without the means to earn it was forced into prostitution:

> In our world there is no other virtue than that of money . . . We yield our body as though fulfilling a material function, without shame and without regret. It is a simple matter of business. The only thing that matters is to preserve the former life and all its conveniences . . . not to come down . . . Poor and well-educated girls, if afraid of poverty, had no other recourse than prostitution.[42]

The men who courted her always fled when they discovered she had no dowry. Rejecting marriage as a solution, she turned to the theatre where she had little success as a dancer but was recruited by Dr Fedelmann as a sexual slave for the German secret service. Freya's crimes, which had resulted in the death of Ulysses' son, were unforgivable. But by abasing herself, she restores his masculine authority, shifting the power within their relationship.

Ibanez's novel contributed much to the mythology of Mata Hari, vaguely following the contours of Margaretha Zelle MacLeod's life that led her into casual prostitution. Her father's bankruptcy, her mother's death and Rudolph MacLeod's brutality, which forced her to reject domestic values, also explained her willingness to join the German spy masters. On a deeper level, the spy-courtesan was a convenient receptacle for men's desire to blame women for the horrors of war.[43] She represented a catalogue of anxiety; 'the scourges on which biological fear was focused, the venereal, alcoholic, consumptive degenerate prostitute appeared to be the symbol of all threats facing society.'[44]

During the war, she became the worst kind of war profiteer. Freya/Mata Hari sold sex and stole secrets that would endanger thousands of lives, to maintain her decadent desires. While marriage in *fin-de-siècle* France was evolving away from regarding the bourgeois woman as a commodity, Mata Hari's betrayal was a ritual enactment of a husband's fear about his wife.[45] Just as the nurse's snowy white uniform hid a vicious power-broker, a spouse's endearing smile might easily mask her murderous desire. Marital ties were still based on an exchange of cash, not love. The spy-courtesan's double identity symbolized the male fear of female treachery that deserved the most brutal punishment.[46]

Another early novel which took Mata Hari as its central character was written by the propagandist Henry de Halsalle, who also linked themes about moral and sexual degeneracy with the female spy. De Halsalle produced the first quasi-biography of Mata Hari in 1917. He claimed that a musician named Henry Dubois had given him a detailed account of his long-standing romance with the famous Dutch dancer. Dubois had conveniently kept a diary which included conversations with Mata Hari who regarded him as a 'father confessor' to the crimes she committed on her espionage missions.

Earlier that year, de Halsalle had also published the adventures of *A Secret Service Woman: Being Confessions, Experiences and Opinions of Olga von Kopf, the Famous International Spy*. He claimed Fräulein von Kopf had given him a complete manuscript of her experiences in German intelligence. She had retired in disgust, left the country and now resided at the Hotel Pannaci, Sea Bright, New Jersey. In 1918, following 'highly appreciative reviews in the English periodicals', Olga kindly obliged de Halsalle with another manuscript revealing her more recent activities as a lady spy for the British secret service in the US. Both 'biographies' were thinly veiled works of fiction.

De Halsalle's novels, however, became a platform for his eugenic theories that equated female sexual passion with retarded social evolution. The Germans' primitive ethics were reflected in their spy training school for women which forced its subjects to set aside their conscience and swear their allegiance to the Kaiser.[47] Olga, whose mother was English, was saved from this Teutonic nightmare when her Anglo-Saxon blood asserted itself and forced her to reject the German spies' nefarious methods. But Mata Hari's 'Oriental' parentage – she had a Dutch father and Japanese/Javanese mother, according to de Halsalle – naturally lent itself to skulduggery. Her 'Eastern Empress' looks, her hypnotic eyes and capricious, fickle, vain and vengeful temper, made her a perfect agent.[48]

De Halsalle used Mata Hari's colourful tapestry of her mythical life in an Indian temple that so infatuated Parisian journalists in 1905, to explain her appeal to men. Offstage, however, de Halsalle portrayed Mata Hari as an 'Oriental' who perpetuated a double deception: she passed as an enemy agent and as a white woman in European society, hiding her Asian origins. She was even forced to use a 'preparation that would make a negress white' to travel to England disguised as Lady Surfham. 'Mata Hari, I knew in my heart, regretted her somewhat dark skin,' Henry Dubois, the story's narrator, comments. 'She was never pleased when she heard it alluded to. This I noticed on more than one occasion.'[49] Her beauty entwined with her evil, which aroused men as it horrified them, was traced to her 'Oriental' blood.

This inherently corrupt nature, according to de Halsalle, would move her to a murderous passion. The novel perpetuated the myth that Mata Hari had killed the Javanese servant who poisoned her son Norman in 1899. She took Rudolph MacLeod's service revolver, threw a shawl over her head and shot the murderer at his home, in cold blood.[50] Mata Hari returned to Europe with Non after this incident, leaving her daughter at a Marseilles convent while she pursued a dancing career as a cover for her espionage operations. She executed several coups for Germany, including enlisting Irish Republican James Connolly's support for a German invasion of Britain. Her only failure came when she attempted to play a nurturing role; disguised as Madame von Houtin, she nursed at a Liège hospital but soon left because the wounded soldiers depressed her.

Her final assignment was in Madrid where she secured information about the Allies' secret weapon, the tank. 'How a woman was able to detect one of the greatest inventions of modern warfare . . . is a mystery,' commented Henry Dubois.[51] All of these claims were imaginary but her discovery of the tank was given credibility through news reports. Although the French press never reported that Mata Hari knew about this new weapon, which was first used on 15 September 1916 on the Somme, the story was widely circulated in America. *The New York Times* claimed that when she was arrested in Paris, 'a contributing circumstance . . . [was] the fact that she was seen there with a young British officer attached to the "tank" service.'[52] *The Literary Digest* labelled her 'Mata Hari – Vampire of a real tank drama' in their 13 October 1917 issue and a year later *Variety* magazine's obituary claimed that 'the charge preferred against her was that of obtaining drawings of the tanks and of passing them on to Berlin with other information'.[53] In fact, the German secret service had learned about the Allies' new weapon from a British prisoner-of-war who had escaped, unharmed, from an exploding tank on the Western Front. He also provided details about his work in a tank factory, describing the weapon's design, construction and rate of production.[54]

However, the rumour that Mata Hari was responsible for sending this vital information to the enemy elevated her importance as an enemy agent which helped to justify her execution. The seductive *femme fatale* of Edwardian fiction now had a deadly serious counterpart, a fully fleshed vixen who was responsible for massive destruction. But there was little difference between de Halsalle's novels and contemporary press reports.[55] Whether it was Charles-Henry Hirsch, Vicente Ibanez or de Halsalle, each novel contributed to the legend, weaving gossip, supposition and fantasy to evaluate her life.[56] Journalists and romance writers reinforced the conviction that Mata Hari was a traitoress who was justly executed for betraying France.

Although her guilt was never questioned, the precise nature of her crime was often disputed. While Massard's account emphasized her calculated seduction of high officials, the Spanish author Enrique Gomez Carillo defended her reputation as a courtesan. This biography, however, evolved along a circuitous route. In 1919 the café gossip in Madrid and Paris claimed that Gomez Carillo's wife, Raquel Meller, was responsible for Mata Hari's arrest two years earlier. Meller was a dancer whose triumphant debut in Paris that year prompted Liane de Pougy's high praise; the Spaniard was 'fragile, tall and magnificent . . . a great artiste'.[57] The tantalizing rumour connected the new star with the notorious Mata Hari, adding an extra frisson to her act. The gossips reported that during the war Meller had been jealous of the Dutch dancer's professional reputation and Gomez Carillo's attentions to her. In retaliation, Meller sent the French secret service a false telegram incriminating Mata Hari as a spy. The Spanish senator Junoy, who had enjoyed a brief affair with the Dutch dancer in Madrid, was supposed to have made this accusation which reached the New York press in 1926.[58]

Years after Mata Hari's execution, so the story went, Meller was overcome with such remorse that she sought an audience with the Pope to absolve her sin. Although Meller denied these claims, they persisted until she wrote to a Barcelona newspaper that 'my visit to the Vatican is very ordinary: my meeting with the Pope is uniquely concerned with feelings of a private nature.'[59] Meanwhile, Gomez Carillo was prompted to vindicate Mata Hari after another article repeated the rumour about Raquel Meller and the incriminating telegram. Carillo's article brought hundreds of enquiries from his readers about the story, which inspired him to publish *Le Mystère de la vie et de la mort de Mata Hari* (The Mystery of the Life and Death of Mata Hari) in 1923. However, his book became a passionate defence of the courtesan whose role within post-war society was rapidly fading. He advised any mistress to remember that if she 'loves the man to whom she gives herself, her acts are natural; when, on the other hand, she thinks only of the reward, they are artificial.'[60]

While Carillo praised Mata Hari for her frank sexuality and skill as a courtesan, he defended her against the unwritten charges which had condemned her to death. General Boucabeille had dismissed her as 'a common prostitute', André Mornet scorned her as a 'Messalina' and Captain Bouchardon mocked her affair with the elderly Maître Clunet. Underlying her interrogation during the Third Tribunal trial in 1917 was the desire to punish a sexually independent woman who had rejected bourgeois marriage. Since Carillo had decided to celebrate Mata Hari as a sexual rebel, it was no coincidence that Raquel Meller was rumoured to have played the jealous wife.

As for the truth about the case, Gomez Carillo suggested that until the French government published their dossier on Mata Hari, it would be impossible to judge her culpability. In 1928 Camille Pitollet published a pamphlet about Carillo supporting this argument. She agreed with Carillo's theory that the documents relating to Mata Hari remained closed because they revealed the extent of the Spanish King Alfonso's sympathy with the Germans. Since the German attachés regularly sent messages from Madrid to Berlin without difficulty during the war, Alfonso must have turned a blind eye to their espionage activities.[61] However, since neither writer persuaded the French cabinet to open the files, the legend was fuelled by speculation.

Interest in the still unresolved case was fed not only by news reports, plays and novels about Mata Hari, but documented spy histories as well. In 1920 Captain Ferdinand Tuohy, the former British intelligence agent, and Sidney Felstead, a semi-official historian of German espionage in Britain, published their accounts of the spy-courtesan. Felstead, who had seen the MI5 files, described Mata Hari as 'the only woman who could advance legitimate claims to being the beautiful spy of fiction'.[62] She seduced men with 'the spell of her Oriental mysticism and their souls were hers', claimed Felstead, taking up a theme which appears in de Halsalle's novel. However, he invented a plausible (although erroneous) explanation for her arrest in 1917: she had been caught with incriminating documents which revealed her as a German spy.

Felstead repeated the claim that Mata Hari was a 'half-breed' with a Javanese mother whose genes were responsible for her becoming 'an exponent of a weird form of Oriental dancing which greatly pleased the pleasure-sated inhabitants of many continental capitals'.[63] But these racist assumptions enjoyed official sanction as they emanated from a historian of intelligence. Tuohy's history, published the same year, also received an enthusiastic review in the *Times Literary Supplement* as 'one of the rare books about espionage written by an insider'.[64] However, while he concurred with Felstead that Mata Hari gained her 'cunning and diplomatic obsequiousness' from her *Japanese* mother, she was neither beautiful nor a dangerous spy. 'But that,' Tuohy deduced, 'detracts in no way from the psychological interest attaching to her tale – it rather enhances it.'[65]

Tuohy was the only espionage writer of the period to acknowledge this. But it did not prevent him from concocting another version of the 'Oriental' courtesan-spy. Early biographies drew on Mata Hari's numerous interviews in Paris, repeating her inventions about Buddhist temples and Eastern rituals where she was taught to 'charm and deceive men'.[66] The espionage writers also exaggerated the already inflated claims about her efficiency as an agent. Thomas Coulson OBE, a regimental intelligence officer in Ireland, England and France, who published a fully researched biography a decade later, credited her with 'reduc[ing] the Second Bureau – the nerve centre of the French army – to temporary impotence'.[67] Such lofty claims worked both ways: Coulson implied that an enemy agent had struck a blow at a critically important Allied secret service. In reality, neither party could lay claim to determining the course of the war.

While the French government refused to argue its case against Mata Hari, it also remained silent on statements issuing from Germany. In 1929 the head of counterespionage in the Ministry of the Reichswehr during the war categorically denied that Mata Hari was ever an agent for his service. Major General A.D. Gempp, in an article entitled 'In the corridors of Espionage', wrote that numerous stories were invented about the German secret service, including those about the 'tragic dancer Mata Hari'. Although she 'did nothing for the service of German Information, [she] was remarkably exploited' in the press.[68] The following month French newspapers interpreted Gempp's statement as 'Mata Hari was Shot Without Reason'.[69] A Berlin correspondent reported that Gempp had discovered, after studying the Reichswehr's dossiers, no proof that the celebrated dancer ever worked for them during the war and was thus executed unjustly. However, the writer cautioned that it was impossible to know how Gempp formed his conclusion and why, suddenly, he made this announcement.

The Paris edition of the *New York Herald* reprinted the story on 6 February claiming new evidence for Mata Hari's innocence. This report had Gempp announcing that detailed research in the German archives revealed that she was never employed by the Reichswehr. Three days later the *Nieuwe Rotterdamsche Courant* ran their version, adding that although the Germans continued to protest Mata Hari's innocence, nothing had been proved.[70] But the French public were no less swayed by revelations from their compatriots. As Marthé Richard, who had been a successful double-agent for the Deuxième Bureau, told a journalist in 1933: 'I knew Mata Hari well when I worked for the French in Madrid during the war. She was a fine dancer, but to my mind she had not the nerve or the intelligence required to do secret service work.'[71]

The following year Paul Allard published his investigation of why the French public wanted to believe in Mata Hari's guilt when they never knew the evidence against her. After Allard's request to see the dossier was denied, he interviewed everyone connected with the case who was still alive including Richard, Maître Clunet's wife, Mata Hari's brother J.H. Zelle, Georges Ladoux, Pierre Bouchardon, Adolphe Messimy and General Boucabeille. Allard discovered that none of her original prosecutors were entirely convinced of her guilt. Even Colonel Lecroix, the keeper of the military archives who had read the Mata Hari files, found they contained 'no palpable, tangible, absolute and irrefutable proof'.[72] Allard concluded, 'I still do not know what Mata Hari has done!'

Another French writer, Georges Marlio, took up Allard's challenge to prove Mata Hari's innocence. 'Even the Germans have confessed that [she] never supplied them with any information during the war,' Marlio wrote in *Le Petit Journal* in 1936. He had long suspected that she was a victim of patriotic passion and knew a Spanish doctor who supplied the evidence. While staying in Madrid in 1918 he met Dr Puellès who claimed to have treated Mata Hari for an unspecified illness during the war.[73] The doctor pleaded with her not to return to France since they both knew she was on the French list of suspected spies. 'I am going to return,' she told Puellès, 'because I have nothing to reproach myself for, and therefore, nothing to fear.' He believed her innocence and naïvety, but not her guilt, had condemned her.

Marlio also quoted the first telegram which was intercepted at the Eiffel Tower between Madrid and Berlin, stating that 'H21 was a good agent before the war but has sent no information since the war'. He questioned whether, on this evidence alone, Mata Hari should have been tried in a military court. If she had faced a civil trial, perhaps she would not have been imprisoned at all. However, he concluded that Mata Hari was 'a victim of the mystical ferocity of the crowds who . . . demanded corpses; one held onto the explanation and the excuse that we were defeated by treason.' He wondered whether the politicians who had sent Mata Hari to die at Vincennes on that icy October morning were haunted by her fate.[74]

Marlio employed that motif which had run through the cultural landscape of the period like a dark thread – the war. Nine million had died and twenty-one million were left wounded; what had been won?[75] The temptation to resurrect a heroic, romantic figure, who had revelled in momentary pleasures, was palpable. To reverse the 'mystical ferocity' of the blood-baying crowds, journalists conjured up sightings of the famous spy-courtesan. The nymph Mata Hari was dancing again.

In 1929 the Paris press carried a story about a mysterious woman washed up on a Bordeaux beach. Inconsistencies in police reports provoked a rumour that she was Mata Hari whose influential friends had saved her from the firing squad twelve years before. The woman, who claimed to have fallen from the British steamer *Eagle*, first told her rescuers at Montalivet that her name was Gloria MacAlister, then she confessed she was really Benita Adamson from the Latvian capital, Riga. 'Higher authorities' had dispatched plain-clothes police to investigate and they announced she was a vagrant, serving a sentence at the military Fort de Ha.

The case aroused local suspicion because tramps and women were never sentenced to military prisons. Different photos of the castaway were issued to journalists who noticed that the subject's apparent age, knowledge of languages and personal appearance bore a striking resemblance to Mata Hari. A steamer had also been sighted, riding at anchor along the coast with its lights extinguished, as if waiting for something. 'It is quite possible that we are finding here a continuation of the drama of the famous Dutch dancer, who should have died . . . at Vincennes,' commented the Amsterdam magazine, *Het Leven*. Although Jonkheer Loudon's plea for mercy on Mata Hari's behalf was officially denied, 'throughout the years opinions have been uttered in many books and magazines – and in popular opinion, it was held – that the execution at Vincennes had been . . . a theatrical act, a comedy.'[76] Many believed that Mata Hari's highly placed friends had locked her away in Fort de Ha until she could safely leave.

Her protectors had organized an escape that had gone horribly wrong at the last minute. She had tried to swim to the *Eagle* but had collapsed with exhaustion, only to be washed up on the beach. The French authorities categorically denied these rumours and, according to the *Daily Mail*, 'the whole story is scouted in French official circles as a wild dream.'[77] But in Holland where 'there are countless people who still believe in her escaping her grave', *Het Leven* said the incident merely added to the mystery.

In later versions of the resurrection story, Mata Hari's daughter rises to her mother's defence. A year after the incident at Bordeaux, an English newspaper claimed that Miss Janine McLeod [sic] was launching several libel actions in the Paris courts. Under French law, Miss McLeod was entitled to sue on her behalf those publishers and authors who had defamed her mother's name. The *Empire News* reported that the daughter possessed evidence which proved Mata Hari's innocence. Alluding to the Malvy/Messimy controversy, Miss McLeod was quoted as stating that these documents were never produced because her mother was protecting an important Frenchman. 'War passions have died down, and whereas the production of these documents fourteen years ago might have involved the Minister in trial for treason, the most he could be accused of now would be indiscretion.'[78] The fact that, in reality, Non had died in August 1919 had not dampened the desire to raise Mata Hari from the grave.

The stories about Mata Hari's daughter had the effect of making her tragedy human. After two decades the 'Messalina' could be presented as a mother whose death was still mourned. An English newspaper in 1931 claimed that her daughter 'Marie' was the result of an affair with a man who was the great passion of her life. 'Love, passionate, sincere and overwhelming . . . shone as unmistakable gold against the dross of her innumerable affairs.' 'Marie' had been raised in a Spanish convent which Mata Hari had returned to in 1916, risking imprisonment to 'obey only the supreme urge of her mother love'. The hard-hearted courtesan was gradually acquiring a softer, more feminine edge. Like her mother, 'Marie' was a temperamental beauty who would soon learn the secret of Mata Hari's last letter written at Saint-Lazare on the morning of her execution.[79] There was now the tantalizing prospect that 'Marie' might follow in her mother's footsteps.

A few months later a woman arrested on espionage charges in Paris enacted this plot precisely. Under interrogation by the French police on 14 August 1931, Dora Olga Ostrogov confessed that Mata Hari, who Ostrogov believed was falsely accused of spying for the Germans, was her mother. She had given her lawyer a letter from Mata Hari in which the dancer solemnly denied the espionage charges against her.[80] There were no further reports about Ostrogov, which suggests she was subsequently released without charge. But her case reveals how prevalent the fantasy had become.

Ostrogov's arrest also coincided with the release of the eponymously-named MGM film based on Mata Hari's life, starring Greta Garbo and Ramon Novarro. It was the era of the Gold Digger – a modernized courtesan – who dreamed of escaping the reality of economic depression by marrying money. The new generation of celluloid vamps, from Theda Bara (an anagram for ARAB DEATH) to Pola Negri, hearkened back to Mata Hari's Oriental extravaganzas. 'Filmland is looking East for its plots,' commented the critic John K. Newham in the *Dancing Times*. 'The Western world has been ransacked for ideas.'[81] The mythic sensuality of the Orient was once again the container for unexpressed sexual desires. In England, director Harry Lachman's film *Insult* caught the crest of the new fashion, featuring Ranee Rama, praised for possessing 'the most expressive hands of any Eastern dancer', in a 'Siamese Love Dance'. The Garbo film followed suit with the Scandinavian actress in 'a remarkably spectacular Idol Dance'.[82] Mata Hari's kohl-laden eyelids, diaphanous veils and jewelled breastplates were once again associated with a fashionable hedonism.

The film also prompted a strange revelation in the German press. Following the debut of Garbo's film, a magazine printed a letter Mata Hari had written to a former lover, Baron Fredi Lazarini, from a Frankfurt hotel at the outbreak of war. Lazarini was an Austrian cavalry officer who died in battle the night that Mata Hari wrote to him at his country's Ministry of War. To prove this extraordinary coincidence, the journal published an official list of losses alongside Mata Hari's letter. Her signature, with its characteristic dashes above the second 'a' and the 'i', appears authentic. Even more persuasive is the letter's straightforward questions and beguiling tone. As Mata Hari wrote:

> After many years I've suddenly been thinking about you for a whole night. God knows how it came about! Don't take offence that I'm writing to you – but there's something telling me I have to do it and, as you know, we Indian women are often that way. Are you still married? In that case, pretend I haven't written to you, but if it's not so, write to me . . . The whole night you've been so clear and distinctive in front of my eyes, tell me how you are and forgive me.[83]

Since 'Indian women' were believed to be closer to nature and therefore more capable of extrasensory perception, the letter fed into the mythology about Mata Hari's hypnotic talents. Whether the letter was authentic or not, its timely appearance added yet another romantic dimension to the story.

Meanwhile, the Zelle brothers, Mata Hari's only surviving relations, objected to the Greta Garbo film and the ensuing interest it aroused. They thought the liberties taken with the facts – especially the scene where Mata Hari murders a Russian general – libellous and attempted to stop the film's European distribution.[84] The family agreed it was time to redress the balance. Otto Pierson, chairman of the Franco/Dutch Society, received a letter on 10 May 1932 from J.D. Huyer, an Amsterdam lawyer, hired by the Zelles to investigate whether the film could be stopped. 'While it is above all doubt that [Mata Hari] hadn't killed a Russian general anyway, these brothers feel very aggrieved about this film.' To set the record straight, they needed access to the archive that Colonel Lecroix guarded.[85]

While Mr Huyer realized he was unlikely to be granted permission to read the dossier on Mata Hari, he thought it might be possible to purchase Maître Clunet's notes. The elderly lawyer had died several years before but his successor had been contacted. Since Mata Hari's brothers were all victims of the world economic depression, they had deputized Huyer to ask Mr Wynaendts, a Dutch lawyer in Paris, if he could raise support for their sister among his compatriots in France. The brothers enquired whether the Franco/Dutch Society or its members would be willing to pay 500 guilders to Maître Clunet's successor for the notes on Mata Hari's case. Mr

Wynaendts claimed the possibilities for a retrial were currently very optimistic.[86]

However, the Zelle brothers were unsuccessful on both counts. An Amsterdam court dismissed their attempt to ban the film as libellous on 25 October 1932.[87] The case was never reopened and it was not until 1962 that two French historians, Alain Presles and François Brigneau, were given access to Mata Hari's dossier.[88]

Even now, there remains one outstanding question about Mata Hari's involvement with German intelligence during the war. A Major von Roepell wrote to Major General Gempp on 24 November 1941 stating that Mata Hari had been recruited for the German intelligence service by Baron von Marbach, a Knight of St John, trained at Frankfurt and that she 'definitely spied for Germany'.[89] The fortuitous publication of her missive to Baron Lazarini puts her in Frankfurt on 25 August 1914, which could have been the period when she underwent the training that von Roepell mentions. Yet according to an official travel document, Mata Hari was in Frankfurt on 15 August 1914 and, under interrogation by Bouchardon, she claimed to have left Berlin two days later.[90]

It is doubtful that a fantastic espionage career has gone undocumented. Mata Hari was notoriously vague about dates and it was possible she simply remained longer in Frankfurt than she remembered. It is also curious that Major von Roepell would have waited twelve years to refute Gempp's public statement denying Mata Hari's involvement in the secret service. If she had been recruited by Baron von Marbach, there is no corresponding evidence of information she sent to him or anyone else in German intelligence. As her disregard for caution in sending letters to Ladoux through the post testifies, whatever she learned at Frankfurt, it certainly wasn't discretion.

The interest in the life of Margaretha Zelle MacLeod, aka Mata Hari, does not lie in her career as an espionage agent. The icon of spy-courtesan which linked her to the intellectual hostesses of the French Third Republic was formed in a particular historical moment during the Great War. She symbolized women's danger, their treacherous desires hidden beneath their rallying cry as mothers of the nation or self-sacrificing nurses. Many men believed they had paid the price in blood for the war while these vain creatures had profited from the bloodshed. The *fin-de-siècle*'s nightmare, phallic woman, had momentarily triumphed. Yet the fear of female betrayal, and the anxiety which it provoked, endured.

When the Mata Hari dossier was finally opened in the French archives, the wartime investigation appeared shoddy, revealing Ladoux's and Bouchardon's obsessive demand for punishment without sufficient evidence. During the 1960s her name became a phrase; a 'real Mata Hari' was a temptress of mystery, intrigue and, possibly, danger. She was celebrated as an enlightened advocate of free love while, in the West, she was invoked to make enemy female agents from Stalingrad, Saigon or Istanbul recognizable. More than ever, the Cold War would spawn the adage that 'sex is a dangerous weapon in the arsenal of espionage operations'.[91] But the human frailties that Mata Hari's story exposed have recently begun to surface; as Washington journalist Michael Dobbs has written, 'The exploits of the spy-seductress are best described as tragi-comedy.'[92]

EPILOGUE

There is a wide-ranging association of war with sexuality, complex,
intricate, intimate and at every level.

A.L. ROWSE[1]

THE TRAGI-COMEDY OF THE SPY-COURTESAN has always been camouflaged
by the history played out behind the scenes. The story of Mata Hari's
execution during the First World War had meaning as a triumph over female
evil. After 1918, however, there were subtle shifts in the iconography of the female
spy that reflected the changing political situation in Europe and North America.
The 'Red' rapidly replaced the 'Hun' as enemy and the espionage writers who
succeeded Georges Ladoux and Basil Thomson battled with a new generation
of ideological spies. G.E.R. Gedye reminded *New York Times* readers in 1930
that contemporary espionage budgets in every Western country far exceeded
those before the war – the spy business was booming.[2] In Britain, the greatest
efforts of the Secret Intelligence Service were devoted to Soviet operations. Its
staff vowed to preserve the Empire while at home they maintained an ordered
society and protected class privilege; intellectuals and radicals had become a
prime target for SIS internal investigations.[3]

As the nature and targets of intelligence changed, so did the espionage
fantasy. According to press reports of the 1930s, the modern female spy was
more likely to be a serious college graduate than a courtesan. Glittering *dames*
who seduced diplomats at champagne suppers had given way to hard-bitten
ladies with degrees in chemistry bent on decoding complicated formulations of
the latest weapons' technology. This new *femme fatale* was a competent driver,
a DIY expert and usually an efficient photographer; as Janet Flanner wrote in
1940, 'the government that employs her is less interested in her boudoir than
in her brain.' Flanner noticed that the majority of female agents arrested in the
past decade were respectably married – to other spies.[4]

Flanner compared Mata Hari, the courtesan, with Madame Lydia Stahl,
the Russian who was sentenced for espionage in Paris in 1935. 'These two,'
she wrote, 'are the perfect and opposing prototypes of the two sorts of female
spy, cerebral and sensual, which our modern times have developed.' Unlike
Mata Hari and her amateur adventures, however, Stahl had collected several degrees, including a doctorate of law at the Sorbonne, before adopting
intelligence as her career. Fluent in English, French, German, Russian and
Finnish, she was accused of heading an international spy ring which specialized
in extracting armaments statistics from French experts. But the comparison
between Mata Hari and Stahl encompassed what were believed to be similar
methods. Stahl, then aged forty-eight, was the mistress of Professor Louis
Martin, a code expert for the French Naval Ministry. She expanded her
network that supplied the Soviet Union with information by employing young

women and married couples to extract dossiers from unsuspecting military scientists.[5]

Stahl was accused of having recruited eight women into her spy ring including a French schoolmistress, a dentist and a graduate of Vassar College. Madeline Mermet, the teacher, and Chana Salman, part of a husband-and-wife team, both gave birth while in prison and appeared in court with babes in their arms. Mermet had aroused suspicion because she was thought to be living above her means and, when arrested, had ten thousand-franc notes sewn into her petticoat. The women were each sentenced to three years and allowed to keep their children in prison with them. The American couple, Marjorie and Robert Switz, who had met at college in New York, turned state's witness against Stahl's network and were eventually acquitted. However, Stahl protested against the injustice of her five-year sentence, saying she knew none of the accused.[6]

Lydia Stahl's calculated moves contrasted sharply with Mata Hari's story of seduction which seemed increasingly tame and innocently glamorous. However, stories about this new breed of 'Red Spy' also signalled that the enemy now practised espionage with a chilling professionalism. But the press reports of Stahl with her well-cut suits, shining blonde hair and direct manner were also reminiscent of the threatening phenomenon of the New Woman. In the inter-war years, as women throughout the former Allied nations gained the vote and moved increasingly into 'male' professions, the anxieties about this change could be safely explored in the female spy's filmic or fictional portrayal.

The memory of the war had also begun to fade by the thirties as its horrors were eclipsed by atrocities in Spain, Italy, Ethiopia and the Soviet Union. 'Mata Hari' was still a by-word for female betrayal; her name was invoked to describe the methods of contemporary women spies. Since 1919, female agents were described in US secret service files as the 'same type as Mata Hari', and reports of Rose Littke's trial in 1932 suggested her espionage methods had outdone those of the Dutch dancer. Despite their recently acquired intellectual status in the 1930s, female agents were still associated with sexual scandal as Littke's story illustrates. *The New York Times* reported: 'The adventures of Mme de Littke who recently . . . brought to a climax two separate plots of treason, one against the Magyar Regency and the other against the Republic of Poland, surpass those of the Dutch Mata Hari, even when related by that executed spy's most sensational biographer.'[7] Littke, who worked for the Polish secret service in Hungary, had posed as a dancer 'in search of a friend', to become the mistress of a clerk on the Hungarian general staff.

Littke, however, was eventually arrested in Budapest on 24 June 1932 after her lover, Captain Ruttkay, of Admiral Horthy's bodyguard, shot himself in her apartment. Since Littke had purchased a gun the day before and the bullets matched those found in Ruttkay's body, she was accused of orchestrating his suicide. It was further revealed that during the two years the couple lived together, Littke had sent reports about Ruttkay, a Czech spy, to the Hungarian and Polish secret services. The Budapest papers speculated that he had shot himself after learning about Littke's betrayal. However, when Littke was finally tried in February 1933, Captain Ruttkay's widow testified that she had lived happily with her husband until 'Frau Littke came into his life'. Shortly before his death, his wife claimed, he had promised to leave his mistress and she believed the affair had triggered his suicide.[8]

Even the Communist women spies could be categorized as 'leftist Mata Haris' who used their wiles to further their cause. The Romanian police in 1934 were warning customs officials about the activities of 'the Red Venus', an extremely beautiful woman spy who worked for the Soviets in the Balkans. A woman who fitted this description was picked up in Constanta, Romania, and while officials searched her trunks, she attempted to swallow a letter. But unlike the simpering courtesans, these female agents were trained for such situations. The Red Venus 'fought desperately when officers attempted to interfere, using boxing tactics and jujitsu; she was overpowered only after a long resistance.' Among other things found in her luggage was a letter from Soviet officials recommending the bearer to Communists in Constanta as 'one of the best workers for the cause of the Soviets'. Along with a typewriter were discovered 'many articles carried by professional spies'.[9] At least one female foreign correspondent ran into difficulty for this very reason; typewriters, shorthand notes and books were regarded as suspiciously intellectual for a lady traveller.[10]

Although press reports attempted to mould the spy to reflect the New Woman, the erotic fantasy still won out. H.Z. Torres argued in 1935 that 'the legendary spy – a siren with eyes as blue as cornflowers and hair the colour of corn tassel . . . or a Mata Hari . . . is as outmoded as yesterday's "thriller".' Yet the beautiful siren who muddles the minds of innocent men through her exotic, hothouse sexuality had endured. It wasn't until the Second World War, when stories began to emerge of women's involvement in the Resistance, that the *femme fatale* faced any serious rival as a cultural icon in this sphere.

In France, the African-American dancer Josephine Baker was haunted by Mata Hari's legacy. However, to join the resistance Baker first had to overcome the prejudices of the officers in General de Gaulle's Free French forces; Jacques Abtey, head of military counter-intelligence in Paris, thought she might prove to be another Mata Hari. Baker had to convince Abtey that the similarities were merely superficial: 'whereas Mata Hari had been an adventuress drifting around the world without a home, interested above all in her own comfort, [she] was fiercely and to the point of self-sacrifice devoted to France.'[11] Colonel Paillole, who directed military counter-intelligence in Marseilles, also believed the Mata Hari myth and had, at first, shared Abtey's reservations about Baker. However, she convinced both men of her strength and commitment; she became de Gaulle's 'ambassador, his propaganda arm in North Africa'.[12]

It wasn't just spy-chiefs who bought the legend. Many biographies about Allied women agents reveal the extent to which the spy-courtesan informed their concept of the intelligence services. Violette Szabo, an Englishwoman who joined the Special Operations Executive French section in 1942, had grown up reading about Mata Hari. According to her biographer, R.J. Minney, she was an avid fan of adventurous women spies. 'She read two or three books on Mata Hari and used to go round to the public library to ask for more. [Her parents] wondered at the flights of fancy of this child of fourteen. Was this the sort of role in which she fancied herself with her recurrent daring and her innocent devilry?'[13] The infatuation continued when Szabo joined the ATS in 1941 and at a New Year's pantomime she performed, in a hastily improvised skirt and bra, 'what might roughly be described as the Dance of the Seven Veils'.[14] It seemed that Mata Hari's combination of exoticism and danger had a bewitching resonance for another generation at war.

When Szabo was recruited into the SOE, the mythology of Mata Hari's experience coloured her expectations. As Minney explains:

> Violette and some of the others . . . were convinced in their own minds that they were about to become spies. But in fact, beyond the assumption of an alias and later the evolution of a new identity, with their normal backgrounds completely obliterated, there was nothing in the training approximating even remotely to any preconceived ideas one had of Olga Polowsky and other famous spies of song or story.[15]

The training schools attributed to the celebrated female agents of music-hall song and story simply didn't exist. However, the spy's lessons in seduction formed an essential element in the espionage fantasy that authors such as Henry de Halsalle, William Le Quex and Georges Ladoux had created decades before. But since the secret services refused to divulge how their recruits were trained, Violette Szabo had culled her information from what was available in the public library. If the SOE could not describe what being a spy was, Violette was content with her own definition.

After the war, films and biographies about those who worked in Allied intelligence suggested all the romance of R.P. Weston and Bert Lee's 1935 song, 'Olga Pulloffski, the Beautiful Spy'. But autobiographies by women who had been in the Resistance often challenged its association with glamour. These authors rarely described using their sexuality as a bargaining tool for information but there were several instances of men who had. Suzanne Warenghem, a Frenchwoman who helped Allied soldiers to escape from France, was betrayed by her lover. She met Paul Cole, who claimed to be a former Scotland Yard detective and agent of the British intelligence service, through a network that helped Allied soldiers to escape from occupied Europe. They worked together in northern France in 1941 and married the following year. In reality, Paul was a British sergeant who had deserted to become a Gestapo informer, but Suzanne didn't discover this until much later on. The French police arrested them together in Lyons and informed Suzanne that her husband was a traitor who planned to denounce her to the Germans. However, since her innocence was difficult to establish during wartime, she was considered guilty by association and spent six weeks in solitary confinement in a Lyons prison.[16]

Suzanne once jokingly scolded herself for being 'no Mata Hari', when she failed to get information from a taciturn German officer. The idea of sleeping with the enemy for espionage purposes seemed faintly ridiculous to a woman who had been so bitterly deceived by her lover. In any case, it was never assumed that a man might decide to use his sexuality – à la Mata Hari – with a woman. A male agent might have gained a reputation as a Romeo but this was never equated with a crime against the state. Hélène Champlain, however, who was an operative in the Office of Strategic Services (OSS), recalled how much more easily men used women. During a mission near Marseilles, she fell in love with an American, Lieutenant Peter Pearson, with whom she had a brief affair. But when they met again in Grenoble, he refused to acknowledge her presence, provoking her to conclude: 'I had yet to learn that no love prevails when the taste of a new adventure and exciting danger is awoken in a man.'[17]

However, Champlain was well aware that women who had relations with the enemy were regarded as the worst collaborators. She was shocked to witness a group of Frenchwomen being paraded in Fréjus with shaven heads and swastikas painted on their foreheads: 'I wanted to run away, ashamed as if I were the cause of this distasteful and wretched parade,' she wrote. 'I had always thought of France as the most civilized and cultured nation and yet, something like this was happening here. I realized then, that when uncontrollable hate and ignorance engulf men, the worst actions are committed.'[18] (The reality in France was that only a small percentage of the population participated in the Resistance movement.)[19] But the greatest punishment was reserved for those women who had played both roles: brave Resistance worker and Gestapo mistress.

Although there is conflicting evidence about the guilt of Mathilde Carré, a Frenchwoman condemned to death on espionage charges in 1949, her story resembles Mata Hari's. In fact, the title of her 1960 autobiography described her as 'the most remarkable woman spy since Mata Hari'. Carré, known as the Cat, was a radio operator working for the *interallié* network. She regularly sent messages to Britain until she was arrested by the Gestapo in 1941 and threatened with death if she did not divulge information about the *interallié*. Carré admitted, however, that she committed a double crime: she supplied the Germans with names and became the lover of Gestapo officer Hugo Bleicher. As she explained, sleeping with Bleicher meant survival:

> It was pure animal cowardice, the reaction of a body which had survived its first night in prison, had suffered cold, felt the icy breath of death and suddenly found warmth once more in a pair of arms . . . even if they were the arms of the enemy.[20]

Carré would later write that she felt so powerless, her 'feminine wiles' became her only form of revenge. Her affair with Bleicher was the most effective way of persuading him to trust her and facilitate her escape. Meanwhile the Abwehr (the German secret service) continued to transmit radio messages to Britain signing them under her code-name, the Cat. Eventually, she was allowed to organize a phoney Resistance network which enabled her to reach London where she told MI5 everything she knew about the Abwehr's operations, even supplying plans and photographs. However, she was arrested on orders from the French government in exile and taken to Aylesbury prison where she was kept with four other women spies.

After three years, Carré was transferred from Britain to France but did not stand trial until 1949. As the prison began to empty of female prisoners incarcerated on war-related crimes, she noticed that only those who had once had German lovers remained. In January 1949, a jury of former Maquis members condemned Carré to death for betraying thirty-five members of the French Resistance to the Germans. She wrote afterwards to her lawyer, Albert Naud, that she was guilty only of 'having tried to reason like a man, instead of following my feminine intuition'.[21] On 4 May 1949 her sentence was reduced to hard labour for life but on 1 July 1962 she was released.

Like Hélène Champlain, Carré felt that there was a special category of crime reserved for women during wartime which revealed men's deepest fears about the other sex. 'I must never forget that men (particularly the French) do not love an equal,' she wrote, 'and since I feel no inclination to be a slave – unless it be to God – I must outgrow them.'[22] The notion that a woman might switch sides – betraying the state and her metaphorical father/patriarch – was symbolized by those female spies who had become double-agents. The legend of Carré, 'the diabolical spy with green eyes', filled column inches in the French press and was made into a film, *La Chatte*, with Françoise Arnoul and Bernard Blier, in 1958. But the theme which popularized this story owed as much to Mata Hari's spy-courtesan as the complex relations between the sexes which the war had refashioned.

After the Berlin blockade, when the British and Americans believed the Soviet Union was once again their prime enemy, the *femme fatale* resurfaced as a handmaiden to the godless Communists. In Hollywood, Lola Lane starred in *Miss V from Moscow* while Sally Eilers played an innocent corrupted in *They Made Her a Spy* and Fay Wray graced the screen as *Madame Spy*. But the blonde, patriotic girl next door was also found fighting on the right side of the secret war. Ann Dvorak starred as 'America's "Mata Hari" of the South Pacific' in the 1951 epic, *I Was an American Spy*.[23] The consistency of the spy-courtesan's story had begun to blur and even true-hearted, patriotic women were shown vamping the enemy in the cause of truth and justice.

During the McCarthy era in the United States, a wave of spy scares had rekindled wartime interest in the subject. Before Pearl Harbor, American housewives had been kept up to date with the 'exploits of famous women spies' and in 1942 *Good Housekeeping* magazine ran a series entitled 'When and What to Report to the FBI'. By 1950 espionage writers were turning their hand once again to quasi-history which claimed to document the threat spies posed to the free world. By now Mata Hari seemed a relic from an innocuous age and it was her daughter who enjoyed yet another reincarnation.

The Austrian-born writer, Kurt Singer, with a reputation as 'a leading expert in international espionage', created Banda MacLeod in 1951. Singer claimed that Mata Hari had had an affair with a Javanese man and given birth to an illegitimate daughter while living in the Dutch East Indies at the turn of the century. This child was raised by relatives but at a young age she married a Dutch official, Wilhelm van Deeren, who was forty years her senior.[24] After his death in 1935, van Deeren left her a modest fortune and her house became known as a salon for politicians, intellectuals and journalists. When the Japanese invaded the islands in 1941, Banda was treated as a Dutchwoman and forced to reopen her salon as a listening post for the occupying forces. Colonel Abdul, a leader in the Indonesian independence movement, approached her to work for his cause, she fell in love and began spying on the Japanese for the nationalists.

But since Banda's lover was twenty years younger (shades of Captain Masloff), he left her for a younger woman. To nurse her broken heart, she accepted an assignment to travel to the United States, lecturing about Indonesian independence in 1948. While on tour she was recruited by the CIA, and headed for China disguised as a Red Cross nurse. In Shanghai she changed her white uniform for a tight-fitting dress to work in a hostess bar. (If she was Mata Hari's daughter, Banda would have been at least forty-eight years old by this time, and an improbable cocktail waitress.) Code-named Sunflower, she gained access to Mao and the Communist leaders, and sent warnings about the 'Red dictator' from Chungking, before making her way to North Korea where she predicted that an invasion was impending. As Wilhelmina van Deeren she settled into the British Mission House in Maengsong, but the Koreans discovered her real identity. She was executed by a firing squad at exactly the same time her mother 'reputedly' died: 5.45 a.m.

However, aside from miscalculating the time of Mata Hari's death (it was 6.15 a.m.), the premise of Singer's story is false. While it is possible that Mata Hari conceived another child in Java, it could hardly have escaped comment in the close-knit Dutch colony. Furthermore, Rudolph MacLeod's frank revelations about his relationship with Mata Hari in Charles Heymans' biography suggest he would not have hidden such damning evidence. Neither is there any documentary proof to support Singer's claim. Espionage writer Bernard Newman, who knew the story had wide currency in the United States and Indonesia, concluded in 1956 that there was a Banda MacLeod but she probably wasn't Mata Hari's daughter.[25]

Yet this suggestion appears to have equally little basis in fact. Professor Leigh Williams, an American specialist in Indonesian history for the period, wrote in answer to my query, 'I cannot recall ever hearing of Banda MacLeod.' Williams explained that there was no record of Mao knowing a mysterious Indo-Dutch spy and it was extremely unlikely since 'he was watched quite closely by numerous reporters and associates'. He added that a spy in 1950 would have avoided Chungking because it was a 'backwater of history, without espionage potential'.[26] Historian Robin Winks looked through a Yale University collection of papers from a professor who was very active in Java and Sumatra in 1948–50 and was widely believed to have worked for the CIA. Winks confirmed that Banda MacLeod does not appear among these papers.[27]

Despite the lack of evidence, the story has enjoyed a long run in espionage mythology. In 1954 it appeared as a full-page feature, 'Daughter of Mata Hari', in Charles Franklin's 1969 *Spies of the Twentieth Century*, and as a Fleet Street wire service article in 1971 entitled 'Mata Hari's Daughter, Secret Agent'. By 1987 Banda was still listed in Donald McCormick alias Richard Deacon's *Spyclopaedia* as 'Mata Hari's daughter'. 'This is a convenient title for a character who remains something of a mystery and whose identity has never been confirmed,' writes Deacon. 'She has been . . . named as Banda Macleod [sic], (known by General Sir Philip Christison when he was serving in the Far East in World War II and afterwards Allied Commander Netherlands East Indies).'[28] However, Sir Philip Christison politely replied to me, 'I was puzzled by your letter . . . I have no idea how my name can have come into this case as I have never heard of Banda Zelle MacLeod.'[29] The desire to believe in Mata Hari's resurrection has, as always, transcended the burden of proof.

By the 1960s the Dutch dancer/spy was given yet another lease of life. This time, Mata Hari's sexual mythology was unearthed and reconstructed for the swinging sixties. Biographer Sam Waagenaar identified the parallel between Mata Hari's daring, on-stage strip-tease in *la belle époque* and the post-war break with moral taboos. 'She nearly undressed in public, this was something unbelievable and can be compared somewhat with the 1960s university revolution when people did whatever they wanted and got away with it.'[30] Another wave of Hollywood films and Broadway productions followed. Wolf Mankowitz wrote a musical based on Mata Hari's life for actress Vivien Leigh in 1963 and then approached Shirley Bassey for the role because 'she has the voice, the savagery, the looks and the body'. Bassey turned it down along with Lena Horne and Georgia Brown.[31]

A film starring Jeanne Moreau and co-written by François Truffaut, *Mata Hari*, opened in 1965 to less than enthusiastic reviews. However, Moreau's performance was praised for turning the *'femme fatale* into a period piece', while her husband-director Jean-Louis Richard admitted this Mata Hari was 'a product of my imagination'.[32] An attempt at a big-budget musical in 1967 proved equally unsuccessful. However, Broadway producer David Merrick's 'lavishly clad and insanely expensive' production suggested that the spy-dancer had resonance for a contemporary audience. Its star Marisa Mell was hailed as 'the only visible successor to Marilyn Monroe' but it lost $850,000 in its pre-Broadway tour. When it opened in New York in 1968 as 'Ballad of a Firing Squad', with an anti-war message, it fared only marginally better.[33]

Mata Hari had become a woman for all seasons. During the 1970s actor David Carradine financed his own film project based on her life. 'I have this obsession with the subject and I want to do it my way,' he told a journalist in 1978. 'Mata Hari lived in her own make-believe world and that is how we are shooting this film.' Since the story would cover fifteen years of Mata Hari's life, Carradine cast his sixteen-year-old daughter Calista in the starring role, and planned to film her over several years. Calista was quoted as saying, 'Like me and my father, Mata Hari does nothing that is expected of her. She is a real rebel, trying all the time to make something of herself.'[34] The Dutch avant-garde dancer, as she had become, was the perfect vehicle for the swinging, sexually liberated sixties and audiences were expected to sympathize with Mata Hari's desire to challenge society's expectations.

While Mata Hari began to be seen as a victim of circumstance in Britain and the United States, she was still regarded with mixed emotions in the rest of Europe. When her home town of Leeuwarden decided to unveil a commemorative statue on the centenary of her birth in 1976, several leading citizens boycotted the ceremony. They still regarded Mata Hari as a blight on Friesian womanhood and feared that publicity about the unveiling might create the wrong impression. Their anxieties were fuelled by such down-market American articles as a widely read piece entitled 'Holland's happy-hooker hoofer-heroine got herself in Dutch'; in other words, the story of how a Dutch dancer-prostitute got herself into trouble.[35] To the tabloid press, Mata Hari has maintained her reputation as a Notorious Woman, shrouded in secrecy.

But has the spy-courtesan survived into the late twentieth century? By 1990 the old-style James Bond bimbette with the naughty-joke name and bursting bosom has given way to Pam Bouvier who dresses in jeans, tennis shoes, little make-up and no jewellery. Carey Lowell, who plays Bouvier in *Licence to Kill*, explained that 'the relationship between my character and Bond is a contemporary one . . . Pam Bouvier is very self-sufficient and very competitive with Bond. We spar with each other and Bond rather likes it.'[36] But while the playboy agent had acquired a proto-feminist partner, on screen the spy-courtesan had also been transformed into a new form of phallic woman. Jeanne Moreau – a Mata Hari film veteran – recently made an ironic appearance in Luc Besson's *Nikita* as an instructor in the feminine arts to the eponymous punk-junkie-turned-terrorist. Trained as a hired killer for the French secret service, Nikita (Anne Parillaud) must learn how to wear slinky black dresses, apply lipstick and charm men before venturing back into the world to kill them.

In this update of the dangerous woman, Nikita wields a high-powered rifle and explodes with exuberant passion in bed with her soulful lover, Jean-Hugues Anglade. But although Nikita packs the biggest weapon around, she finds that her murderous assignments, which she keeps secret, increasingly impinge on her relationship. After a particularly gruesome botched assassination, she ditches her 007 career and goes into hiding, leaving her lover to explain her absence to the French secret service. Yet unlike the spy-courtesan of yore, this *femme fatale* feels betrayed by her boss, the Henry-Higgins-like instructor Bob, who effected her transformation back into womanhood. All she really wants is a quiet life with her boyfriend. She yearns to embrace the domesticity that Mata Hari was portrayed as rejecting at every opportunity.

Off-screen, the spy-courtesan has never been far from the spotlight. Reports about the KGB using women or gay men as plants within foreign embassies became so prolific in the 1970s that a new term, 'sexspionage', was coined. According to former FBI officer Robert Lamphere, 'there is an old adage in the FBI to the effect that there has never been an espionage case in which sex did not play a part.'[37] The story of the Bonn secretaries who were convicted of spying for the GDR, and released in 1990, reveals that the ancient themes are still at work.

Margret Hoke, who served five West German presidents, was charged in 1985 with leaking classified foreign policy and military information to the GDR. In a dramatic reversal of the usual 'honey-trap' scenario, Hoke had become the lover of Franz Becker, who she did not realize was a KGB agent. They maintained a relationship for thirteen years while Hoke supplied him with intelligence service dossiers, documents on Bonn's tactics on security issues and NATO opinions, from her office. 'That he was six years younger than me disturbed me at first, but he always seemed to dispel my doubts,' testified the fifty-two-year-old Hoke. 'He told me he wasn't interested in younger women.'[38] The most recent secretary to be tried, Elke Falk, fell in love with a KGB officer she met through a lonely hearts advertisement at the age of twenty-eight. However, during her 1989 trial, she stressed that she 'wouldn't like him maybe to have even more trouble over there'. Altogether, an estimated twenty-five secretaries were believed to have fallen for the charms of Eastern agents and were tried in German courts.[39]

In the wake of Hoke's trial, Bonn issued a poster which was pinned up in government offices throughout West Germany. It showed a svelte blonde woman smiling seductively above the caption, 'The smile of espionage?' A confidential telephone number was listed for employers who suspected their secretaries. (It seemed ironically reminiscent of the British Second World War poster which suggested any attractive woman was a spy and warned men 'Keep Mum, She's Not so Dumb!') The women working in the West German government offices complained that the poster campaign fostered 'an atmosphere of suspicion and mistrust'. Some secretaries found their phones were tapped and their private lives placed under constant surveillance.[40]

However, the Hoke case had demonstrated that it was not young, attractive secretaries who were vulnerable to the GDR's agents, but what the West German press called *die grauen Mause*, the grey mice. They were usually single women, portrayed as lonely, living in one-roomed flats in a dull city. These 'spinsters' appeared as pathetic creatures, reduced to finding their lovers through newspaper advertisements and swallowing the lie that a younger man might find them attractive. When the seduction scenario is reversed, the older woman seems unnatural, hardly the heroic figure around whom a spy thriller might be built.

The reaction to these stories also reveals that the internal dynamic in the spy-courtesan story revolves round the existing tension between the sexes. Whether it's Gustav Steinhauer's detective, Herbert Yardley's fictional Nathaniel Greenleaf or John Le Carré's Smiley, the perspective has always been male. The seductive *femme* moves the plot along, sparks the action and speeds along the conclusive battle between good and evil. Mata Hari falls at Vincennes, 'Red Venus' is locked away and Bond's bad girl is eaten alive by piranhas. But the protagonist is rarely female, she plays a crucial role but never tells the story; the adventure still speaks to its male audience.

Mata Hari remains as a potent cultural icon, conjuring up a more innocent age and a vibrant celebration of life. Our contemporary interest in a woman who so definitely rejected the expectations society seemed destined to thrust upon her has resonance for our shifting mores. Her 'Oriental' mystique and its appeal to a *fin-de-siècle* audience provides valuable insight into nineteenth-century exoticism. The mythology which accompanied her amateur adventure in espionage also reminds us how inextricably fantasy was woven into the constructed world of the secret war. From her lonely, cramped cell at Vincennes, her letters spoke eloquently of the female conundrum within it. For how can women ever defend themselves against those crimes for which there are unwritten rules and for which they will never be charged but often persecuted? Mata Hari made the mistake of writing her own code and expecting the world to play along.

NOTES

INTRODUCTION
pages 1–7

1. Mata Hari to Lieutenant André Mornet, n.d., *Dossier Mata Hari*, Service Historique de l'Armée de Terre, hereafter, SHAT.
2. Alain Presles and François Brigneau, 'Le Dossier Secret de Mata Hari', *Le Nouveau Candide*, 15–22 March, 1962.
3. Mata Hari to Mornet, op. cit., SHAT.
4. Pierre Bouchardon, *Souvenirs* (Paris: Albin Michel, 1953), p. 325-8.
5. Emile Massard, *Les Espionnes à Paris* (Paris: Albin Michel 1922), p. 70.
6. Léon Bizard, *Souvenirs d'un Médecin de Saint-Lazare* (Paris: Albin Michel 1923), p. 88.
7. Emile Massard, 'La véridique histoire de Mata Hari – L'Expiation', *La Liberté*, 13 December, 1921.
8. *Le Gaulois*, 16 October, 1917.
9. George Wickes, *The Amazon of Letters: The Life and Loves of Natalie Barney* (London: W.H. Allen, 1977), p. 93.
10. Ibid., p. 94.
11. Letter from Natalie Barney to Sam Waagenaar, n.d., mentioned in interview with Waagenaar, April 1990.
12. Bernard Newman, *Inquest on Mata Hari* (London: Robert Hale, 1956), p. 43.
13. Paul Allard, *Les Enigmes de la Guerre* (Paris: Editions de Portiques, 1934), p. 173.
14. Phyllis Rose, *Jazz Cleopatra: Josephine Baker in Her Time* (London: Chatto and Windus, 1989), pp. 186/7.
15. *International Herald Tribune*, 3 October, 1964.
16. Raphael Gould to J.N.B. Hill, MS Fr 132, Houghton Library, Harvard, MA, hereafter, HL.
17. *New York Times*, 23 January, 1977, section 10, p. 5.
18. 'La Mata-Harisme', *Crapouillot*, 15 November, 1952, pp. 39–42.
19. J.M. Spaight, *Air Power and War Rights* (London: Longman, 1924), p. 25.
20. Newman, op. cit., p. 105.
21. Dr Magnus Hirschfeld, *The Sexual History of the Great War* (New York: Panurge Press, 1934), p. 239.
22. Newman, op. cit., p. 82.
23. Lt-Col. Oreste Pinto, *The Spycatcher Omnibus: The Spy and Counter-Spy Adventures of Lt-Col. Oreste Pinto* (London: Hodder and Stoughton, 1969), p. 308, fifth printing.
24. Sir Vernon Kell, *Security Intelligence in War. Lecture Notes*, 1934, Imperial War Museum, hereafter, IWM. Kell MSS.
25. Herbert O. Yardley, *The Blonde Countess* (London: Faber, 1934), p. 288.

CHAPTER 1 THE CHILD-BRIDE
pages 8–30

1. Georges du Parcq, *Secrets of the French Police* (London: Jarrolds, 1934), p. 59.
2. Margaretha Zelle MacLeod alternately called herself Lady MacLeod, Mrs MacLeod or Mata Hari and after her divorce in 1906, Madame Zelle. To avoid confusion, however, I have referred to her as Margaretha during her marriage to MacLeod and as Mata Hari when she took that name in Paris.
3. Charles S. Heymans, *La Vraie Mata Hari: Courtisane et Espionne* (Paris: Editions Prométhée, 1930), p. 18. At the end of May 1895 Margaretha wrote to Rudolph, 'Pardonne-moi mon ignorance mais dis-moi, jusqu'on une pareille chemise doit-elle descendre, au-dessus ou au-dessous du genou? . . . Et ce pantalon, est-il du même modèle que mon pantalon blanc?'

Wherever possible, I have referred to the original documents of Mata Hari's case and have had material from the Dutch Foreign Ministry and legation archives translated into English. However, Heymans' biography, which I read in French, was originally published in Dutch, the language in which the MacLeod correspondence was originally written. Since the letters therefore have been translated from Dutch into French and back into English, certain nuances and subtleties of the language may have been lost.

4. Elaine Showalter, *Sexual Anarchy: Gender and Culture at the Fin de Siècle* (London: Bloomsbury, 1991), p. 21 for discussion of attitudes towards female sexuality.

5. Sam Waagenaar, *The Murder of Mata Hari* (London: Arthur Barker, 1964), p. 33.

6. Adam Zelle, *Mata Hari, Mme M.G. MacLeod-Zelle: A History of the life of My Daughter And my grievances against her ex-husband, With portraits, documents, facsimiles and supplements* (Amsterdam: C.L.G. Veldt, 1906), quoted in *Mercure de France*, 1 January, 1923, pp. 242–3.

7. Waagenaar, op. cit., p. 33 and Zelle, op. cit., p. 241.

8. Waagenaar, op. cit., p. 36.

9. Quoted in Erika Ostrovsky, *Eye of Dawn: The Rise and Fall of Mata Hari* (New York: Dorset Press, 1978), pp. 116–17.

10. Heymans, op. cit., p. 22; Waagenaar, op. cit., pp. 10–11, Bernard Newman, *Inquest on Mata Hari* (London: Robert Hale, 1956), p. 179.

11. Polly Binder, *The Truth About Cora Pearl* (London: Weidenfeld and Nicolson, 1986), p. 28.

12. Madame Zelle McLeod [sic], New Scotland Yard, 16 November, 1916, Public Record Office, hereafter, PRO Metropolitan Police, hereafter, MEPO file 3–2444.

13. Heymans, op. cit., p. 42.

14. Ibid., p. 48.

15. Ibid., p. 51.

16. Waagenaar, op. cit., p. 38.

17. Ibid., p. 41.

18. Zelle, op. cit., p. 243.

19. Heymans, op. cit., p. 60.

20. Ibid., p. 43.

21. Ibid., p. 43.

22. Leo Faust, 'Notes et Documents d'Histoire', *Mercure de France*, 1 January, 1923, p. 239.

23. 'Mata Hari racontée par l'homme qui a fit la condamner', *Paris Match*, 22 August, 1953.

24. Mata Hari interrogation by Captain Bouchardon, 15 February, 1917, SHAT.

25. Henry Jean-Baptiste Joseph de Marguérie, interview by Bouchardon, 12 June, 1917, SHAT.

26. *The Lady's Realm*, Vol. xxiv, May to October 1908, p. 552 and Diana Cooper, *The Rainbow Comes and Goes* (London: Rupert Hart-Davis, 1958), p. 87.

27. 'The Parisians of Paris', *The King*, 4 February, 1905, p. 610.

28. Ibid.

29. Ibid.

30. Waagenaar, op. cit., p. 46.

31. Edward Said, *Orientalism* (London: Penguin, 1985), p. 1.

32. Said, op. cit., p. 182.

33. 'Paris fancies and fashions', *The Gentlewoman*, 25 March, 1905, p. 434.

34. 'Bloc-Notes Parisien – Matahari', *Le Gaulois*, 17 March, 1905.

35. Quoted in Dr. Léon Bizard and Jane Chapon, *Histoires de la Prison de Saint-Lazare, du Moyen-Age à Nos Jours* (Paris: E. de Boccards, 1925), p. 256.

36. Waagenaar, op. cit., p. 53.

37. Major Thomas Coulson, *Mata Hari: Courtesan and Spy* (London: Harper, 1930), p. 21.

38. Judith Walkowitz, *Prostitution and Victorian Society: Women, Class and the State* (London: Cambridge University Press, 1980), p. 247: 'The white-slavery and child-prostitution scandals had all the symptoms of a cultural paranoia overtaking Britain in the late nineteenth century . . . '

39. In 1905, Princess Caraman Chimay caused a furore in Paris after performing in a flesh-

coloured body-stocking. Mata Hari Collection, Frysk Letterkundich Museum en Dokumintaes-jesintrum, Leeuwarden, Holland, hereafter FLMD.

40. Camille Pitollet, *Mercure de France*, 15 July, 1922, p. 505.

41. *Le Figaro*, 20 August, 1905.

42. *Journal de St Petersburg*, 16 April, 1905, FLMD.

43. 'Mata Hary', *Variety*, 3 May, 1918.

44. Astruc letter quoted in Waagenaar, op. cit., p. 81. As she wrote to Astruc from The Hague, 'There are no two women who can give this impression of seduction,' in Gabriel Astruc, *Le Pavillon des Fantômes: Souvenirs* (Paris: Grasset, 1929), p. 38.

45. Rana Kabbani, *Europe's Myths of Orient: Devise and Rule* (London: Pandora Press, 1986), p. 69.

46. Quoted in George Wickes, *The Amazon of Letters: The Life and Loves of Natalie Barney* (London: W.H. Allen, 1977), p. 92.

47. Waagenaar, op. cit., p. 92.

48. Wickes, op. cit., p. 94.

49. Modris Eksteins, *Rites of Spring: The Great War and the Birth of the Modern Age* (Toronto: Lester and Orpen Dennys, 1989), p. 82.

50. Waagenaar, op. cit., p. 77.

51. Ibid., p. 73.

52. See for example, Eksteins, op. cit., p. 27: 'With every season Diaghilev became more daring. The eroticism became more overt . . . in *Cléopatre* in the 1909 season – the tale about a queen who seeks a lover willing to die at dawn after a night of love – with its wild bacchanal scene of quickening *tempi*, great leaps of the Ethiopians, tossing flesh, and waves of silk and gold.'

53. Maud Allan, *My Life and Dancing* (London: Everett and Co., 1908), p. 10.

54. Eksteins, op. cit., p. 25.

55. Allan, op. cit., p. 77.

56. Judith Lynne Hanna, *Dance, Sex and Gender: Signs of Identity, Dominance, Defiance and Desire* (London: University of Chicago Press, 1988), p. 27.

57. Showalter, op. cit., p. 150.

58. Joris-Karl Huysmans, *Against the Grain*, translated by John Howard, introduction by Havelock Ellis (New York: Dover, 1969), p. 53.

59. Allan, op. cit., p. 78.

60. Eksteins, op. cit., p. 83.

61. Percival Pollard, 'The Regnant Wave of the Sensational Dance', *New York Times*, 23 August, 1908.

62. Ibid.

63. Ibid.

64. *Intermédiare des Chercheurs et Curiseux*, 30 September, 1906, pp. 485–7.

65. Alain Corbin, *Women for Hire: Prostitution and Sexuality in France after 1850*, translated by Alan Sheridan, (London: Harvard University Press, 1990), p. 213.

66. *Who's Who in Theatre; A Biographical Record of the Contemporary Stage* (London, 1912).

67. *The Lady's Realm*, October 1908, Vol. xxiv, p. 38.

68. Regenia Gagnier, *Idylls of the Marketplace: Oscar Wilde and the Victorian Public* (Aldershot: Scolar Press, 1986), p. 203 for Pigott quote.

69. Allan, op. cit., p. 99.

70. *Who's Who in Theatre*, op. cit.

71. *New York Times*, 16 August, 1908.

72. Ibid.

73. Allan, op. cit., p. 117.

74. Carl E. Schorske, *Fin-de-Siècle Vienna: Politics and Culture* (New York: Random House, 1981), p. 224.

75. Allan, op. cit., p. 107.

76. Quoted in Waagenaar, op. cit., p. 75.

77. Allan, op. cit., p. 125.

78. Ibid., p. 127.

79. Cooper, op. cit., p. 88.

80. 'Salome Craze', *The Sketch*, 24 June, 1908, p. 9.

81. *New York Times*, 16 August, 1908; Percival Pollard noted in the *New York Times*, 23 August, 1908, that in Germany, the sketch writers satirized Isadora Duncan: 'The humorists found plenty of material in her classic intentions and in her pretensions that she was illustrating Attic lore and legend; they announced solemnly that in the following years her dances would exhibit the Dictionary of Logarithms, the Parliamentary Record and the Tariff.'

82. Hanna, op. cit., p. 33.

83. Scala Theatre Programme, 7 October, 1908, Victoria and Albert Theatre Museum Collection.

84. Quoted in Hanna, op. cit., p. 134.

85. Michael de Cossart, *Ida Rubenstein (1885–1960), A Theatrical Life* (Liverpool: Liverpool University Press, 1987), p. 10.

86. Ibid., p. 12.

87. Ibid., pp. 14 and 21 and Eksteins, op. cit., p. 25.

88. 'Coquelin and Charity', *The Era*, 3 October, 1908.

89. Margaretha's marriage was dissolved on 26 April, 1906 by the Tribunal of Arnhem, *Mercure de France*, 1 January, 1923, p. 245 and information about Kiepert, Mata Hari's investigation with Bouchardon, 15 February, 1917, SHAT.

90. In Mata Hari Scrapbooks, FLMD.

91. Henry Channon, *The Ludwigs of Bavaria* (London: Lehmann, 1952), quoted in *Evening Standard*, 1 September, 1952.

92. Binder, op. cit., p. 33.

93. Jean Cocteau, *Paris Album, 1900–1914* (London: W.H. Allen, 1956), p. 49.

94. Binder, op. cit., p. 31 and Janine Alexandre-Debray, *La Pavia: ses amants, ses maris* (Paris: Librarie Académique Perrin, 1986), p. 185.

95. Dr Magnus Hirschfeld, *The Sexual History of the World War* (New York: Panurge Press, 1934), p. 239.

CHAPTER 2 THE BIRTH OF EROTIC ESPIONAGE
pages 31–46

1. 'Olga Pulloffski, the Beautiful Spy', written by R.P. Weston and Bert Lee (London: Francis, Day and Hunter, Ltd, 1935). My thanks to the British Music Hall Society for this reference. Quoted with permission from EMI Music Publishing.

2. *Mercure de France*, 15 July, 1922.

3. Charles S. Heymans, *La Vraie Mata Hari: Courtisane et Espionne* (Paris: Editions Prométhée, 1930), p. 116.

4. Ibid., p. 114.

5. Mata Hari Scrapbooks, FLMD. Mata Hari was so accepted into French society that she was even invited to perform at a soirée on 29 January, 1909 in honour of the 'nouveaux décorés' of the Legion of Honour in the salons of the Hotel Continental, Paris.

6. MS Fr 132, HL.

7. Gabriel Astruc, *Le Pavillon des Fantômes: Souvenirs,* (Paris: Grasset, 1929), p. 39.

8. Emile Massard, *Les Espionnes à Paris* (Paris: Albin Michel, 1922), pp. 19–20, emphasis in original.

9. Charles Castle, *Folies Bergère* (London: Hamish Hamilton, 1982), p. 54.

10. MS Fr 132 HL.

11. Russell Howe, *Mata Hari – The True Story* (New York: Dodd Mead, 1986), p. 53.

12. MS Fr 132, (15), HL.

13. Astruc, op. cit., p. 39.

14. 'Lady MacLeod dances . . . ', *The Tatler*, 24 September, 1913.

15. Jean Overton Fuller, *Noor-un-Nisa Inayat Khan (Madeleine)* (London: Barrie and Jenkins, 1979), p. 32.

16. bMS Am 1553, HL.

17. *Comoedia Illustré*, March 1913, p. 961.

18. Castle, op. cit., p. 54.

19. Erté, *Things I Remember* (London: Peter Owen, 1975), p. 25.

20. Liane de Pougy, *My Blue Notebooks*, translated by Diana Athill (London: André Deutsch, 1977), p. 99.

21. Misia Sert, *Two or Three Muses: The Memoirs of Misia Sert*, translated from the French by Moura Budberg (London: Museum Press,*New 1953), pp. 148–9*.

22. Fuller, op. cit., p. 36.

23. Catherine von Casselaer, *Lot's Wife: Lesbian Paris, 1890–1914* (Liverpool: Janus Press, 1986), p. 106 and 'The Spread of Bohemianism in English Society', the *New York Times*, 16 August, 1908.

24. Massard, op. cit., p. 27.

25. Howe, op. cit., pp. 54/55 and Sam Waagenaar, *The Murder of Mata Hari* (London: Arthur Barker, 1964), p. 93.

26. Waagenaar, op. cit. p. 93.

27. Bram Dijkstra, *Idols of Perversity: Fantasies of Feminine Evil in Fin de Siècle Culture* (Oxford: University Press, 1986), p. 357.

28. Heymans, op. cit. p. 133.

29. Howe, op. cit., p. 33.

30. Léon Bizard, *Souvenirs d'un Médecin de Saint-Lazare* (Paris: Albin Michel, 1923), p. 85.

31. 'Les mangeuses d'hommes' was the name given to courtesans by bourgeois wives.

32. Olivier's letter to Mata Hari, from Mata Hari Scrapbooks, FLMD.

33. Heymans, op. cit., p. 341.

34. Playbill from Trianon, Palermo, Sicily, Mata Hari Scrapbooks, FLMD.

35. *The Bystander*, 10 June, 1914.

36. bMS Am 1553, HL.

37. De Pougy, op. cit. p. 30.

38. *New York Times*, 23 August, 1908.

39. Phyllis Rose, *Jazz Cleopatra: Josephine Baker in Her Time* (London: Chatto and Windus, 1989), p. 155.

40. Letter from Margaretha Zelle to MacLeod, 15 October, 1902, quoted in Heymans, op. cit., p. 344.

41. Quoted from the introduction to Alphonse Lemonnier's novel, *Les Femmes du Théâtre*, in Joanna Richardson, *The Courtesans: The Demi-Monde in Nineteenth-Century France* (London: Weidenfeld and Nicolson, 1967), p. 227.

42. Alain Corbin, *Women for Hire: Prostitution and Sexuality in France after 1850*, translated by Alan Sheridan (London: Harvard University Press, 1990), p. 133.

43. Paul Allard, *Les Enigmes de la Guerre* (Paris: Editions de Portiques, 1934), pp. 184–5.

44. Quoted in Waagenaar, op. cit., p. 111.

45. Mata Hari, interrogation by Captain Bouchardon, 15 February, 1917, SHAT.

46. Sam Waagenaar puts Mata Hari in Frankfurt on 15 August when she received an official travel permit from the Consul General of the Netherlands. However, the letter to Baron Lazarini appears to contradict this.

47. bMS Am 1553 (3), HL.

48. Ibid.

49. Bouchardon interrogation, 15 February, 1917, SHAT. Added to this were immediate financial problems since the theatre contract guaranteed her a salary of 48,000 marks or 60,000 francs. Mata Hari Scrapbooks, FLMD.

50. Maurice Rickards, *Posters of the First World War* (London: Evelyns, Adams and Mackay, 1968), plate 36.

51. Colonel James Edmonds, MO5, 'Intelligence Systems in Germany', 9 February, 1909, in IWM, Kell MSS.

52. Heymans, op. cit., p. 132.

53. Sert, op. cit., p. 146.

54. Alfred Morain, *The Underworld of Paris: Secrets of the Sûreté* (London: Jarrolds, 1930), p. 215.

55. Basil Thomson, *Queer People* (London: Hodder and Stoughton, 1922), pp. 14–16.

56. Nicholas Hiley, 'Decoding German Spies: British Spy Fiction 1908–18', in *Intelligence and National Security*, Vol. 5, October 1990, p. 56 and Jan Brunvand, *The Vanishing Hitchhiker: American Urban Legends and their Meanings* (New York: Pan Books, 1983) p. 23.

57. Captain Vernon Kell, 'War Delusions and Scares', IWM Kell MSS.

58. Diary, Miss W.L.R. Tower, 20 August, 1914, IWM.

59. Misc. 522, diary, IWM.

60. Robert Stephenson Smyth, Baron Baden-Powell, *Aids to Scouting for NCOs and Men* (London: Gale and Powell Military Series, 1914), pp. 140–1.

61. Felix Gross, *I Knew Those Spies* (London: Hurst and Blackett, 1940), p. 63.

62. Diary, Miss R.A. Neal, Hamburg, 7 August, 1914, IWM.

63. Daisy Williams, 'Adventures in Germany, May–September 1914', IWM.

64. Sert, op. cit., p. 148.

65. Marthé Richer (alias Richard), *I Spied for France*, translated from the French by Gerald Griffin (London: Long, 1935), pp. 26–36. Marthé Richard's married name was Richer, but after Georges Ladoux published her biography in 1932, she was known publicly as Richard, the name he had given her as a spy.

66. Heymans, op. cit., p. 124.

67. Mata Hari to unnamed consul, 10 October, 1916, bMS Am 1553, HL.

68. Jean-Jacques Becker, *The Great War and the French People*, translated from the French by Arnold Pomerans (Dover, New Hampshire: Berg Publishing, 1985), pp. 40–1.

CHAPTER 3 FINAL PERFORMANCES
pages 47–64

1. Major Georges Ladoux, *Marthé Richard, the Skylark: The Foremost Woman Spy of France* (London: Cassell, 1932), p. 19.

2. Bouchardon interrogation of Mata Hari, 15 February, 1917, SHAT.

3. bMS 1553, HL.

4. Sam Waagenaar, *The Murder of Mata Hari* (London: Arthur Barker, 1964), p. 134.

5. Emile Massard, *Les Espionnes à Paris* (Paris: Albin Michel, 1922), p. 27.

6. Testimony of Henry Marguérie, 13 June, 1917, SHAT.

7. Waagenaar, op. cit., p. 134.

8. Misia Sert, *Two or Three Muses: The Memoirs of Misia Sert*, translated from the French by Moura Budberg (London: Museum Press, 1953), pp. 149–50.

9. Metropolitan Police (MEPO) file, 3-2444, W531, PRO.

10. Jonkheer Loudon to DeMarees van Swinderen, 27 April, 1916, Nederlandse Gezantschap in Groot-Brittanie (en Ierland), 1813–1932 (849), Algemeen Rijksarchief, hereafter NGG-B, AR.

11. Swinderen to Loudon, ibid., NGG-B, AR.

12. Major General Sir Vernon Kell, *Security Intelligence in War*, 1934, IWM Kell MSS.

13. Lady Constance Kell, *Secret Well Kept*, unpublished manuscript, IWM Kell MSS.

14. Bouchardon interrogation of Mata Hari, 21 February, 1917, SHAT.

15. Ibid.

16. Ambassade de la République Française en Espagne to van Royen, 17 June, 1916, Dutch legation in Spain, AR.

17. PRO MEPO 3-2444.

18. Bouchardon interrogation of Mata Hari, 21 February, 1917, SHAT.

19. 'Scandales et Trahisons', *Le Gaulois*, 20 March, 1918.

20. Ladoux, op. cit. p. 8.

21. Massard, op. cit. p. 57.

22. Joanna Richardson, *The Courtesans: The Demi-Monde in Nineteenth-Century France* (London: Weidenfeld and Nicolson, 1967), pp. 4 and 125.

23. Tarlet and Monier's surveillance report; she was seen with the French lieutenant on

14 August, 1916; Henry Marguérie on 18 August, 1916; James Plunkett and Edwin Cecil O'Brien on 21 August, 1916; James Stewart Fernie on 31 August, 1916; General Baumgarten on 31 August, 1916 and British captain on 21–22 August, 1916, SHAT.

24. Captain Louis Pineau's interview with Captain Vladimir de Masloff, 19 May, 1917 and Bouchardon's interrogation of Mata Hari, 21 February, 1917, SHAT.

25. Tarlet and Monier's surveillance report; Mata Hari visited the Commissariat de Police on 31 July, 1916 to ask for a 'sauf-conduit' for Calais and the Prefecture of Police on 3 August, 1916, asking for a 'Carnet d'Etranger' to spend 21 days at Vittel. SHAT.

26. Captain Georges Ladoux testimony, 3 May, 1917, SHAT.

27. Georges Ladoux, *Mes Souvenirs*, (Paris: Les Editions de France, 1937), pp. 140–3 and Mata Hari's comments on Ladoux, PRO MEPO file 3-2444, op. cit.

28. Georges Ladoux, *Les Chasseurs d'espions. Comment j'ai fait arrêter Mata Hari* (Paris: Les Editions du Masque, 1932), pp. 231–4, emphasis added.

29. Ibid., p. 232.

30. Ibid., p. 233.

31. Ibid., pp. 233/4 and Mata Hari interrogation by Captain Bouchardon, 15 February, 1917, SHAT.

32. Mata Hari interrogation by Bouchardon, 23 February, 1917, SHAT.

33. Ibid.

34. Ladoux, op. cit., pp. 236–44.

35. Ibid.

36. *Le Matin*, 29 May, 1937.

37. Alain Corbin, *Women for Hire: Prostitution and Sexuality in France after 1850*, translated by Alan Sheridan (London: Harvard University Press, 1990), pp. 174–5.

38. Quoted in Joanna Richardson, op. cit., p. 4.

39. Monier and Tarlet's surveillance report, 14 October, 1917, SHAT.

40. Mata Hari to unnamed consul, Paris, 13 October, 1916, bMS 1553, HL.

41. Testimony of Henri Rapférer (sic): actual spelling of his name is Raphérer, 11 May, 1917, SHAT. Reference to Raphérer's identity from Russell Howe, *Mata Hari – The True Story* (New York: Dodd Mead, 1986), p. 202.

42. Corbin, op. cit., p. 135.

43. Mata Hari interrogation by Bouchardon, 24 February, 1917, SHAT. On 14 July, 1917 Mata Hari gave Mornet a list of the dates on which she sent Ladoux letters concerning her intelligence gathering: Sept.–Oct., 1916 (from Paris); Nov. 1916 (from London); Dec. 1916 (from Madrid) and Jan. 1917 (from Paris).

44. Ladoux's testimony, 3 May, 1917, SHAT and Emile Massard, 'La Veritable Histoire de Mata Hari', *La Liberté*, 8 December, 1921.

45. Mata Hari interrogation by Bouchardon, 24 February, 1917, SHAT.

46. British List of Suspects, Zelle, Margaretha Geertruida, in *Name Index to Correspondence of the Military Intelligence Division of the War Department Staff, 1917–1941*, National Archives, Washington, DC, hereafter NA, NND 740058.

47. *Mata Hari: Eye of the Day*, BBC Television, 1964, and Margaretha Zelle MacLeod, New Scotland Yard, 15 November, 1916, PRO MEPO 3-2444.

48. MEPO 3/2444 W531.

49. Mata Hari interrogation by Bouchardon, 24 February, 1917, SHAT.

50. Howe, op. cit., p. 108 for Grant reminiscences and PRO, MEPO 3/2444.

51. Christopher Andrew, *Secret Service: The Making of the British Intelligence Community* (London: Spectre, 1986), p. 180.

52. Basil Thomson, *Queer People* (London: Hodder and Stoughton, 1922), pp. 182/3.

53. W.H. Thompson, ex-Detective-Inspector, *Guard from the Yard* (London: Jarrolds, 1938), p. 57.

54. Margaretha Zelle MacLeod, New Scotland Yard, 15 November, 1916, PRO MEPO 3-2444.

55. Thomson, op. cit., p. 181.

56. Ibid.

57. Ibid.

58. M.G. Zelle MacLeod to DeMarees van Swinderen, Netherlands Minister, London, 13 November, 1916, NGG-B, AR.

59. PRO MEPO, op. cit.

60. Madame Zelle McLeod [sic], New Scotland Yard, 16 November, 1916, PRO MEPO 3-2444.

61. Ibid. However, Thomson was certainly bluffing at this stage since there is nothing in either the PRO MEPO files nor the Dutch legation's that supports this.

62. Ibid.

63. Thomson, op. cit., p. 183.

64. PRO MEPO 3-2444, op. cit.

65. Mata Hari interrogation by Bouchardon, 24 February, 1917, SHAT.

66. PRO MEPO 3-2444, op. cit.

67. Mata Hari interrogation by Bouchardon, 24 February, 1917, SHAT.

68. Thomson wrote two letters on 16 November to DeMarees van Swinderen stating that she 'has been detained here on suspicion that she is a German agent ... the passport she carries bears signs of being tampered with.' Basil Thomson to His Excellency the Netherlands Minister, 16 November, 1916. NGG-B, AR.

69. Thomson, op. cit., p. 183.

70. Ladoux, *Chasseurs d'espions*, op. cit., pp. 50, 52, 256.

71. British List of Suspects, op. cit., National Archives, Washington, DC, NND 740058 and MEPO file 3/2444 W531.

72. Thomson wrote to the Dutch legate, van Swinderen, on 16 November, 1916: 'Enquiries are being made as quickly as possible by cable and [Madame Zelle MacLeod] will not be detained longer than is necessary. If, however, she proves to be a person suspected of un-neutral acts, it may be necessary to take further action against her.'

73. NGG-B.

74. DeMarees van Swinderen to Dutch legation in Madrid, 1 December, 1916, Dutch Legation in Spain, AR.

75. This is how Mata Hari recalled her conversation with Thomson to Bouchardon, 24 February, 1917, SHAT.

76. PRO MEPO 3-2444/W531.

77. PRO MEPO 3-2444, op. cit.

78. Mata Hari interrogation by Bouchardon, 28 February, 1917, SHAT.

79. Ibid.

80. Ladoux's testimony, 3 May, 1917, SHAT.

81. Ladoux, *Chasseurs d'espions*, op. cit., p. 246.

82. Pierre Bouchardon, *Souvenirs* (Paris: Albin Michel, 1953), p. 208.

83. Mata Hari's interrogation by Bouchardon, 28 February, 1917, SHAT.

84. Ibid.

85. Marthé Richard quoted in Paul Allard, *Les Enigmes de la Guerre* (Paris: Editions de Portiques, 1934), p. 176.

86. Ladoux, *Marthé Richard, the Skylark*, op. cit., p. 40.

87. Ladoux, 'My Recollections', in Dennis Wheatley (ed.), *A Century of Spy Stories* (London: Hutchinson and Co., 1938), p. 548.

88. Thomas Coulson, 'Mata Hari – the Red Dancer', *The Forum*, February, 1930, p. 124.

89. Ladoux, 'My Recollections', op. cit., p. 581.

CHAPTER 4 SHADOW PLAYS
pages 65–83

1. Cesare Lombroso and William Ferrero, *The Female Offender* (New York: Appleton, 1899), p. 151.

2. Mata Hari interrogation by Captain Bouchardon, 1 March, 1917, SHAT.

3. Monier and Tarlet's surveillance report, 3 January, 1917, SHAT.

4. Mata Hari interrogation by Bouchardon, 1 March, 1917, SHAT.

5. Jean-Jacques Becker, *The Great War and the French People*, translated from the French by Arnold Pomerans (Dover, New Hampshire: Berg Publishing, 1985), pp. 205–6.

6. Quoted in Modris Eksteins, *Rites of Spring: The Great War and the Birth of the Modern Age* (Toronto: Lester and Orpen Dennys, 1989), p. 43.

7. Tarlet and Monier's surveillance report, 3 January, 1917; Mata Hari interrogation by Bouchardon, 1 March, 1917, SHAT.

8. Mata Hari interrogation, 1 March, 1917, op. cit.

9. Tarlet and Monier surveillance report, 8 January, 1917, SHAT.

10. Captain Louis Pineau's interrogation of Captain Vladimir de Masloff, 19 May, 1917, SHAT.

11. Although this series of letters donated to the Houghton Library is anonymous, Mata Hari had given Count van Limburg Styrum, who was attached to the Dutch legation in Paris in 1916, as a reference to Sir Basil Thomson on 16 November, 1916. She had also, in a 16 April, 1917 letter from Saint-Lazare prison to Otto Bunge at the Dutch legation in Paris, mentioned Count van Limburg Styrum as a friend who 'knows me and knows about my close friends in The Hague'. Since Mata Hari was, in the spring of 1917, most anxious to contact the Baron and Anna Lintjens – both of whom Count Styrum seems to have known – this was probably her 'dear consul'. However, I have no concrete proof of the correspondent's identity. Letter from autograph file, HL.

12. Margaretha Zelle MacLeod to 'mon cher consul'; Paris, 10 January, 1917, HL.

13. Inspector Curnier's Report, 10 April, 1917, SHAT.

14. Order of Arrest, 13 February, 1917, SHAT.

15. Alfred Morain, *The Underworld of Paris: Secrets of the Sûreté* (London: Jarrolds, 1930), p. 217.

16. Ibid.

17. Quoted in 'Les Femmes et L'Espionnage,' *Crapouillot*, Paris, 1951, No. 15, pp. 37–44, and Pierre Bouchardon, *Souvenirs* (Paris: Albin Michel, 1953), p. 305.

18. Morain, op. cit., p. 221.

19. Captain Bouchardon to Major Jullien, 15 May, 1917, *Dossier Mata Hari*, SHAT. The letter, written during Bouchardon's investigation, perpetuates the mistaken claim that Mata Hari was the mistress of the 'chief of police' in Berlin whose name was Traugott von Jagow. In reality, her lover was named Griebel, an officer in the police force whom she had met when he had come to inspect the costumes to be worn during her performance at the Metropol.

20. Paul Allard, *Les Enigmes de la Guerre* (Paris: Editions de Portiques, 1934), p. 176. This is a curious recollection by Bouchardon since, during the investigation, he never met Marta Hari at Clunet's apartment.

21. Georges Ladoux, 'My Recollections' in Dennis Wheatley (ed.), *A Century of Spy Stories* (London: Hutchinson and Co., 1938), pp. 547–8 and 581, and PRO MEPO file 3/2444.

22. Commandant Jacques Abtey and Fregutten Kapitan Dr Fritz Outerberg-Gibhardt, *Deuxième Bureau Contre Abwehr* (Paris: La Table Ronde, 1967), p. 181.

23. Ladoux, 'My Recollections', op. cit., p. 545.

24. Georges Ladoux, *Les Chasseurs d'espions: Comment j'ai fait arrêter Mata Hari* (Paris: les Editions du Masque, 1932), p. 247.

25. Ibid.

26. Henri Maunoury, *Police de guerre* (Paris: Editions de la Nouvelle Revue Critique, 1937), pp. 75–6. Maunoury also claimed that Mata Hari often tried to 'solicit' him in his office on the Boulevard du Palais, and was as uncompromising as Bouchardon in his description of her: 'Masculine, male-like with angular features, coffee-coloured complexion, big lips. She had all the accentuated faults of the Northerner without having the corrective charms of long blond tresses, blue eyes or a milky skin. Exuberant she was, without feminine charm and certainly little intelligence.' From *Crapouillot*, op. cit.

27. Allard, op. cit., pp. 180–1.

28. Ladoux, 'My Recollections', op. cit., p. 586.

29. For the interpretation of the radio messages, Russell Howe, *Mata Hari – The True Story* (New York: Dodd, Mead, 1986), p. 139 and the Minister of War's secret report, 21 April, 1917, SHAT.

30. Howe, op. cit., p. 143 and SHAT.
31. Mata Hari interrogation by Bouchardon, 28 February, 1917, SHAT.
32. Mata Hari interrogation by Bouchardon, 13 February, 1917, SHAT.
33. Bouchardon, op. cit., pp. 305–6.
34. Ibid., p. 306.
35. Alain Corbin, *Women for Hire: Prostitution and Sexuality in France after 1850*, translated by Alan Sheridan (London: Harvard University Press, 1990), p. 94.
36. Morain, op. cit., p. 218.
37. Corbin, op. cit., pp. 108/9.
38. Léon Bizard, *Souvenirs d'un Médecin de Saint-Lazare* (Paris: Albin Michel, 1923), p. 45.
39. Morain, op. cit., p. 219.
40. Bouchardon, op. cit., p. 218.
41. Morain, op. cit., p. 218.
42. Bizard, op. cit., p. 46.
43. Sam Waagenaar, *The Murder of Mata Hari* (London: Arthur Barker, 1964), pp. 178 and 179.
44. Mata Hari interrogation by Bouchardon, 15 February, 1917, SHAT.
45. Bouchardon, op. cit., p. 307.
46. Mata Hari interrogation by Bouchardon, 15 February, 1917, SHAT.
47. Mata Hari to Mornet, n.d., SHAT.
48. Mata Hari to Mornet, n.d., SHAT.
49. She had, however, written a letter to the legation on 16 April, 1917, which was received on 22 April stating that, 'for six weeks I have been shut up in Saint-Lazare accused of espionage that I have not committed'. Mata Hari to van Stuers, the Dutch legate, Paris in Ministerie van Buitenlandse Zaken Gezantshap-Paris (1866), 1870–1944, no. 1306, hereafter, MBZG–P, AR.
50. Mata Hari interrogation by Bouchardon, 1 March, 1917, SHAT.
51. Translation of Anna Lintjen's letter 15 December, 1916, and telegram, SHAT.
52. Bouchardon's report, 10 April, 1917, and 22–23 June, 1917, SHAT.
53. Bouchardon report, 5 May, 1917, SHAT.
54. Mata Hari interrogation by Bouchardon, 1 May, 1917, SHAT.
55. Mata Hari interrogation by Bouchardon, 9 March, 1917, SHAT.
56. Mata Hari letter to Bouchardon, 9 March, 1917, SHAT.
57. Bouchardon, op. cit., p. 315 and Dr Socquet quoted in Howe, op. cit., p. 160.
58. Mata Hari interrogation by Bouchardon, 12 April, 1917, SHAT.
59. Ibid.
60. General Sir Walter Kirke diary, 11 October, 1915, IWM. Emphasis in original.
61. Mata Hari to Bouchardon, 16 April, 1917, SHAT.
62. Mata Hari to Bouchardon, 28 April, 1917, SHAT.
63. Pineau interrogation of Masloff, op. cit.
64. Howe provides an extremely convincing analysis of the discrepancy between the three sets of messages – those intercepted at the Eiffel Tower, those given by Ladoux to Dubail and Bouchardon. He suggests that Ladoux had quite obviously altered the evidence to load the case against Mata Hari. Howe, op. cit., p. 166.
65. Bouchardon, op. cit., p. 314.
66. Ibid.
67. Mata Hari interrogation by Bouchardon, 1 May, 1917, SHAT.
68. Marthé Richer (alias Richard), *Ma vie d'espionne au service de la France* (Paris: Les Editions de France, 1935) second edition, p. 220.
69. Bouchardon, op. cit., p. 316; Bouchardon writes that the investigation where he first presented the radio messages was 21 April but the records show the date was actually 1 May.
70. Mata Hari interrogation by Bouchardon, 1 May, 1917, SHAT.
71. Bouchardon, op. cit., p. 315.
72. Marthé Richer (alias Richard), op. cit., p. 222.
73. Jules Cambon 4 April, 1917, SHAT and MBZG–P, AR.

74. Foreign Minister Jonkheer Loudon, to Dutch legate, Paris, MBZG–P, AR.

75. Paris legation to Minister of Foreign Affairs, 23 April, 1917, MBZG–P, AR.

76. Mata Hari to the Dutch legation in Paris, 16 April, 1917, MBZG–P, AR.

77. Margaretha Zelle MacLeod to 'mon cher consul; Paris,' n. d., 1917, autograph file, HL. This may also have been sent to Count van Limburg Styrum, the secretary of the Dutch legation ['our legation'], about whom Mata Hari says in her 16 April letter, 'he knows me and knows about my close friends in The Hague.'

78. Bouchardon on journalists, op. cit., p. 315 and Howe, op. cit., p. 185.

79. Maître Clunet to Captain Bouchardon 4 May, and Captain Bouchardon to Major Jullien, Chief Military Prosecutor, 5 May, 1917, SHAT.

80. Mata Hari's lovers, Mr Mégé, Jean Hallaure, Henry Marguérie, and Henri Raphérer were all interviewed and agreed that they had never discussed military or political matters with her.

81. Mata Hari's interrogation by Bouchardon, 1 May, 1917, SHAT.

82. The Times, 17 May, 1915.

83. Bouchardon, op. cit., p. 323 and 1 May, 1917 interrogation, SHAT.

84. Mata Hari interrogation by Bouchardon, 21 May, 1917, SHAT.

85. M.G. Zelle McLeod [sic] to Bouchardon, 31 May, 1917, SHAT.

86. Mata Hari to Bouchardon, 1 June, 1917, SHAT.

87. Mata Hari to Bouchardon, 5 June, 1917, SHAT.

88. Mata Hari to Bouchardon, 8 June, 1917, SHAT.

89. Bouchardon, op. cit., p. 311.

90. Ibid., p. 323.

91. Mata Hari to Clunet, 28 June, 1917, SHAT.

92. Mata Hari to Dutch legation, 6 July, 1917, SHAT, emphasis in original.

93. Mata Hari to Mornet, 10 July, 1917, and Memo from the Office of Military Justice to the Office of the Chief of Military Justice, n. d., SHAT.

94. Inspector Curnier to Major Jullien, 19 July, 1917, SHAT.

CHAPTER 5 TRIAL AND ERRORS
pages 84–100

1. Emile Massard, Les Espionnes à Paris (Paris: Albin Michel, 1922), p. 36.

2. Edouard Clunet to Dutch consul in Paris, 24 July, 1917, MBZG–P, AR.

3. Alfred Morain, The Underworld of Paris: Secrets of the Sûreté (London: Jarrolds, 1930), p. 219.

4. Ibid.

5. Ibid.

6. Félix Belle, 'Mata Hari Condamnée à Mort', Le Gaulois, 26 July, 1917.

7. Emile Massard, 'La Véritable Histoire de Mata Hari', La Liberté, 7 December, 1921.

8. Massard, Les Espionnes, op. cit., pp. 32 and 36.

9. Judgement of 25 July, 1917, SHAT.

10. Ibid.

11. Massard, 'La Véritable Histoire de Mata Hari', op. cit.

12. Ibid.

13. Ibid.

14. Alain Presles and François Brigneau, 'Le Dossier Secret de Mata Hari', Le Nouveau Candide, 22 March, 1962.

15. Massard, 'La Véritable Histoire de Mata Hari', op. cit.

16. Ibid.

17. Marthé Richer (alias Richard), I Spied for France, translated from the French by Gerald Griffin (London: Long, 1935), pp. 218–21.

18. Morain, op. cit., p. 217.

19. Massard, 'La Véritable Histoire de Mata Hari', op. cit.

20. Morain, op. cit., p. 210.

21. Jean-Jacques Becker, The Great War and the French People (Dover, New Hampshire:

Berg Publishing, 1985), pp. 218–19.

22. Judgement of 25 July, 1917, SHAT.

23. Paul Allard, *Les Enigmes de la Guerre* (Paris: Editions de Portiques, 1934), p. 184 and written depositions in *Mata Hari dossier*, SHAT.

24. Allard, op. cit., p. 184.

25. 'Mata Hari et le Ministre, Une lettre de M. Messimy', *La Liberté*, 20 April, 1926, front page.

26. 'Cherchez la femme', *Handlesblad*, 21 April, 1926.

27. Massard, *La Liberté*, 10 December, 1921.

28. Sam Waagenaar, *The Murder of Mata Hari* (London: Arthur Barker, 1964), p. 258.

29. Judgement of 24 July, 1917, SHAT.

30. Massard, *Les Espionnes*, op. cit., p. 36.

31. Judgement of 25 July, 1917, SHAT.

32. Massard, *La Liberté*, 11 December, 1921.

33. Judgement of 25 July, 1917, SHAT.

34. 'Ordre d'exécution, Le gouverneur militaire de Paris', 25 July, 1917, SHAT.

35. Massard, op. cit., and *Le Matin*, 25 July, 1917.

36. Modris Eksteins, *Rites of Spring: The Great War and the Birth of the Modern Age* (Toronto: Lester and Orpen Dennys, 1989), p. 28 and Saint-Lazare description, Morain, op. cit., p. 22.

37. Sanche de Gramont, *The French: Portrait of a People* (New York: Putnam, 1969), pp. 390–1.

38. Louis Schneider, 'Les Femmes exécutées', *Le Gaulois*, 16 October, 1917.

39. Quoted in Waagenaar, op. cit., p. 266.

40. Massard, *Les Espionnes*, op. cit., p. 63.

41. Waagenaar, op. cit., p. 160.

42. Even before Mata Hari's trial, stories had appeared in the French press about the charges made against her. So the efforts to censor news about the trial by Bouchardon, General Dubail and Major Jullien proved to be ineffective.

43. Maurice de Waleffe, 'Après le chatiment de l'espionne', *Le Journal*, 27 July, 1917.

44. 'A Woman Spy's Fate', *Daily Sketch*, 1 August, 1917. It is an interesting comment on the Deuxième Bureau's record on informing its Allies about the prosecution of suspected spies. The MEPO 3-2444/W531 file records that the British authorities were informed about Mata Hari's death sentence through the British press.

45. Dutch Foreign Minister Loudon to van Stuers, Paris, 28 July, 1917, MBZG–P, AR.

46. Clunet to van Stuers, 2 August, 1917, 16 August, 1917 and 17 August, 1917, MBZG–P, AR and 'Tribunaux', *Le Matin*, 18 August, 1917.

47. The Under-Secretary of State to the Minister of War, 11 September, 1917, SHAT.

48. Loudon, to van Stuers, 31 August, 1917, MBZG–P, AR.

49. Mata Hari, M. Zelle MacLeod to van Stuers, 22 September, 1917, MBZG–P, AR.

50. 'Dancing Girl to be Shot – Mata Hari loses appeal in France', *Daily Chronicle*, 27 September, 1917.

51. 'Le Pouvoir de Mata Hari', *Le Figaro*, 28 September, 1917.

52. Van Stuers notes, 28 September, 1917, MBZG–P, AR.

53. Dr Magnus Hirschfeld, *The Sexual History of the World War* (New York: Panurge Press, 1934), p. 260.

54. Loudon to Dutch legation, Paris, 13 October, 1917, MBZG–P, AR.

55. PRO FO395/103/197559 (1917).

56. Allard, op. cit., p. 178.

57. Morain, op. cit., p. 224.

58. Since Mata Hari was tried in a military rather than a civil court, this article in any case would not have applied.

59. Massard's description from Massard, *La Liberté*, 12 December, 1921.

60. Massard, *La Liberté*, 13 December, 1921.

61. Russell Howe, *Mata Hari: The True Story* (New York: Dodd Mead, 1986), p. 264.

62. Pastor Arboux letter, 9 February, 1918, SHAT.

63. Ibid.

64. Morain, op. cit., p. 225.

65. M. Georges Godot, 'La Mort de Mata Hari', *Paris Match*, 12 October, 1953.

66. Howe claims the officers in charge had been told to choose four sergeants, four corporals and four privates so the enlisted men of all ranks would witness a German spy's execution. However, the officer in charge, concerned about the effects on his less experienced men of seeing a woman shot, selected twelve sergeants; he ordered four to pretend to be corporals and four to pose as privates. Howe, op. cit., p. 12.

67. Allard, op. cit., p. 177.

68. Morain, op. cit., p. 225.

69. Godot, op. cit. Godot, who was a member of the firing squad, contradicts both Bouchardon's account in his *Souvenirs* and Paul Allard's report. He claims that he passed the body, rent with wounds, which more than three bullets had passed through.

70. Massard, *La Liberté*, 13 December, 1921, and Bouchardon, op. cit., pp. 325–8.

71. *Le Gaulois*, 16 October, 1917.

72. Ibid.

CHAPTER 6 THE AFTERMATH
pages 101–118

1. Gustav Steinhauer, edited by S.T. Felstead, *Steinhauer: The Kaiser's Master Spy as told by Himself* (London: John Lane, 1930), p. 151.

2. *The People*, 23 April, 1933.

3. Warrington Dawson in Major Georges Ladoux, *Marthé Richard, the Skylark: The Foremost Woman Spy of France* (London: Cassell, 1932) and 'Le Capitaine Ladoux inculpé', *Le Petit Journal*, 20 March, 1918.

4. Marthé Richer (alias Richard), *I Spied for France*, translated by Gerald Griffin (London: Long, 1935), p. 283.

5. Captain Ferdinand Tuohy, *The Secret Corps: A Tale of 'Intelligence' on all Fronts* (London: Murray, 1920), p. 42.

6. D. Manning, diary 19 March, 1915–6 February, 1919, unpublished MSS, IWM.

7. Ibid.

8. Harold Stainton, *A Personal Narrative of the War*, unpublished MSS, IWM. A report from the French chamber revealed the extent of the spy scare: up to 1 January, 1916, fifty-five people had been shot in the military zone, nine in the interior and 100 were serving sentences of penal servitude. There were also fifty-three concentration camps for aliens and suspects throughout regions close to the Western Front. A man near Béthune was shot by the French in November, 1914 for having a telephone in his house and another in June, 1915 for keeping carrier pigeons for the enemy.

9. 'German Spies in the West', *Daily Express*, 16 January, 1917.

10. For a variation on this story see Captain David Fallon, 'The Ways of the Spies', *New York Herald*, magazine of the war section, 6 January, 1918, p. 11. Fallon describes a Belgian peasant girl who 'daily supplied us with the European edition of the Herald', who collected information for her father and turned it over to the Germans. They were caught, the father was tried and the girl 'sentenced to imprisonment for life'. However, Fallon gives no place names, dates, or other specific details.

11. Diary of Captain Walter Kirke, 23 December, 1914, IWM.

12. Tuohy, op. cit., p. 42 and *The Times*, 3 November, 1915.

13. *New York Times*, 27 October, 1907 and 2 April, 1915.

14. *The Times*, 23 February, 1916.

15. 'Vigilant' [Christopher Sykes], *Secrets of Modern Spying* (London: John Hamilton, 1930), p. 188, *The Times*, 22 December, 1916 and Hirschfeld, op. cit., p. 260.

16. There was also the case of Mrs Louise Mathilde Smith, née von Zastrow, who served three years' penal servitude for sending 'information of little value' to her family in Switzerland in 'General revision of sentences on German spies', WO 32/4898, PRO. Mrs Louise Sophy

Caroline Herbert, a German-born curate's wife, was charged in Darlington under the DORA for writing to her relatives in Switzerland in 1915, 'Information for the Enemy', *The Times*, 21 October, 1915.

17. Martha Earle, CRIM 1/176/1, PRO.
18. Dr Magnus Hirschfeld, *The Sexual History of the World War* (New York: Panurge Press, 1934), see chapter on 'prostitution', pp. 154–68; Alain Corbin, *Women for Hire; Prostitution and Sexuality in France after 1850*, translated by Alan Sheridan (London: Harvard University Press, 1990), pp. 334–6.
19. Steinhauer, op. cit., p. 177.
20. Thomas Coulson, 'Mata Hari – the Red Dancer', *The Forum*, January, 1930, p. 63.
21. Henry de Halsalle and C. Sheridan Jones, *The German Woman and Her Master* (London: T. Werner Laurie, 1916), p. 44.
22. Quoted in Catherine von Casselaer, *Lot's Wife: Lesbian Paris 1890–1914* (Liverpool: Janus Press, 1986), p. 118.
23. Ibid., p. 172.
24. De Halsalle, op. cit., p. 42.
25. MacLeod Yeardsley, Diary, p. 198. IWM.
26. Arnold White's *The Hidden Hand* (London: Richards, 1917) was published in the hope of convincing the King of England to 'repudiate personal relations with His Majesty's cousin, the head of the Hohenzollerns, and that for the future, sovereigns of these realms will mate with Queens of British or Irish stock.'
27. De Halsalle and Jones, op. cit., p. 45.
28. Corbin, op. cit., pp. 307–8.
29. *The Times*, 10 May, 1916.
30. Captain David Fallon, 'The Ways of the Spies', *New York Herald*, 6 January, 1918.
31. Hamil Grant, *Spies and Secret Service: The Story of Espionage, Its Main Systems and Chief Exponents* (London: Richards, 1915), p. 25.
32. Tuohy, op. cit., p. 8.
33. 'A Woman on Secret Service', *The Graphic*, 17 October, 1914.
34. Film was an equally important disseminator of these images; Britain's first spy film was produced in 1899 and by 1911 there were eleven such thrillers screened. Female spies were featured in; *The Submarine Plans* (1921); *An Adventuress Outwitted* (1912); *The Heart of a Woman* (1912); *OHMS* (1913); *Huns of the North* (1913) and *Two Little Britons* which portrayed two children of the British Secretary for Foreign Affairs in Brussels 'unmasking an ideal spy – their teacher!' From Denis Gifford, 'Silent Spies', in *The Journal of the Society of Film and Television Arts*, No. 24, Summer 1966, pp. 6–10.
35. 'Mystia the Witch', *Lot-O'-Fun*, No. 448, 10 October, 1914.
36. Nicholas Hiley, 'Decoding German Spies: British Spy Fiction, 1908–18', in Wesley K. Wark (ed.), special issue on 'Spy Fiction, Spy Films and Real Intelligence', *Intelligence and National Security*, Vol. 5, October 1990, No. 4, pp. 55–79.
37. Christopher Andrew, *Secret Service: The Making of the British Intelligence Community* (London: Spectre, 1986), p. 71.
38. Phillip Knightley, *The Second Oldest Profession: The Spy as Bureaucrat, Patriot, Fantasist and Whore* (London: André Deutsch, 1986), p. 23.
39. Ladoux, op. cit., p. 20.
40. Felix Gross, *I Knew Those Spies* (London: Hurst and Blackett, 1940), p. 36.
41. Steinhauer, op. cit., p. 199. Steinhauer's pseudonym may have been a joke; Leeuwarden is the name of Mata Hari's home town.
42. Ibid., p. 199.
43. Ladoux, op. cit., p. 22.
44. H.R. Berndorff, *Espionage*, translated by Bernard Miall (London: Nash and Grayson, 1930).
45. Winifred Ludecke, *Behind the Scenes of Espionage: Tales of the Secret Service* (London: Harrap, 1929), p. 225.
46. Captain Ferdinand Tuohy, *This is Spying: Truth and Fiction about Secret Service* (London: World's Work, 1938), p. 41.

47. *Times Literary Supplement*, 27 May, 1920.
48. Steinhauer, op. cit., p. 50.
49. H.C. Peterson, *Propaganda for War: The Campaign Against American Neutrality* (Norman: University of Oklahoma Press, 1939), p. 157.
50. 'Has Uncle Sam Caught One of the Kaiser's "Vampire" Spies?', *San Francisco Sunday Chronicle*, 27 January, 1918.
51. Ibid.
52. In a letter to the US Attorney General, Elizabeth Nix wrote on 24 April, 1918, 'Five and a half weeks ago all the New York papers and papers all over the United States and abroad for days headlines, that the Department of Justice had captured a gang of German spies and plotters.' Department of Justice, File no. 9-19/1601, NA.
53. 'Two women in luxury', *New York Herald*, 19 March, 1918. Information about this case also taken from 'Arrest 4 as Spies; 2 Women Accused', *New York Times*, 19 March, 1918.
54. See, for example, Hirschfeld, op. cit., p. 251.
55. Clairmont was alleged to have been suffering from stomach cancer. However, he appeared to have made a remarkable recovery and was investigated by the Department of Justice in December 1921 while staying at the Hotel Commodore in New York. File no. 9-19/1601, NA.
56. 'Madame Storch, Spy leader, dies on Ellis Island', *New York Herald*, 31 March, 1918.
57. 'Madame Storch dead; was held as spy', *New York Times*, 31 March, 1918.
58. 'Charges Spies Work in Airship Factory', *New York Times*, 31 March, 1918; the same issue reported that 'secret service agents are expected to make a roundup of those women who there is reason to believe are active in the spy service of the Kaiser'. Senator Overman had proposed the death penalty for espionage in the senate; disloyalty was reported to be growing among German-American clergy; and a mob of 500 in Coshocton, Ohio forced twenty-five alleged pro-Germans to kiss the stars and stripes and say 'to hell with the Kaiser'.
59. Elizabeth Nix to J.W. Gregory, Ellis Island, New York, 24 April, 1918, file no. 9-19/1601, NA.
60. All quotes taken from Witt K. Cochrane, New York to Attorney General, 16 April, 1918, ibid. file, NA.
61. Washington to Berlin, January–May, 1915, intercepted telegrams, ADM 137/3963, PRO.
62. John L. O'Brian, Special Assistant to the Attorney General for War Work, to Honorable William M. Calder, Washington, DC, 12 September 1918, NA.
63. Herbert O. Yardley, *The American Black Chamber* (Indianapolis: Bobbs-Merrill Co., 1931), p. 90.
64. Intercepted German Diplomatic Telegrams, Berlin-Washington, 26 January, 1915 (b103)-13040, ADM 137/4047, PRO.
65. Reinhard R. Doerries, *Imperial Challenge: Ambassador Count Bernstorff and German-American Relations, 1908–1917*, translated by Christa D. Shannon (London: University of North Carolina Press, 1989), p. 75.
66. Francis Caffey, Attorney General, to O'Brian, 16 May, 1918, Dept. of Justice, file no. 9-19/119/190637, NA.
67. 'Marie Victorica, German Spy, Dead', *New York Times*, 13 August, 1920.
68. Statement of Marie K. DeVictorica [sic]. Ibid. file.
69. 'Hold Young Woman as Master Spy's Aid', *New York Times*, 28 April, 1918.
70. Marie de Victorica von Kretschman to Mitzi, 20 July, 1919, Department of Justice, ibid. file, NA.
71. Ibid.
72. Marie de Victorica von Kretschman to Geheimrath Schramm, 21 July, 1919. Ibid. file. The Justice Department strongly criticized New York's Enemy Alien Bureau in 1918 for 'the blunder made in allowing the Victorita [sic] story to get to the newspapers'.
73. 'Marie Victorica, German Spy, Dead', *New York Times*, 13 August, 1920.
74. 'Hold Young Woman as Master Spy's Aid', *New York Times*, 28 April, 1918.
75. Yardley, op. cit., p. 110.
76. Ibid., p. 119.

77. One example is found in a letter to a 'most reverend father' from Marie de Victorica, 20 July, 1919, ibid. file: 'Never had the officials of the Department of Justice permitted themselves to be prejudiced against an enemy whom they had at the first times of their investigations a perfect right to believe dangerous.'

78. Mitzi letter, op. cit., and Statement of Marie K. DeVictorica [sic], ibid. file.

79. Herbert O. Yardley, *The Blonde Countess* (London: Faber, 1934), p. 86. Yardley's novel was made into an MGM film entitled *Rendezvous* (1935), starring William Powell and Rosalind Russell and later remade as *Pacific Rendezvous* in 1942. The original, according to film writers Larry Langman and David Ebner, was 'singled out as the first spy film to introduce a dose of wit'. Larry Langman and David Ebner, *Encyclopedia of American Spy Films* (London: Garland Park, 1990), p. 332.

80. Ibid., p. 293.

CHAPTER 7 A BATTLE FOR HEARTS, MINDS AND RECRUITS
pages 119–128

1. *Daily Mirror*, 22 October, 1915.

2. 'Nuestros Amigos Los Frances', *ABC Domingo*, 21 October, 1917.

3. FO395/103/197559 (1917) PRO.

4. 'The Execution', *El Parlamentario*, 25 October, 1917.

5. *La Tribuna*, 18 October, 1917, quoted in *Mercure de France*, 15 April, 1920, p. 272.

6. *La Protesta*, 7 April, 1918, in Cuban Postal Censorship, Havana, NND 740058, NA. A photograph of Mata Hari in costume and others with captions praising the Germans and condemning Allied actions, were considered suspicious enough for the censor to ban *La Protesta* from the island.

7. *Le Figaro*, 28 March, 1916 and 'Cavell oranges', *Daily Express*, 18 April, 1916.

8. *Daily Express*, 30 June, 1918 and 19 September, 1918.

9. US Military Attaché, Holland, 8 March, 1919, NND 740 058, NA.

10. Louise Thuliez, *Condemned to Death* (London: Methuen, 1934), p. 150.

11. Colonel Sir Vernon Kell, 'Lecture on Security Intelligence in the Field', n.d., p.6, IWM Kell MSS.

12. *Daily Express*, 10 July, 1915 and FO 395/103/197559, PRO.

13. George Barton, *The World's Greatest Military Spies* (Boston: Page, 1917), p. 84.

14. *Daily Express*, 25 October, 1915.

15. Archibald Bodkin to Director of Public Prosecutions, 16 November, 1915, DPP1/32 xc 3332 PRO.

16. Archibald Bodkin to DPP, 16 November, 1915, DDP 4/51, PRO, Chancery Lane.

17. J.C. Silber, *The Invisible Weapons* (London: Hutchinson, 1932), p. 58.

18. *The Times*, 18 February, 1916 and 24 March, 1916.

19. Admiral Sir William James, *The Eyes of the Navy: A Biographical Study of Admiral Sir Reginal Hall* (London: Methuen, 1955), p. 36.

20. Hugh Gibson to Brand Whitlock, in *The Execution of Miss Cavell at Brussels*, presented to the House of Parliament, October, 1915.

21. A.E. Clark-Kennedy, *Edith Cavell: Pioneer and Patriot* (London: Faber, 1965) pp. 216–18.

22. Ibid., p. 224.

23. Ibid., p. 225.

24. Louise Thuliez, *Condemned to Death* (London: Methuen, 1934), p. 163.

25. Baron Oscar von der Lancken, *Thirty Service Years*, quoted in *New York Times*, 9 November, 1930.

26. H.R. Berndorff, *Espionage*, translated by Bernard Miall (London: Nash and Grayson, 1930), p. 221.

27. *Daily Telegraph*, 18 October, 1915.

28. *Daily Express*, 18 October, 1915 and *Morning Post*, 21 October, 1915.

29. *Daily Express*, 21 October, 1915.

30. *Daily Express*, 22 October, 1915.

31. *Daily Mirror*, 23 October, 1915.
32. *Daily Mirror*, 29 October, 1915.
33. *Morning Post*, 24 December, 1915.
34. *Daily Express*, 15 November, 1916.
35. *The Diary of P. Macleod Yearsley*, circa 1938, unpublished MSS IWM, p. 146.
36. Berndorff, op. cit., p. 227.
37. Captain Ferdinand Tuohy, *The Secret Corps: A Tale of 'Intelligence' on All Fronts* (London: Murray, 1920), p. 22.
38. I am grateful to Dr Nick Hiley for these references.
39. Quoted in *Daily Express Clippings Service*, unidentified English newspaper, 3 November, 1915.
40. General Sir Walter Kirke's diary, 16 October, 1914 to 29 April, 1915, unpublished MSS, IWM.
41. Dr Magnus Hirschfeld, *The Sexual History of the Great War* (New York: Panurge Press, 1934), pp. 52–65.
42. For an account of the British war nurse's experience see Vera Brittain, *Testament of Youth* (London: Virago, 1978) and for the experience of an English ambulance driver see Helen Zena Smith, *'Not So Quiet . . . ' Stepdaughters of War* (London: Albert Marriott, 1930).
43. Tuohy, op. cit., p. 115.
44. 'Vigilant' (Christopher Sykes), *Secrets of Modern Spying* (London: John Hamilton, 1930), pp. 185–7.
45. Hirschfeld, op. cit., p. 250.
46. *Daily Express*, 13 October, 1917.
47. Kirke diary, op. cit., 25 April, 1916 and 8 June, 1916.
48. Hirschfeld, op. cit., p. 261.
49. 'Sister Beatrice Seeking Vindication', *The Gazette*, 7 December, 1915; 'Gives Career of Sister Beatrice', *The Gazette*, 9 December, 1915; 'Mrs Bartlett Gets Exoneration as Spy', *New York Times*, 14 July, 1929.
50. Hirschfeld, op. cit., p. 265.

CHAPTER 8 THE LEGACY
pages 129–44

1. Herbert T. Fitch, *Traitors Within: The Adventures of Detective Inspector Herbert T. Fitch* (London: Hurst and Blackett, 1933), pp. 99–100.
2. 'Olga Pulloffski, The Beautiful Spy', by R.P. Weston and Bert Lee, (London: Francis, Day and Hunter, Ltd, 1935).
3. Paul Allard, *Les Enigmes de la Guerre* (Paris: Editions de Portiques, 1934), p. 199.
4. Valerien Svetloff, 'The Execution of Mata Hari', *Dancing Times*, November 1927, pp. 193–7.
5. Carlos Knight, 'Fifty Thousand Spies', *True Stories* (London: W.C. Merrett, 1938), p. 48.
6. Camille Pitollet, *Mercure de France*, 15 May, 1920, pp. 272–7.
7. Ibid., p. 276, Rachilde quoted from *Mercure de France*, 15 January, 1919.
8. Pitollet's article from *Mercure de France* was picked up in the English press and appeared under the title, 'Mata Hari's Last Lover', in *The Weekly Dispatch*, 16 July, 1922.
9. *Daily Star*, 16 September, 1936. *Liverpool Post*, 13 October, 1936, which picked up the report from the French press.
10. Loudon, 27 November, 1917 telegram to the Dutch legate, Paris, Embassy at Paris, 1866–1940 (1306), MBZG–P, AR.
11. 'Spy Drama Revealed', *News of the World*, 9 March, 1924.
12. Raoul Deboissigne, 'Mata Hari: Queen of Spies', *Sunday Express*, 30 October, 1927.
13. Albert de Courville, 'Butterflies on the Wheel of Chance', *Sunday Express*, 18 December, 1927.
14. Georges Godot, 'La Mort de Mata Hari', *Paris Match*, 12 October, 1953.
15. Sam Waagenaar, *The Murder of Mata Hari* (London: Arthur Barker, 1964), p. 277, and E.J. van der Veen and W.G. van der Veen, to the Dutch legate in Paris, 4 December, 1917, MPZG–P, AR.

16. Liane de Pougy, *My Blue Notebooks*, translated by Diana Athill (London: André Deutsch, 1977), p. 87.

17. Charles Heymans, *La Vraie Mata Hari. Courtisane et Espionne* (Paris: Editions Prométhée, 1930), p. 394.

18. Catherine von Casselaer, *Lot's Wife: Lesbian Paris 1890–1914*, (Liverpool: Janus Press, 1986), p. 172 and George Wickes, *The Amazon of Letters: The Life and Loves of Natalie Barney* (London: W.H. Allen, 1977), p. 268.

19. 'Les Femmes et L'Espionnage', *Crapouillot*, Paris, 1951, No. 15, pp. 37–44 and Joanna Richardson, *The Courtesans: The Demi-Monde in Nineteenth-Century France* (London: Weidenfeld and Nicolson, 1967), p. 105.

20. 'Mata Hari et le Ministre, Une lettre de M. Messimy', *La Liberté*, 20 April, 1926, front page.

21. 'Cherchez la femme', *Handelsblad*, 21 April, 1926.

22. E. de Peretti de la Rocca, Ministère des Affaires Etrangères, to Jonkheer J. Loudon, Dutch minister in Paris, 3 February, 1923, MPZG–P, AR.

23. Extract from *Les Espionnes à Paris*, de la Rocca correspondence, MPZG–P, AR.

24. G. Fournier, the Deuxième Bureau, to the military attaché at the Dutch legation in Paris, 6 February, 1923, MPZG–P, AR.

25. Minister of Foreign Affairs, The Hague, to Loudon, 21 February, 1923, MPZG–P, AR.

26. Minister of Foreign Affairs, Paris, to the Dutch legation, Paris, 14 January, 1918, MPZG–P, AR.

27. Rudolph MacLeod to Jonkheer Loudon, 10 April, 1919, MPZG–P, AR.

28. Henry Lecouturier to Loudon, 10 May, 1918, MPZG–P, AR.

29. Ibid. and French Minister of Foreign Affairs to Loudon, 9 March, 1918, MPZG–P, AR.

30. Rudolph MacLeod to Loudon, 10 April, 1919 and Minister of Foreign Affairs to Dutch legation, Paris, 9 May, 1919, MPZG–P, AR.

31. Russell Howe, *Mata Hari: The True Story* (New York: Dodd, Mead, 1986), p. 255.

32. 'Une pièce scandaleuse', *La Liberté*, 8 December, 1921.

33. 'Une lettre de l'auteur de la "Danseuse Rouge"', *La Liberté*, 9 December, 1921.

34. 'Une déclaration de M. Binet-Valmer', *La Liberté*, 11 December, 1921.

35. 'La Danseuse Rouge', *La Liberté*, 13 December, 1921.

36. *New York Times*, 17 June, 1922.

37. *La Liberté*, 8 December, 1921.

38. *Intermédiare*, Vol. 85, Col. 402, 10 May, 1922.

39. Vicent Blasco Ibanez, *Mare Nostrum*, translated from the Spanish by Charlotte Brewster Jordan (London: Constable, 1920), p. 152.

40. Ibid., p. 218.

41. Ibid., p. 333.

42. Ibid., pp. 406–7.

43. Ibanez's novel *Mare Nostrum* was made into a film of the same name starring Alice Terry, in 1926.

44. Alain Corbin, *Women for Hire: Prostitution and Sexuality in France after 1850*, translated by Alan Sheridan (London: Harvard University Press, 1990), p. 332.

45. Bram Dijkstra, *Idols of Perversity: Fantasies of Feminine Evil in Fin de Siècle Culture* (Oxford: University Press, 1986), p. 355.

46. For a discussion about changes within bourgeois marriage in France during this period, see Corbin, op. cit., pp. 331–2.

47. Henry de Halsalle, *A Secret Service Woman: Being Confessions, Experiences, and Opinions of Olga von Kopf, the Famous International Spy* (London: T. Werner Laurie, 1917), p. 34.

48. Henry de Halsalle, *The Life Story of Madame Zelle: The World's Most Beautiful Spy* (London: Skeffington and Sons, 1917), p. 13.

49. Ibid., p. 69.

50. Ibid., p. 13.

51. Ibid., p. 177.

52. 'Woman Dancer Shot by French as a Spy', the *New York Times*, October 16, 1917.

53. 'Mata Hary' [sic], *Variety*, 3 May, 1918.

54. Phillip Knightley, *The Second Oldest Profession: The Spy as Bureaucrat, Patriot, Fantasist and Whore* (London: André Deutsch, 1986), p. 42.

55. The November 1927 issue of *Dancing Times* picked up de Halsalle's theme of Mata Hari's mixed parentage to explain her proclivity towards espionage. 'Her being an adventuress had something to do with the "oriental neurasthenia" of her mixed blood.' Valérien Svetloff, 'The Execution of Mata Hari', *Dancing Times*, November, 1927, pp. 193–7.

56. Other early novels based on Mata Hari's life included: Louis Dumur's *Les Défaitistes*, in which she played the role of 'Oriental siren'. Dumur, who had consulted Emile Massard about her death, first published his account in *Mercure de France*, in 1922. Marcel Nadaud, who published a three-part series in *Le Petit Journal* on Mata Hari with André Fage, had written a novel about her, *Zisha; Danseuse Espionne* (Albin Michel, 1920); Elinor Glyn's novel with a spy-heroine named Harrietta Boleski, *The Price of Things*, was published in 1919.

57. De Pougy, 31 January, 1920, op. cit., p. 87.

58. *New York Evening Graphic*, 6 February, 1926.

59. Charles Heymans, *La Vraie Mata Hari: Courtisane et Espionne* (Paris: Editions Prométhée, 1930), p. 365.

60. Quoted in Bernard Newman, *Inquest on Mata Hari* (London: Robert Hale, 1956), p. 79.

61. Heymans, op. cit., p. 175.

62. Sidney Theodore Felstead, *German Spies at Bay: Being an Actual Record of the German Espionage in Great Britain during the years 1914–1918 compiled from Official Sources* (London: Hutchinson, 1920), p. 90.

63. Ibid., p. 90.

64. *Times Literary Supplement*, 27 May, 1920.

65. Captain Ferdinand Tuohy, *The Secret Corps: A Tale of 'Intelligence' on all Fronts* (London: Murray, 1920), p. 23.

66. Ibid., p. 25.

67. Thomas Coulson, 'Mata Hari – the Red Dancer', *The Forum*, January, 1930, p. 3.

68. *Kolnische Zeitung* on 31 January, 1929, quoted in Heymans, op. cit., p. 383.

69. *Paris-Midi*, 5 February, 1929.

70. Quoted in Heymans, op. cit., p. 394.

71. 'Mata Hari had not the Nerve to be a Spy', Paris correspondent, *Daily Express*, 26 January, 1933.

72. Paul Allard, *Les Enigmes de la Guerre* (Paris: Editions de Portiques, 1934), p. 175.

73. *Le Petit Journal*, 4 March, 1936; Dr Puellès implies that he treated Mata Hari for a sexually transmitted disease.

74. 'H-21, très bon agent d'avant-guerre', *Le Petit Journal*, n.d., from MBZG–P.

75. Modris Eksteins, *Rites of Spring: The Great War and the Birth of the Modern Age* (Toronto: Lester and Orpen Dennys, 1989), pp. 252–3.

76. 'Is Mata-Hari nog in leven?', *Het Leven*, 21 August, 1929.

77. 'Is Mata Hari Still Alive?', *Daily Mail*, 3 September, 1929.

78. 'Shot Spy: Daughter's Fight', *Empire News*, 16 November, 1930.

79. 'Convent Beauty Soon to Learn Secret of the Loveliest Spy', *The People*, 20 April, 1931.

80. 'Executed in Error', Paris report, 16 August, 1931.

81. John K. Newnham, 'The Screen Goes Eastern', *Dancing Times*, July 1932, pp. 347–50.

82. *Dancing Times*, August 1932, for review of Greta Garbo's 'Mata Hari'.

83. 'Lieber Fredi!', undated article from German-language periodical and original letter, Mata Hari, Grand Hotel, Frankfurter-Hof, Frankfurt, to Baron Fredi Lazarini, c/o Feldpost 87, 25 August, 1914, bMS, AM 1553 HL.

84. The first known film about Mata Hari was a silent picture released in 1922 which authentically re-enacted the execution scene, and the second was *The Red Dancer* by Continental Productions starring Magda Sonia which was released in 1927.

85. J.D. Huyer, Amsterdam, to Otto Pierson, chairman of the 'France-Holland' Friendship Society, Paris, 10 May, 1932, MBZG–P.

86. Ibid.

87. 'Mata Hari film', *Daily Express*, 25 October, 1932.

88. They produced their findings in 'Le Dossier secret de Mata Hari', *Le Nouveau Candide*, 1, 8, 15, 22 March, 1962. For British coverage see 'The Truth About Mata Hari', *Evening Standard*, 17 January, 1964.

89. Military Archives, Freiburg, iB. Translation from German by John MacLaren to whom I am indebted for this reference.

90. Waagenaar, op. cit., p. 120.

91. 'Call-boy Scandal reminds analysts of sex's role in spying', *Washington Times*, 4 July, 1989.

92. Michael Dobbs, 'Sexpionage: Why We Can't Resist Those KGB Sirens', *Washington Post*, 12 April, 1987.

EPILOGUE
pages 145–54

1. Quoted in John Costello, *Love, Sex and War: Changing Values, 1939–45* (London: Pan Books, 1986), p. 12.

2. G.E.R. Gedye, 'Even in Peace the Spies are at Work', *New York Times Magazine*, 12 January, 1930.

3. Phillip Knightley, *The Second Oldest Profession: The Spy as Bureaucrat, Patriot, Fantasist and Whore* (London: André Deutsch, 1986), p. 85.

4. Janet Flanner, *An American in Paris: Profile of an Interlude Between Two Wars* (London: Hamish Hamilton, 1940), p. 345.

5. Ibid., p. 350.

6. 'Mother Sentenced in Spy Trial', *Daily Express*, 18 April, 1935.

7. 'Mata Hari outdone by Polish girl spy', *New York Times*, 26 June, 1932.

8. 'Woman on Trial in Budapest Death', *New York Times*, 21 February, 1933.

9. 'Russian beauty is seized as spy', *New York Times*, 7 September, 1934.

10. A case in point is that of the American journalist Jane Anderson. This correspondent from Georgia was held in prison in Madrid on espionage charges in 1936. 'American Woman Freed of Espionage in Spain', *New York Times*, 11 October, 1936.

11. Phyllis Rose, *Jazz Cleopatra: Josephine Baker in Her Time* (London: Chatto and Windus, 1990), p. 184.

12. Ibid., p. 202.

13. R.J. Minney, 'Carve Her Name With Pride: The Story of Violette Szabo', in *The Secret War* (London: Octopus Books, 1983), pp. 504/5. Minney's biography first appeared in 1964.

14. Ibid., p. 534.

15. Ibid., p. 552.

16. Gordon Young, *In Trust and Treason: The Strange Story of Suzanne Warren* (London: Edward Hulton, 1959). Suzanne was born Warenghem which the British War Office later anglicized to Warren.

17. Hélène Champlain, *The Secret War of Helen de Champlain* (London: W.H. Allen, 1980), p. 210.

18. Ibid., p. 188.

19. Robert O. Paxton, *Vichy France* (New York: Knopf, 1972), p. 292, quoted in Rose, op. cit., p. 181.

20. Mathilde-Lily Carré, *I Was 'the Cat': The Truth About the Most Remarkable Woman Spy Since Mata Hari – by Herself* (London: Souvenir Press, 1960), p. 115.

21. Ibid., p. 204.

22. Ibid., p. 173.

23. Michael Barson (ed.), *Career Girls* (New York: Pantheon Books, 1990).

24. Kurt Singer, *Spies Over Asia* (London: W.H. Allen, 1956), p. 100. According to Singer, van Deeren was a 'high government official' who worked as a double British/Japanese agent. However, there is no mention of anyone by this name in the PRO files for this period.

25. Bernard Newman, *Inquest on Mata Hari* (London: Robert Hale, 1956), p. 149.

26. Professor Leigh Williams, Brown University, Rhode Island, letter to author, 21 February, 1990.

27. Professor Robin Winks, Yale University, New Haven, letter to author, 29 January, 1990.

28. Richard Deacon (Donald McCormick), *Spyclopaedia* (London: Futura, 1987), p. 218.

29. General Sir Philip Christison, Melrose, letter to author, 28 September, 1989.

30. Conversation with author at his home in Rome, March, 1989.

31. *Daily Express*, 8 May, 1964.

32. *Daily Telegraph*, 12 February, 1965 and Cynthia Grenier, *International Herald Tribune*, 3 October, 1964.

33. *Evening News*, 1 November, 1967.

34. Victor Davis, 'A Rebel Finds His Cause', *Daily Express*, 6 July, 1978.

35. Anthony Mann, 'A Pedestal for Mata Hari', *Sunday Telegraph*, 27 March, 1983.

36. Jane Gordon, 'Bond Bombshells', *Elle*, June 1990.

37. Quoted in Chapman Pincher, *Traitors: The Labyrinths of Treason* (London: Sidgwick and Jackson, 1987), p. 89.

38. 'Secretary to West German leaders admits spying for love', *Washington Times*, 16 June, 1987.

39. Marianne Quoirin, 'Two lonely secretary-spies come out of the cold', *German Tribune*, 7 January, 1990 (reprinted from the *Kolner Stadt-Anzeiger*, Cologne, 21 December, 1989).

40. Christine Toomey, 'Spinsters who spy for love', *Sunday Times*, 30 August, 1987.

SELECTED SOURCES

Broadmoor, Berkshire, Broadmoor Hospital Medical Records,
  Medical records of Lizzie Luise Wertheim (5 February, 1918–30 July, 1920)
Cambridge, MA, the Houghton Library, Harvard University
  bMS Am 1553
  Manuscripts presented by James Hill, MS Fr 132/54M-145
The Hague, Algemeen Rijksarchief
  Ministry of Foreign Affairs; 2 May, 1918, no. 129
  Dutch legation Spain; 2 May, 1946, no. 284
  Dutch legation Great-Britain; 2 May, 1944, no. 849
The Hague, Ministerie van Buitenladse Zaken
  Archive of the Embassy at Paris, 1866–1940, No. 1306 (Mata Hari)
Leeuwarden, Mata Hari Foundation at the Frysk Letterkundich Museum en Dokumintaes-
jesintrum
  H.W. Keikes Collection
  Mata Hari Scrapbooks
London, Colindale Newspaper Library
  Daily Express clipping file – Edith Cavell/Mata Hari
London, Imperial War Museum
  Papers: Millicent Battrum, Edith Cavell, Brigadier T.I. Dun, Mrs Amy Nora Foote,
  Sybil Harry, Miss Constance Annie Hill, Sir Vernon Kell, KBE, and Lady Constance
  Kell: 'Secret Well Kept' (unpublished MS), General Kirke diaries, Sgt A.H.J. Lane, D.
  Manning, Misc. 522 diary, Miss R.A. Neal diary, Alfred E. Schultz, Harold Stainton, Miss
  Winifred Tower diary, Daisy Williams, P. Macleod Yearsley diary
London, Public Record Office
  Eva de Bournonville (CRIM 1/538) (DPP4/51) (DPP1/32 x 3332) (WO32/4894);
  Martha Earle (CRIM 1/176/1); Maud Gould (CRIM 1/145/2); Mrs Lizzie Luise
  Wertheim (WO 32/4898) (DPP1/32/3328) (FO 372/1424/T 206364); Margaretha
  Zelle aka Mata Hari (MEPO 3/2444) (MEPO 3/2444/7) (FO395/103/197559/1917)
Los Angeles, CA, Department of Special Collections, University of California
  Espionage and Secret Service Archive, Series E, box E 917, No. 79; Box 918, file 80.81
  Mennevee Collection
Paris, Service Historique de l'Armée de Terre, Château de Vincennes
  Dossier Mata Hari
Stanford, CA, Hoover Library
  Kent Shumate seminar paper (Stanford, 1947)
Washington, DC, National Archives and Record Administration
  General Records, Department of Justice (Record Group 60); MID-9140-815-1; MID-
  10130-165; MID-10314-423-1-2
  Military Reference Branch
  *Name Index to the Correspondence of the Military Intelligence Division of the War Department
  Staff*, British List of Suspects, NND 740058

SELECTED
BIBLIOGRAPHY

ON MATA HARI

Major Thomas Coulson, *Mata Hari: Courtesan and Spy* (London: Harper, 1930)

Charles S. Heymans, *La Vraie Mata Hari, Courtisane et Espionne* (Paris: Editions Prométhée, 1930)

Russell Howe, *Mata Hari – The True Story* (New York: Dodd, Mead, 1986)

Edmond Locard, *Mata Hari* (Lyons: Editions de la Flamme, 1954)

René Masson, *Pavane pour une espionne* (Lyons: Presses de la Cité, 1965)

Ronald Miller, *Mata Hari* (Geneva: Edito-Service, SA, 1970)

Bernard Newman, *Inquest on Mata Hari* (London: Robert Hale, 1956)

Erika Ostrovsky, *Eye of Dawn: The Rise and Fall of Mata Hari* (New York: Dorset Press, 1978)

Sam Waagenaar, *The Murder of Mata Hari* (London: Arthur Barker, 1964)

Adam Zelle (translated from the Dutch), *The History of the Life of my Daughter and my Grievances against her Ex-Husband* (Amsterdam: C.L.G. Veldt, 1906)

REMINISCENCES AND RELATED BIOGRAPHIES

Janine Alexandre-Debray, *La Pavia: ses amants, ses maris* (Paris: Librarie Académique, 1986)

Maud Allan, *My Life and Dancing* (London: Everett and Co., 1908)

Gabriel Astruc, *Le Pavillon des Fantômes: Souvenirs* (Paris: Grasset, 1929)

Polly Binder, *The Truth About Cora Pearl* (London: Weidenfeld and Nicolson, 1986)

Léon Bizard, *Souvenirs d'un Médecin de Saint-Lazare* (Paris: Albin Michel, 1923)

Léon Bizard and Jane Chapon, *Histoires de la Prison de Saint-Lazare, du Moyen-Age à Nos Jours* (Paris: E. de Boccards, 1925)

Pierre Bouchardon, *Souvenirs* (Paris: Albin Michel, 1953)

Mathilde-Lily Carré, *I Was 'the Cat': The Truth About the Most Remarkable Woman Spy Since Mata Hari – by herself* (London: Souvenir Press, 1960)

Charles Castle, *Folies Bergère* (London: Hamish Hamilton, 1982)

Hélène de Champlain, *The Secret War of Hélène de Champlain* (London: W.H. Allen, 1980)

Alexander Clark-Kennedy, *Edith Cavell: Pioneer and Patriot* (London: Faber, 1965)

Jean Cocteau, *Paris Album, 1900–1914* (London: W.H. Allen, 1956)

Diana Cooper, *The Rainbow Comes and Goes* (London: Rupert Hart-Davis, 1958)

Michael de Cossart, *Ida Rubenstein (1885–1960), A Theatrical Life* (Liverpool: Liverpool University Press, 1987)

Erté, *Things I Remember* (London: Peter Owen, 1975)

Janet Flanner, *An American in Paris: Profile of an Interlude Between Two Wars* (London: Hamish Hamilton, 1940)

R.J. Minney, 'Carve Her Name with Pride: The Story of Violette Szabo', in *The Secret War* (London: Octopus Books, 1983)

Jean Overton-Fuller, *Noor-un-Nisa Inayat Khan (Madeleine)* (London: Barrie and Jenkins, 1979)

Liane de Pougy, *My Blue Notebooks*, translated by Diana Athill (London: André Deutsch, 1977)

Phyllis Rose, *Jazz Cleopatra: Josephine Baker in Her Time* (London: Chatto and Windus, 1990)

Misia Sert, *Two or Three Muses: The Memoirs of Misia Sert*, translated by Moura Budberg (London: Museum Press, 1953)

Louise Thuliez, *Condemned to Death* (London: Methuen, 1934)

George Wickes, *The Amazon of Letters: The Life and Loves of Natalie Barney* (London: W.H. Allen, 1977)

Edwin T. Woodhall, *Detective and Secret Service Days* (London: Jarrolds, 1934)

Gordon Young, *In Trust and Treason: The Strange Story of Suzanne Warren* (London: Edward Hulton, 1959)

ON ESPIONAGE

Commandant Jacques Abtey and Fregutten Kapitan Dr Fritz Outerberg-Gibhart, *Deuxième Bureau Contre Abwehr* (Paris: La Table Ronde, 1967)

Paul Allard, *Les Enigmes de la Guerre* (Paris: Editions de Politiques, 1934)

Christopher Andrew, *Secret Service: The Making of the British Intelligence Community* (London: Spectre, 1986)

Robert Stephenson Smyth Baden-Powell, *Aids to Scouting for NCOs and Men* (London: Gale and Powell Military Series, 1914)

George Barton, *The World's Greatest Military Spies* (Boston: Page, 1917)

Richard Baxter, *Guilty Women* (London: Quality Press, 1943)

Patrick Beesly, *Room 40: British Naval Intelligence 1914–1918* (Oxford: University Press, 1984)

H.R. Berndorff, *Espionage*, translated by Bernard Miall (London: Nash and Grayson, 1930)

Robert Boucard, *Les Dessous des Archives secrètes* (Paris: Les Editions de France, 1929)

Pierre Bouchardon, *Souvenirs* (Paris: Albin Michel, 1953)

Richard Deacon (Donald McCormick), *Spyclopaedia* (London: Futura, 1987)

Sidney Theodore Felstead, *German Spies at Bay: Being an Actual Record of the German Espionage in Great Britain during the years 1914–1918 compiled from official sources* (London: Hutchinson, 1920)

Herbert T. Fitch, *Traitors Within: The Adventures of Detective Inspector Herbert T. Fitch* (London: Hurst and Blackett, 1933)

Hamil Grant, *Spies and Secret Service: The Story of Espionage, its Main Systems and Chief Exponents* (London: Richards, 1915)

Felix Gross, *I Knew Those Spies* (London: Hurst and Blackett, 1940)

Henry de Halsalle and C. Sheridan Jones, *The German Woman and Her Master* (London: T. Werner Laurie, 1916)

Hugh Cleland Hay, *40 OB or How the War Was Won* (London: Hutchinson, 1932)

Vernon Hinchley, *Spy Mysteries Unveiled* (London: George Harrap, 1963)

Admiral Sir William James, *The Eyes of the Navy: A Biographical Study of Admiral Sir Reginald Hall* (London: Methuen, 1955)

Phillip Knightley, *The Second Oldest Profession: The Spy as Bureaucrat, Patriot, Fantasist and Whore* (London: André Deutsch, 1986)

Georges Ladoux, *Les Chasseurs d'espions: Comment j'ai fait arrêter Mata Hari* (Paris: Editions du Masque, 1932)

Georges Ladoux, *Marthé Richard, the Skylark: The Foremost Woman Spy of France* (London: Cassell, 1932)

Georges Ladoux, *Mes Souvenirs* (Paris: Les Editions de France, 1937)

Georges Ladoux, 'My Recollections', in Dennis Wheatley (ed.), *A Century of Spy Stories* (London: Hutchinson and Co., 1938)

Winifred Ludecke, *Behind the Scenes of Espionage: Tales of the Secret Service* (London: Harrap, 1929)

Emile Massard, *Les Espionnes à Paris* (Paris: Albin Michel, 1922)

Henri Maunoury, *Police de guerre* (Paris: Editions de la Nouvelle Revue Critique, 1937)

Alfred Morain, *The Underworld of Paris: Secrets of the Sûreté* (London: Jarrolds, 1930)

Georges du Parcq, *Secrets of the French Police* (London: Jarrolds, 1934)

Lt-Col. Oreste Pinto, *The Spycatcher Omnibus: The Spy and Counter-Spy Adventures of Lt-Col. Oreste Pinto* (London: Hodder and Stoughton, 1969)

Marthé Richard, *Ma vie d'espionne au service de la France* (2nd edition, Paris: Les Editions de France, 1935)

Marthé Richard, *Espions de guerre et de paix* (Paris: Les Editions de France, 1938)

Marthé Richer (alias Richard), translated by Gerald Griffin, *I Spied for France* (London: Long, 1935)

Kurt Singer, *Spies Over Asia* (London: W.H. Allen, 1956)

Gustav Steinhauer, edited by S.T. Felstead, *Steinhauer: The Kaiser's Master Spy as told by himself* (London: John Lane, 1930)

W.H. Thompson, *Guard from the Yard* (London: Jarrolds, 1938)

Basil Thomson, *Queer People* (London: Hodder and Stoughton, 1922)

Ferdinand Tuohy, *The Secret Corps: A Tale of 'Intelligence' on All Fronts* (London: Murray, 1920)

Ferdinand Tuohy, *This is Spying: Truth and Fiction about Secret Service* (London: The World's Work, 1938)

'Vigilant' (Christopher Sykes), *Secrets of Modern Spying* (London: John Hamilton, 1930)

Arnold White, *The Hidden Hand* (London: Richards, 1917)

Charles Wighton, *The World's Greatest Spies* (London: Odhams Press, 1962)

ON CULTURAL HISTORY

Michael Barson (ed.), *Career Girls* (New York: Pantheon Books, 1990)

Jan Brunvand, *The Vanishing Hitchhiker: American Urban Legends and their Meanings* (New York: Pan Books, 1983)

Catherine von Casselaer, *Lot's Wife: Lesbian Paris, 1890–1914* (Liverpool: Janus Press, 1986)

Alain Corbin, translated by Alan Sheridan, *Women for Hire: Prostitution and Sexuality in France after 1850* (London: Harvard University Press, 1990)

Bram Dijstra, *Idols of Perversity: Fantasies of Feminine Evil in Fin de Siècle Culture* (Oxford: University Press, 1986)

Regenia Gagnier, *Idylls of the Marketplace: Oscar Wilde and the Victorian Public* (Aldershot: Scolar Press, 1986)

Judith Lynne Hanna, *Dance, Sex and Gender: Signs of Identity, Dominance, Defiance and Desire* (London: University of Chicago Press, 1988)

Rana Kabbani, *Europe's Myths of Orient: Devise and Rule* (London: Pandora Press, 1986)

Joanna Richardson, *The Courtesans: The Demi-Monde in Nineteenth-Century France* (London: Weidenfeld and Nicolson, 1967)

Edward Said, *Orientalism* (London: Penguin, 1985)

Carl E. Schorske, *Fin-de-Siècle Vienna: Politics and Culture* (New York: Random House, 1981)

Elaine Showalter, *Sexual Anarchy: Gender and Culture at the Fin de Siècle* (London: Bloomsbury, 1991)

Judith Walkowitz, *Prostitution and Victorian Society Women: Class and the State* (London: Cambridge University Press, 1980)

ON THE FIRST WORLD WAR

Jean-Jacques Becker, translated by Arnold Pomerans, *The Great War and the French People* (Dover, New Hampshire: Berg Publishing, 1985)

Modris Eksteins, *Rites of Spring: The Great War and the Birth of the Modern Age* (Toronto: Lester and Orpen Dennys, 1989)

Dr Magnus Hirschfeld, *The Sexual History of the Great War* (New York: Panurge Press, 1934)

Samuel Hynes, *A War Imagined: The First World War and English Culture* (London: Bodley Head, 1990)

Maurice Rickards, *Posters of the First World War* (London: Evelyns, Adams and Mackay, 1968)

J.M. Spraight, *Air Power and War Rights* (London: Longman, 1924)

SPY NOVELS

Elinor Glyn, *The Price of Things* (London: T. Werner Laurie, 1919)

Henry de Halsalle, *The Life Story of Madame Zelle: The World's Most Beautiful Spy* (London: Skeffington and Sons, 1917)

Henry de Halsalle, *A Secret Service Woman: Being Confessions, Experiences, and Opinions of Olga von Kopf, the Famous International Spy* (London: T. Werner Laurie, 1917)

Henry de Halsalle, *A Woman Spy: Being Further Confessions of Germany's Principal Secret Service Woman, Olga von Kopf* (London: Skeffington, 1918)

Vicent Blasco Ibanez, translated by Charlotte Brewster Jordan, *Mare Nostrum* (London: Constable, 1920)

Georges Ladoux, *The Kaiser's Blonde Spy: An Historical Romance of the Secret War* (London: Hutchinson, 1934)

Temple Thurston, *Portrait of a Spy: The Story of Mata Hari* (London: Queensway, 1918)

Lael Tucker, *The Eye of the Lion* (Boston: Little Brown, 1964)

Herbert O. Yardley, *The Blonde Countess* (London: Faber, 1934)

ARTICLES (BY DATE)

'The Parisians of Paris', *The King*, 4 February, 1905

'Bloc-Notes Parisien – Matahari', *Le Gaulois*, 17 March, 1905

'Paris Fancies and Fashions', *The Gentlewoman*, 25 March, 1905

Le Figaro, 20 August, 1905

Intermédiare des Chercheurs et Curieux, 30 September, 1906

The Lady's Realm, Vol. xxiv May–October, 1908

'Salome Craze', *The Sketch*, 24 June, 1908

'The Spread of Bohemianism in English Society', the *New York Times*, 16 August, 1908

Percival Pollard, 'The Regnant Wave of the Sensational Dance', the *New York Times*, 23 August, 1908

'Coquelin and Charity', *The Era*, 3 October, 1908

Comoedia Illustré, March, 1913

'Lady MacLeod dances . . . ', *The Tatler*, 24 September, 1913

Le Figaro, 28 March, 1916

Daily Express, 18 April, 1916

Félix Belle, 'Mata-Hari Condamnée à Mort', *Le Gaulois*, 26 July, 1917

Maurice de Waleffe, 'Après le châtiment de l'espionne', *Le Journal*, 27 July, 1917

'A Woman Spy's Fate', the *Daily Sketch*, 1 August, 1917

'Dancing Girl to be Shot – Mata Hari loses appeal in France', *Daily Chronicle*, 27 September, 1917

'Le Pouvoir de Mata Hari', *Le Figaro*, 28 September, 1917

Louis Schneider, 'Les Femmes exécutées', *Le Gaulois*, 16 October, 1917

'A Woman on Secret Service', *The Graphic*, 17 October, 1917

La Tribuna, 18 October, 1917

El Parliamentario, 25 October, 1917

'Mata Hary', *Variety*, 3 May, 1918

Mercure de France, 15 April, 1920

Mervyn Lamb, 'On Hazardous Service', *Blackwood's Magazine*, July–December, 1920, pp. 751–70

Emile Massard, 'La Véritable Histoire de Mata Hari', *La Liberté*, 7 December, 1921; 8 December, 1921; 10 December, 1921; 12 December, 1921; 13 December, 1921

'Une pièce scandaleuse', *La Liberté*, 8 December, 1921

'Une lettre de l'auteur de la "Danseuse Rouge"', *La Liberté*, 9 December, 1921

'Une déclaration de M. Binet-Valmer', *La Liberté*, 11 December, 1921

'La Danseuse Rouge', *La Liberté*, 13 December, 1921

Camille Pitollet, 'Mata Hari, la "dame aux blanches fourrures" et la trappiste de la Cartuja de Miraflores', *Mercure de France*, 15 July, 1922

Leo Faust, 'Notes et Documents d'Histoire', *Mercure de France*, 1 January, 1923

'Spy Drama Revealed', *News of the World*, 9 March, 1924

'Mata-Hari et le Ministre, Une lettre de M. Messimy', *La Liberté*, 20 April, 1926

'Cherchez la femme', *Handelsblad*, 21 April, 1926

Valérien Svetloff, 'The Execution of Mata Hari', *Dancing Times*, November 1927

Albert de Courville, 'Butterflies on the Wheel of Chance', *Sunday Express*, 18 December, 1927

'Is Mata Hari nog in leven?', *Het Leven*, 21 August, 1929

'Is Mata Hari Still Alive?' *Daily Mail*, 3 September, 1929

'Shot Spy: Daughter's Fight', *Empire News*, 16 November, 1930

'Convent Beauty Soon to Learn Secrets of the Loveliest Spy', *The People*, 20 April, 1931

John K. Newnham, 'The Screen Goes Eastern', *Dancing Times*, July 1932

'Mata Hari had not the Nerve to be a Spy', *Daily Express*, 26 January, 1933

Le Petit Journal, 4 March, 1936

Carlos Knight, 'Fifty Thousand Spies', *True Stories*, 1938

'Les Femmes et l'Espionage', *Crapouillot*, No. 15, 1951

M. Georges Godot, 'La Mort de Mata Hari', *Paris Match*, 12 October, 1953

Alain Presles and François Brigneau, 'Le Dossier Secret de Mata Hari', *Candide* 8–15 March, 1962; 16–23 March, 1962

INDEX